Current Biochemical Approaches to Learning and Memory

Monographs in Modern Neurobiology
edited by Walter B. Essman

PSYCHOPHARMACOLOGY
An Introduction to Experimental and Clinical Principles
Luigi Valzelli

NEUROCHEMISTRY OF CEREBRAL ELECTROSHOCK
Walter B. Essman

**CURRENT BIOCHEMICAL APPROACHES
TO LEARNING AND MEMORY**
Edited by Walter B. Essman and Shinshu Nakajima

Current Biochemical Approaches to Learning and Memory

Edited by **Walter B. Essman**
Queens College of the City University of New York
and

Shinshu Nakajima
Dalhousie University
Halifax, N.S., Canada

SPECTRUM PUBLICATIONS, INC.
Flushing, New York

DISTRIBUTED BY THE HALSTED PRESS DIVISION OF
JOHN WILEY & SONS
New York   Toronto   London   Sydney

Spectrum Publications, Inc.
75-31 192 Street, Flushing, New York 11366

Distributed solely by Halsted Press Division, John Wiley & Sons, Inc., New York

Library of Congress Cataloging in Publication Data

Essman, Walter B
   Current biochemical approaches to learning and memory.

   1. Memory. 2. Learning ability. 3. Brain chemistry. I. Nakajima, Shinshu, joint editor. II. Title. [DNLM: 1. Brain chemistry. 2. Learning. 3. Memory. WL300 E78c 1973]
QP406.E78   612'.82   73-18009
ISBN 0-470-24566-2

CONTRIBUTORS

G. V. Abuladze
Institute of Physiology
Siberian Department of the USSR
Academy of Sciences
Novosibirsk, USSR

Samuel Bogoch
Dreyfus Medical Foundation and
Foundation for Research on the Nervous System,
New York and Boston, Mass. U.S.A.

Walter B. Essman
Departments of Psychology and Biochemistry
Queens College of the City University of New York
Flushing, N.Y., U.S.A.

E. J. Fjerdingstad
Anatomy Department B
University of Aarhus
Aarhus, Denmark

M. A. Gilinsky
Institute of Physiology
Siberian Department of the USSR
Academy of Sciences
Novosibirsk, USSR

R. Yu. Ilyutchenok
Institute of Physiology
Siberian Department of the USSR
Academy of Sciences
Novosibirsk, USSR

Ivan Izquierdo
Department of Pharmacology
Faculty of Chemical Sciences
National University of Córdoba
Córdoba, Argentina

Shinshu Nakajima
Department of Psychology
Dalhousie University
Halifax, N.S.
Canada

Yasuzo Tsukada
Department of Physiology
School of Medicine
Keio University
Tokyo, Japan

Luigi Valzelli
Section of Neuropsychopharmacology
Mario Negri Institute for
Pharmacological Research
Milan, Italy

Preface

The concept around which the contributions to this volume developed came about at a time when the editors were inviting symposium participants for the XXth International Congress of Psychology. That symposium, "Biochemical Correlates of Learning and Memory", was held at the Congress in Tokyo in 1972, where some of the contributors to the present volume participated. Since the symposium, each author has had the opportunity to revise, update, or integrate his chapter, the result being the present monograph.

Although there have been several symposium volumes, compilations, and works concerned with the general theme of learning and memory and biochemical methodologies or concepts related to these processes, there was a rationale governing the development of the present volume. One point of concern was an attempt to avoid duplication of issues and/or text that has previously appeared, and another was to develop the concept of the volume around a number of distinguished scientists whose recent work and ideas might best represent biochemical approaches to learning and memory.

The reader will find that this volume is not an introduction to one set of relationships between biochemistry and behavior, but rather represents multidisciplinary methodologies wherein biochemical parameters are varied and biochemical changes are measured. The behavioral methodologies and results are similarly varied. One goal of this volume was to provide a potential stimulus to further research with the hope that some further meaningful insights are derived, making some of the complexities of behavior more accessible to biochemical investigation.

The editors wish to express their appreciation to the contributors, who, in spite of postal strikes, distance, and language differences, managed to meet both editorial and publisher's deadlines with highly original, topical chapters.

Walter B. Essman
Shinshu Nakajima

August, 1973

Table of Contents

CHAPTER 1

Biochemical Studies of Learning and Memory: An Historical Overview

SHINSHU NAKAJIMA
AND WALTER B. ESSMAN

1. CHEMICAL IMPROVEMENT OF INTELLIGENCE: BEFORE 1960

The enhancement of intellectual functions by drug administration has been one of the most formidable tasks presented to the student of the function of the brain. Intelligence was once a miracle, then it was a mystery. When scientists believed to have grasped it, it became a mirage.

One of the earliest manifestations of the mirage was, perhaps, in the applications of and studies with glutamic acid. In 1936, Weil-Malherbe found that the only amino acid oxidized in vitro by brain tissue is l-glutamic acid. Zimmerman and Ross (1944) suggested that feeding this amino acid might enhance several brain functions, including intelligence. They administered l-glutamic acid orally to rats for two weeks, and found that this treatment facilitated maze learning. The findings in laboratory animals were followed by a clinical report (Zimmerman et al., 1947) indicating that the Intelligence Quotients of mentally retarded and epileptic children were improved after feeding with glutamic acid over a period of six months. However, the facilitatory effect observed with rats was not confirmed in subsequent experiments from other laboratories (Hamilton & Maher, 1947; Marx, 1948, 1949; Stellar & McElroy, 1948; Porter & Griffin, 1950; Francis et al., 1951; Zabarenko et al., 1951). Most of the subsequent clinical reports were negative, and some of the positive reports did not have proper controls (Astin & Ross, 1960).

Another chemical substance intensively studied in the early years was cholinesterase (ChE), an enzyme that hydrolyzes acetylcholine (ACh). A group of research workers in the University of California, Berkeley, tested a working hypothesis that the rat's preference for spatial or visual cues in solving a spatial-visual problem (maze) may be related to the activity of ChE in the somatosensory or visual cortex (Krech et al., 1954). The hypothesis was rejected. The animals preferring spatial cues showed a higher ChE activity in the visual and motor areas, as well as in the somatosensory area (Krech et al., 1954).

The Berkeley group then tested the second hypothesis that the general level of cortical ChE activity may be related to the problem-solving ability (Rosenzweig et al., 1960). This hypothesis was also abandoned because the correlation was positive in some of the strains studied, but negative in others. A third hypothesis was that the ability for learning may be related to the concentration of ACh relative to that of ChE. The results finally supported the third hypothesis (Rosenzweig et al., 1960).

Meanwhile, young members of the Berkeley group proceeded in a new direction. McGaugh and Petrinovich (1959) injected rats with a weak solution of strychnine before training them in a maze, and found a facilitation of learning. Strychnine was used because initially it was thought to inhibit ChE activity (Rosenzweig et al., 1960), but McGaugh and Petrinovich (1959) considered its general stimulant effect to be more important.

2. THE EMERGENCE OF MACROMOLECULAR THEORIES

A rudimentary form of macromolecular theory of memory was first proposed by Halstead at the Hixon symposium in 1948 (Halstead, 1951), with an added comment "so little is known about the particular functions of the brain that no speculation can be said to be foolish." He hypothesized that the nucleoproteins in the nerve cells transform themselves from random to organized configurations as a result of neural activity in the process of learning. The hypothesis was heavily influenced by contemporary knowledge of genetics, which emphasized the role of nucleoproteins in the storage of genetic information.

In the ensuing decade, genetics shifted its emphasis from nucleoproteins to nucleic acids. A new field of science, molecular biology, had developed. Yet the new field was too young to influence other fields of science. In the Wisconsin symposium on "Biological and Biochemical Basis of Behavior" (Harlow & Woolsey, 1958), no one was able to foresee the development to come in a few years.

In a paper presented at the Montevideo symposium in 1959 (Fessard et al., 1961), Gerard emphasized the high rate of metabolism in the neuron, and asserted that any enduring modification of neural function must be sustained by continuously self-reproducing macromolecules, nucleic acids or proteins. The macromolecules were officially introduced into the field of memory.

In Sweden, Hydén (1959) was developing methods for measuring the chemical compositions and enzymatic activity in single neurons freshly excised from the mammalian brain. On the basis of his experimental findings, he proposed a theory that a change in the base sequence of ribonucleic acid (RNA) may represent a biochemical basis of memory (Hydén, 1961). Electrochemical events produced by a pattern of nerve impulses may replace one of the RNA bases (purines and pyrimidines). The codified RNA then starts synthesizing a new type of protein, which may facilitate the release of a transmitter substance upon the arrival of the same pattern of impulses.

About the same time, Gaito (1961) formulated a similar theory. He asserted that behavior is a function of genetic potential as it is modified by learning. The modification may occur in the brain as an exchange in position of the nucleosides of desoxyribonucleic acid (DNA) or RNA molecules, or as an alteration of the amino acid sequence in proteins. Electrochemical reaction at the synaptic site may cause these changes, and the molecular changes in turn produce a behavior other than that determined by heredity.

The theories of Hydén (1961) and Gaito (1961) involve an assumption that mnemonic information is stored as an altered monomer sequence in macromolecules. Briggs and Kitto (1962) offered the criticizm that such an alteration is rather difficult to achieve with nerve impulses, and that, even if an alteration is achieved, the new type of proteins would hardly have a functional significance. They proposed an alternative theory in which repetitive stimulation of a neuron leads to an increased synthesis of particular species of RNA molecules, which enhance the synthesis of a set of enzymes required for the formation and degradation of transmitter substances (Briggs & Kitto, 1962). The theory is influenced by the concept of enzyme induction.

3. AN ERA OF DISCOVERIES: 1961-1963

The macromolecular theories generated new lines of research. Discoveries were successively reported from many laboratories, people were excited, and optimism prevailed. There was little time for criticism.

The Swedish scientists continued their microchemical analysis of neurons. Hydén and Egyházi (1962, 1963) trained rats to climb an inclined wire in order to obtain food, and then excised neurons and glia from the vestibular nucleus. After a few days of training, the proportion of adenine in the neuronal RNA increased, and cytosine decreased, while no appreciable change was observed in glial RNA. The same investigators (Egyházi & Hydén, 1961) also attempted to augment RNA synthesis by injecting rabbits with tricyano-amino-propene (TCAP) and found changes in the base compositions of neuronal and glial RNA. Egyházi and Hydén (1961) interpreted these results as representing the synthesis of a particular species of RNA in the neurons while another species was produced in the glia cells.

A direct approach to memory facilitation based on the RNA hypothesis was carried out by Cameron and Solyom (1961). They administered RNA orally or intravenously to geriatric patients, and observed general improvement in the patients' memory. Cook et al. (1963) injected rats with RNA and observed faster learning and slower extinction of a shock escape response.

In contrast to these attempts at the facilitation of learning and memory, studies were also designed to interfere with mnemonic process using antimetabolites. Dingman and Sporn (1961) injected rats with 8-azaguanine and observed an impairment in the learning of a maze task. Since 8-azaguanine is incorporated into cerebral RNA, the experimenters suggested that the behavioral impairment may have resulted from the inhibition of enzyme synthesis.

Flexner et al. (1963) used puromycin to interfere with the RNA-dependent synthesis of proteins. Mice were trained in a maze and several days later the drug was injected directly into the brain. The drug-injected animals demonstrated an impairment in later performance of the learned task. These experimenters were quite aware of the possibility that the drugs may have influenced behavior by mechanisms other than protein synthesis inhibition. Nevertheless, the findings were impressive and provided some strong support for macromolecular theories.

The significance of RNA in memory was also tested in an invertebrate. Corning and John (1961) trained planarians to perform a conditioned response, and then dissected the heads from the tails. The tails allowed to regenerate in pond water retained the conditioned response, but those regenerated in a solution with added ribonuclease did not. In another interesting study conducted with planaria, McConnell (1962) trained planarians on a conditioned response, minced them, and fed them to naive planarians. The worms fed with the trained worms demonstrated the conditioned response. Subsequently, Zelman et al. (1963) suggested that the effective ingredient was RNA in the trained worm.

While these macromolecular experiments were being conducted, the Berkeley group entered into a new phase of research. They (Krech et al., 1960; Rosenzweig et al., 1962) found that mice reared in an enriched environment (with toys and peers in a large cage) developed heavier cerebral cortices containing a higher concentration of ChE as compared with the isolated control animals. The increase in weight was greater than the increase in ChE, thus the specific ChE activity per unit weight of cerebral tissue was reduced. Furthermore, those raised in the enriched environment showed less errors in reversal learning, so that the error scores were highly correlated to the cortical/subcortical ChE ratio (Krech et al., 1960).

A new field of research was clearly established by 1963, following varied approaches but having one purpose, the biochemical study of learning and memory. Dingman and Sporn (1964) examined the findings up to 1963, and concluded that there was no single chemical substance that could be regarded as the engram of memory. They warned of an overemphasis upon biochemical mechanisms, and called attention to the idea of reverberatory circuits.

The reverberatory circuit was first hypothesized by Lorente de Nó (1938) as a model for the retention of neural activity, and later incorporated into the concept of cell assembly by Hebb (1949). A memory stored as reverberating impulses is unlikely to be permanent, because any stimulus that excites or inhibits the neurons in the circuit would easily interrupt the reverberation. Hebb (1949), therefore, assumed that synaptic structure of the neurons involved in the circuit would undergo a morphological change while the neurons are repetitively excited by the reverberating impulses. Thus, a memory is retained by two distinct processes: temporarily by reverberation, and then permanently by a morphological change.

The dual-process theory was supported by experimental findings on retrograde amnesia. Glickman (1961) reviewed the studies in which various treatments (electroconvulsive shock, anoxia, hypothermia, anesthesia, and brain stimulation) were given shortly after learning, and concluded that the resulting retrograde amnesia could best be accounted for by assuming consolidation of a relatively fragile memory trace into a more stable and pernament one. Gaito and Zavala (1964) substituted what was thought to be a morphological change in 1949 with a chemical change in macro-molecules, and integrated the dual-process theory with the macromolecular theory of memory.

4. CHEMICAL ANALYSIS OF LEARNING: CORRELATION STUDIES

For several years, the field of correlational study was dominated by the Swedish group because of their technical excellence in microchemical analysis. The wire climbing task which Hydén and Egyházi (1962, 1963) used in their experiments was quite inadequate for the study of learning effects. Although they had a control group which was passively rotated, the chemical differences between the trained and control animals may have simply reflected the degree in which the vestibular system was stimulated. Therefore, Hydén and Egyházi (1964) introduced a new task. Rats were trained to obtain food by reaching to the bottom of a tube using a nonpreferred forepaw, and the neurons in the motor cortex were analyzed for their RNA base compositions. The cortex contralateral to the trained forepaw was considered to be trained, while the ipsilateral cortex was designated as an untrained control. The neurons from the trained cortex contained more RNA with more adenine and less cytosine as compared with the neurons from the untrainsed side (Hydén & Egyházi, 1964). The effects were relatively small at the early stages of learning, and increased as training continued for many days (Hydén & Lange, 1965). The daily accumulation of the effect suggests that the molecular change lasts more than a day. Nasello and Izquierdo (1969) also reported an increase in hippocampal RNA, which lasted for two days after the last trial of an avoidance training.

Another line of analytical study was initiated by Glassman and his associates, using radioisotopes. Zemp et al. (1966) injected radioactive uridine directly into the mouse brain before a shock-avoidance training, and examined the incorporation of the radioactive precursor into cerebral RNA during the training period. The results indicated that the rate of RNA synthesis was higher in the brain of the trained animals than in the brain of the yoked control animals. The enhanced RNA synthesis was observed in the ribosomal and nuclear RNA. In subsequent experiments, they demonstrated that the major site of enhancement is in the diencephalon and associated structures (Zemp et al., 1967). The effect was confirmed in somewhat different learning situations, in adrenalectomized and hypophysectomized mice, and in the goldfish (Adair et al., 1968a,b; Glassman et al., 1966; Glassman, 1970; Kahan et al., 1970; Coleman et al., 1971; Uphouse et al., 1972a,b). The period of enhanced RNA synthesis lasted about 15-30 min.

It should be noted that intraventricular injection of radioactive precursors results in an uneven incorporation: heavier along the ventricular walls and sharply declining in the distant structures (Altman & Chorover, 1963). Physiological (Grafstein, 1956) and behavioral (Bohdanecka et al., 1967) effects of needle insertion are not negligible either. Yanagiha and Hydén (1971) recently conducted a radioautographic experiment along with their usual analytical experiment. According to their observation, the incorporation of leucine injected directly in the brain was quite irregular: generally heavier in the dorsal regions than in the ventral regions. Dark brown pigmentation, suggestive of hemorrhage, was observed in the dorsal surface of the hippocampus.

Bowman and Strobel (1969) avoided these problems by intravenous injection. They implanted a cannula into the jugular vein of the rat, and injected radioactive cytidine without anesthetizing the animal. A preliminary training on a position discrimination task was given first, then the injection, followed by a series of reversal training sessions. The control group continued the original task without the reversals, thereby maintaining almost equivalent sensory stimulation, motor activity, and motivational level. The reversal training increased RNA synthesis in the hippocampus, but not in any other major structures in the brain.

An ingenious method was developed by Machlus and Gaito (1968a) to determine the amount of RNA unique to a behavioral task. They severed the strands of DNA molecules, and hybridized the split DNA with RNA twice. If the first RNA is complementary to DNA, hybridization does not occur on the second application of RNA. If, however, the first RNA is not totally complementary, then there is room for the second RNA to hybridize and become resistant to ribonuclease. Machlus and Gaito (1968a, b, 1969) incorporated radioactive orotic acid into RNA of experimental (or control) animals, and determined the amount of radioactive RNA hybridized. The experimental group was trained on a shock-avoidance task, while the control group was rotated in a tread mill. Species of RNA that were not in the control animal's brain were found in the experimental animal's brain. More interestingly, however, the control animal's brain did not contain any unique species of RNA that was not found in the experimental animal's brain.

The synthesis of new RNA molecules would certainly lead to changes in subsequent synthesis of proteins, quantitative and qualitative. Altman and Das observed an increase in the incorporation of radioactive leucine into neuronal proteins after a motor exercise (Altman & Das, 1966) and a stressful stimulation (Das & Altman, 1966), but not after visual discrimination learning (Altman et al., 1966).

In contrast, Hydén and Lange (1968) did observe an increase in leucine incorporation into proteins in the hippocampal CA3 pyramidal neurons after the handedness-transfer training. Protein synthesis was enhanced more in the hippocampus contralateral to the trained paw than in the ipsilateral hippocampus of the trained rats. There was no enhancement in the hippocampus of the control animals which continued to use the preferred paw. Hydén and Lange (1970) further separated the hippocampal proteins by electrophoresis, and found increases in the synthesis of two protein fractions (fractions 4 and 5). They also found the third fraction unique to the trained animals, which had the characteristics of S-100 (the brain-specific acidic protein). The unique fraction was present in the animals that were retrained after 14 days of rest, but not in those who had 30 days of rest period. Using radioautography, Beach et al. (1969) examined the incorporation of leucine into proteins after shock-avoidance training. They found the increased protein synthesis in the hippocampus in CA1 area rather than CA3.

The shift of interest from the motor cortex to the hippocampus reflects the findings of electroencephalography. The hippocampus produces a conspicuous pattern of electrical activity, theta waves, in correlation with various patterns of motor activity (Vanderwolf, 1969). Systematic changes in the hippocampal electrical activity was observed during the course of learning (Adey, 1961; Grastyán, 1961) and were thought, in the 1960s, to be related directly to learning rather than to a systematic change in motor activity as a result of learning. Another factor which contributed to investigators' attention to the hippocampus was a report by Scoville and Milner (1957) that bilaterally hippocampectomized patients demonstrate memory deficits. More recent studies, however, indicated that such patients do show good memory of nonverbal tasks (Ervin & Anders 1970). Animal studies, in which the tasks must be nonverbal, have also indicated that the hippocampus is not necessarily a critical focus of memory storage (Douglas, 1967).

Gaito and his associates (Gaito et al., 1968a, b, 1969) measured the relative amount of proteins per unit RNA, and relative amount of RNA per unit DNA, in 10 subdivisions of the rat brain after learning of a shock-avoidance task and a water maze. They observed a relative increase or decrease of proteins in the medial-ventral and medial-dorsal cortices, but not in the hippocampus. Bogoch (1968) examined cerebral protein fractions in pigeons after training them on discrimination tasks. There was a fraction of proteins that increased after learning and remained increased for several months (fraction 11A) and another fraction that increased immediately after learning, then decreased (fraction 10B). Both of these protein fractions were rich in bound carbohydrate moieties. Bogoch (1968), therefore, proposed that memory may be coded in the glycoprotein molecules.

5. BEHAVIORAL ASSAY OF MEMORY SUBSTANCES: TRANSFER STUDIES

The mere fact that a unique substance is produced in the brain as a result of learning does not necessarily mean that such substances constitute the engram. Since the process of learning involves complex activities of the brain, it may result in the production of various substances: some of them may facilitate learning, some may impair it, and some others may have no effect. If the information provided by a learning experience is encoded into the molecular structure as hypothesized by Gaito (1961), then the presence of the encoded molecules in a proper locus in the brain would ensure the occurrence of a learned behavior. Therefore, whether a chemical substance has been encoded or not may potentially be tested by a behavioral assay. This was the basic logic underlying the earlier studies on the transfer of memory.

It is rather unfortunate that the first transfer experiment was conducted with planaria (McConnell, 1962), because in this species conditioning itself is a questionable phenomenon (Halas et al., 1962; Hullett & Homzie, 1966; Reynierse, 1967). Hartry et al. (1964) was able to observe the facilitation of conditioned response in planarians fed with trained planarians, as reported by McConnell (1962). However, they also found that the worms fed with untrained worms exposed to photic stimuli only, or handling only, showed performance superior to naive planarians.

The first series of transfer experiments in mammals were reported in 1965. Babich (1965a) trained donor rats to approach a food cup, extracted crude RNA from the trained donors, and injected it intraperitoneally into naive recipient rats. The recipients demonstrated the approach response. In a subsequent experiment Jacobson et al. (1965) gave a differential training to the donors: an approach response was reinforced if it was made in the presence of visual stimulus, but not if it was made with an auditory stimulus. The recipients demonstrated the differential responses. Babich et al. (1965b) reported a similar transfer of learned response from one species of donors to another species of recipients (hamsters to rats). About the same time, a group of Danish research workers reported the transfer of a light-dark discrimination learning by intracisternal injection of RNA from trained donors to naive recipients (Fjerdingstad et al., 1965; Nissen et al., 1965; Røigaard-Petersen et al., 1968).

These reports of successful transfer were immediately followed by a number of papers from other laboratories reporting failure of confirmation (Gross & Carey, 1965; Byrne et al., 1966; Luttges et al., 1966). Why transfer was successful in some laboratories but not in others has not been resolved. There is a question as to whether the donor's RNA can enter the nervous system or the neurons of the recipients. Luttges et al. (1966) demonstrated that intraperitoneally injected radioactive RNA does not cross the blood-brain barrier. With regard to intracisternal injection, there has been no experimental evidence for distribution or localization.

The presence of encoded molecules may lead to a successful transfer of memory, but a successful transfer experiment does not necessarily prove the presence of encoded molecules. The brain, or any other organ may produce a chemical substance in response to sensory stimulation or motor activity as involved in the learning of a particular task. The substance may remain in the brain, or be taken into the brain, and may possibly facilitate the performance of the learned task. The substance need not be encoded. There have been experiments which advocate the latter possibility.

Ungar and Oceguera-Navarro (1965) observed a transfer of habituation to a sound stimulus by a brain extract. Later, Ungar et al (1968) reported a transfer of passive avoidance learning. The effective substance was found to be synthesized in the brain 12-24 hr after training, and hydrolyzed in the presence of trypsin. They suggested a basic peptide with 6-10 amino acids as a probable effective substance. Albert (1966) trained rats on a shock-avoidance task under a unilateral cortical depression, and then excised cortical tissue from the undepressed, that is, the trained side of the brain. The tissue was homogenized and injected back to the same animals intraperitoneally. The injected rats demonstrated the learned response under a spreading depression of the trained cortex.

In another research strategy, Bohus and de Wied (1966) injected rats with a peptide constituted of the first 10 amino acids of adrenocortico-trophic hormone (ACTH), and observed that the extinction of a shock-avoidance response was retarded. That is, the initial segment of the ACTH molecules had an effect similar to the whole ACTH molecule. Also, a similar peptide in which d-phenylalanine, replaced l-phenylalanine at the 7th position, facilitated the extinction of an avoidance response. Since ACTH is secreted from the adenohypophysis in response to a stressful stimulus, Bohus and de Wied (1966) suggested that the substance effective in transfer of avoidance responses may be the ACTH fragments.

6. PHARMACOLOGICAL FACILITATION OF LEARNING AND MEMORY

The earlier clinical report that exogenous RNA improved memory (Cameron & Solyom, 1961) attracted the interest of many psychiatrists, psychologists, and pharmacologists for the obvious practical reason (Brown, 1966; Cohen & Barondes, 1968 a,b; Corson & Enesco, 1966; Solyon et al., 1966; Wagner et al., 1966; Siegel, 1967, 1968). However, their experimental findings were equivocal: some of them confirmed the facilitation of memory, others did not.

In 1966, research workers at Abbott Laboratories reported that a new drug, magnesium pemoline, increased the activity of RNA polymerase in vitro and in vivo (Glasky & Simon, 1966). A behavioral experiment reported at the same time from the same laboratory (Plotnikoff, 1966) indicated that the oral administration of pemoline facilitated learning and later retention of an avoidance task in the rat. Many behavioral experiments were conducted using this drug, but the results were equivocal (Cyert et al., 1967; Frey & Polidora, 1967; Gurowitz et al., 1967; Lubar et al., 1967; Doty & Howard, 1968; Gaito et al., 1968a; Bianchi & Marazzi-Uberti, 1969; Plotnikoff, 1969). Morris et al. (1967) examined the effect of intraperitoneally administered pemoline upon cerebral RNA synthesis, but they did not find any increase either in the total amount of RNA or in uridine incorporation into RNA after injection. Stein and Yellin (1967) of Abbott Laboratories re-examined the pemoline effect on RNA polymerase in vitro and in vivo. No increase in the enzyme activity was observed either in carcinoma cell culture or in the rat brain.

Another substance believed to enhance RNA synthesis is tricyano-aminopropene (TCAP) (Egyházi & Hydén, 1961). Essman (1966) injected mice with this drug for 3 days, and examined the effect of ECS. The drug-injected animals showed a higher concentration of RNA in the cerebral cortex, and were more resistent to the amnesic effect of electroconvulsive shock (ECS). Brush et al. (1966) could not find any facilitatory effect of this drug on learning or retention of a shock-avoidance task and a maze task. Buckholtz and Bowman, (1970) failed to confirm Essman's findings of ECS resistance or change in RNA concentration.

Facilitation of memory has also been explored outside the framework of macromolecular theory. McGaugh and his associates continued their experiments on the facilitatory effect of strychnine on learning (McGaugh & Thompson, 1962). An important development in their research was made when they discovered that strychnine facilitated learning even when it was injected after each daily training trial (McGaugh et al., 1962). They substantiated their findings with more experiments, and came to the conclusion that strychnine facilitates consolidation of memory (Hudspeth, 1964; McGaugh & Petrinovich, 1965; McGaugh, 1966). The time interval in which the posttrial injection was effective was about 15-30 min, somewhat similar to the time interval in which ECS has an amnesic effect. Prien et al. (1963) were unable to demonstrate the strychnine effect, but the absence of the effect may have been due to the drug dosage. According to McGaugh and Krivanek (1970), strychnine is effective at a low and a high dosage levels, but not at an intermediate dosage.

A word of caution is due. Cooper and Krass (1963) found that proactive facilitatory effect of strychnine lasts more than 72 hr. If the retroactive effect of strychnine is tested within a few days after injection, the results would be inflated by the proactive effect.

A retroactive facilitation similar to the strychnine effect has been found with other analeptic drugs: picrotoxin (Garg & Holland, 1968a), Caffeine (Paré 1961), and pentylene-tetrazol (Irwin & Benuazizi, 1966). An opposite effect (retroactive amnesia) was found with posttrial injection of pentobarbital (Garg & Holland, 1968b). It may be that whereas the neural stimulants facilitated, the anesthetic agent suppressed the formation of a structural or chemical substrate of memory, as McGaugh (1966) hypothesized. It may also be that the effects of the stimulants were conditioned to the learning situation, and that the conditioned excitation facilitated performance in retention testing.

In the meantime, evidence has accumulated that ACh may be one of the transmitter substances in the brain (Reeves, 1966; Hebb, 1970). Carlton (1963) reviewed pharmacological studies using cholinergic and anticholinergic drugs, and proposed a theory that the cholinergic system may play a critical role in learning by selectively antagonizing the effects of reticular activating system, thus suppressing nonreinforced responses.

Deutsch and his associates initiated a series of experiments injecting a cholinergic drug, diisopropyl fluorophosphate (DFP), into the rat hippocampus (Deutsch et al., 1966). The drug prolongs the effect of ACh at the synaptic site by inhibiting the activity of ChE. They trained rats on a discrimination task, and after various time intervals tested them for the retention of the learned task. DFP was dissolved in peanut oil and injected into the hippocampus 24 hr before the retention test. The performance of the task was interfered with if the task had been learned either 30 min or 5 days before the test, but not if it had been learned 3 days or 14 days before the test (Deutsch et al., 1966). The task learned 28 days before the test was improved by DFP injection (Deutsch & Leibowitz, 1966). Similar results were obtained with another cholinergic drug, physostigmine, injected intraperitoneally (Hamburg, 1967). Scopolamine, an anticholinergic drug, had an opposite effect: interference with the 3-day old memory but not with the 7-day old memory (Wiener & Deutsch, 1968).

Deutsch (1971) accounted for these complicated effects of cholinergic and anticholinergic drugs by assuming that the cholinergic postsynaptic sites increase their excitability after learning. According to his explanation, there are two sets of cholinergic neurons. In the first type of neurons, the excitability increases immediately after learning, and then returns to a normal level in a few days. In the second type of neurons, it increases to a maximum in a week or so, then declines after several weeks. If cholinergic drugs are given at the height of the synaptic excitability they block impulse transmission by flooding the synaptic site with ACh; if the drugs are given when cholinergic excitability has returned to a relatively low level, they improve performance. Squire et al. (1971) suggested that the drugs injected intra- peritoneally may have interfered with performance by acting upon the peripheral cholinergic neurons. With regard to the hippocampal injection of DFP, there have not been any electrographic or microscopic studies of its cytotoxic effect.

It is interesting to note that ECS increases the activity of acetylcholinesterase (AChE), ChE specific to ACh. Adams et al. (1969) found that the AChE level increased immediately after ECS, and proposed a hypothesis that the amnesic effect of ECS is due to a high level of ACh in the brain. To test this hypothesis, they injected cholinergic and anticholinergic drugs after ECS treatment, and examined their effect on retrograde amnesia. Scopolamine (anticholinergic) was antagonistic, and physostigmine (cholinergic) was synergistic to ECS. However, there is a problem of dissociation (state-dependent learning). Scopolamine and physostigmine both produce dissociation from the normal state (Overton, 1966), and they are related to the dissociable state produced by ECS (Gardner et al., 1972). In fact, Lewis and Bregman (1972) were unable to find any effect of these drugs on ECS-produced amnesia when they tested their animals 24 hr after drug injection.

Suggestions have been made that adrenergic (Roberts et al., 1970) and serotonergic (Essman, 1968) systems may be involved in memory storage, but their mechanisms remain to be investigated.

7. INTERFERENCE WITH THE FORMATION OF MEMORY TRACES.

Attempts have been made to interfere with memory by inhibiting brain RNA synthesis with an antibiotic actinomycin D. Barondes and Jarvik (1964) were able to achieve an 87% inhibition of cerebral RNA synthesis in mice by intracranial injection of this drug, but the mortality rate was so high that the animals required testing within a short period of time before they began to deteriorate. As far as testing permitted, the animals learned a conditioned suppression of locomotor activity, and retained it well. Similar results were obtained with position discrimination tasks (Appel, 1965; Cohen & Barondes, 1968a,b) and in a conditioned inhibition of bar-pressing response (Goldsmith, 1967).

Agranoff et al. (1967) used goldfish which survived long enough to test for long-term memory. They found that the fish injected with the drug within 1 hr after learning of an avoidance task showed a deficit in the performance of learned response 4 days later. Squire and Barondes (1970) injected actimonycin D into the temporal area of the mouse before or after training them on a discrimination task. In a retention test conducted 27 hr after injection, the performance of learned response was impaired in the animals injected 3 hr before or 1 day after learning, but not in those injected 7 days after learning.

Nakajima (1969) found that injection of actinomycin D into the hippocampal area produced epileptiform electrical activity, and suggested that the behavioral effect of this drug might be based upon abnormal hippocampal discharges. In a subsequent study (Nakajima, 1972), it was found that the behavioral effect of actinomycin was proactive; that is, the drug interfered with the performance of a discrimination task regardless of the time when the task had originally been learned. The time course of the behavioral effect coincided with the development of the electrographic abnormality. Daniels (1971) reported an amnesic effect of actinomycin in the rats in a one-trial approach learning situation, but a question remains as to whether the animals' motivation for water persisted after drug injection.

The effects of protein synthesis inhibitors on memory have been chiefly investigated with three drugs: puromycin, acetoxycycloheximide, and cycloheximide. Mice injected intracranially with puromycin showed deficits in the performance of previously learned tasks (Flexner et al., 1963, 1964, 1965a,b, 1967), even though they could learn and retain new tasks for a period shortly after the injection (Barondes & Cohen, 1966). Similar effects were also found in goldfish (Agranoff & Klinger, 1964; Davis et al., 1965; Agranoff et al., 1965, 1966; Potts & Bitterman, 1967), quails (Mayor, 1969), and salmon (Oshima et al., 1969).

Initially, the puromycin effects were thought to indicate a loss of long-term memory due to the inhibition of brain protein synthesis. However, Cohen et al. (1966) observed abnormal electrographic activity in the hippocampus of the drug-injected animals, and suggested that the behavioral effect may be due to the seizure activity in the limbic system (Cohen & Barondes, 1967). Flexner and Flexner (1968) found that the amnesic effect of puromycin disappeared if physiological saline was injected into the brain regions where puromycin had been injected. Flexner and Flexner (1968) found that the injected puromycin remained in the brain for a long period of time as peptidil puromycin. Roberts et al. (1970) found that injection of adrenergic drugs eliminated the amnesic effect of puromycin. At any rate, the major effect of puromycin is to produce electrographic seizure activity in the limbic system, making the animals incapable of performing certain tasks. The impairment is not immediate, but occurs after a period of several hours, so that the animals appear to have lost the memory of a previously learned task after having demonstrated retention for several hours (see Chapter 7).

Acetoxycycloheximide is another chemical substance that was reported to inhibit protein synthesis (Flexner & Flexner, 1966). The amnesic effect of this substance has been observed by a number of investigators (Flexner et al., 1967; Cohen & Barondes, 1968a,b; Swanson et al., 1969; Serota, 1971; Serota et al., 1972). It should be noted, however, that all the investigators used a substance once supplied through the courtesy of a single manufacturer. It is unfortunate that the substance is not available to other investigators, and the evaluation of the biochemical and behavioral findings using acetoxycyloheximide cannot be made until such time as the drug again becomes available.

Cycloheximide is structurally similar to acetoxycyloheximide. Barondes and Cohen (1967) found that intracranial injection of this drug to the mouse produces suppression of cerebral protein synthesis for about 8 hr.

The injected animals, however, learned a shock-escape T-maze task during the suppression period, and retained it well three days later (Barondes & Cohen, 1967). The same investigators subsequently demonstrated an amnesic effect in mice for an appetitive learning situation following subcutaneous injection with this drug (Cohen & Barondes, 1968a,b). The animals were trained to run for water while 97% of cerebral protein synthesis was suppressed. When they were tested from 6 hr to 7 days later, they did not show any signs of memory. The amnesic effect of subcutaneously injected cycloheximide was further confirmed in a shock-escape T-maze situation (Barondes & Cohen, 1968) and in a passive avoidance situation (Geller et al., 1969, 1970; Randt et al., 1971; Flood et al., 1972). Schneider and Chenoweth (1971) found that subcutaneous injection of cycloheximide resulted in hyperactivity, but Segal et al. (1971) ascertained that the amnesic effect could be separated from the hyperactivity.

The absence of seizure activity, the almost complete suppression of cerebral protein synthesis (94-97%), the ease of subcutaneous injection, and the ease of availability of the drug made cycloheximide the drug of choice for recent studies on memory interference, and the findings with this drug were taken as the most unequivocal demonstrations of the macromolecular basis of memory (Barondes, 1970). Andry and Luttges (1972) compared the amnesic effects of cycloheximide and ECS, and distinguished two kinds of memory: one abolished by ECS but resistant to cycloheximide, and the other resistant to ECS but susceptible to cycloheximide. The former was considered to last about 120 min, the latter completed in about 60 min. These findings strongly supported the dual-process theory of memory.

There are a few conflicting findings. Squire et al. (1970) exposed mice to a novel environment after cycloheximide injection, and found that the animal's habituation to the environment remained normal. The findings indicate that the memory of the environment was retained in the absence of cerebral protein synthesis. Furthermore, the memory apparently lost by cycloheximide has been reported to recover spontaneously (Quartermain & McEwen, 1970) or after a reminder foot-shock (Quartermain et al., 1970). Injection of cycloheximide before the reminder shock abolished the recovery effect (Quartermain et al., 1972). Nakajima (unpublished observation) recently found that cycloheximide does not produce the usual amnesic effect in adrenalectomized mice. The critical effect of subcutaneously injected cycloheximide may be the inhibition of adreno-cortical protein synthesis and not related to brain proteins. It should be recalled that cycloheximide did not produce amnesic effect when injected directly into the brain (Barondes & Cohen, 1967). In an appetitive learning situation also, the previous report of amnesia (Cohen & Barondes, 1968) appears to be based on a confounding effect of this drug on the gastrointestinal system (see Chapter 7). Thus, it is still too early to conclude that cycloheximide produces amnesia by interfering with cerebral protein synthesis.

The aforementioned findings (Roberts et al., 1970) indicating an adrenergic mediation of antagonism toward the effects of puromycin-induced inhibition of cerebral protein synthesis are perhaps related to the suggestion that cerebral protein synthesis and acquisition of adrenergically dependent avoidance behaviors may be dependent upon catecholamine availability (Kety, 1972). This view has been supported behaviorally in that inhibition of catecholamine synthesis with α-methyl-ρ-tyrosine interfered with the acquision of avoidance behavior by mice (Essman, 1970); with regard to cerebral protein synthesis, inhibition with electro-convulsive shock was attenuated when mice were injected intracranially with small amounts of norepinephrine or normetanephrine at critical times prior to ECS. The effect was further localized to synaptic sites for which the ECS-induced protein synthesis inhibition could be attenuated by catecholamines (Essman, 1973).

Another consideration relevant to the present discussion is the cellular site and nature of those proteins, the inhibition of which are relevant to memory processing, storage, and/or retrieval. Potent antimetabolites, while effecting the inhibition of a large range of microsomal and mitochondrial proteins may be proportionately less specific for proteins associated with other subcellular sites for which the synthesis of proteins has been given some attention; namely, membrane sites and components within the synaptosomal unit.

Ideally endogenous changes, particularly alterations in those substrates which may potentially contribute to events regulating protein synthesis, may represent a separate approach to the same general problem. A role for at least one endogenous substrate, 5-hydroxytryptamine (5-HT), a putative transmitter molecule in brain, has been assigned some significance for its parallel changes concomitant with amnesic agents or events and its inhibitory effect upon cerebral protein synthesis (Essman, 1970, 1971, 1972). This relationship has been further developed in Chapter 9, but it may be pointed out additionally that the amnnesic effect of posttraining treatments leading to alterations in brain 5-HT metabolism or concentration and inhibition of cerebral protein synthesis can be significantly attenuated by pretreatment with a number of compounds; these include such agents as nicotine, uric acid, or compounds that reduce 5-HT (Essman, 1973). This effect is also manifest behaviorally as an antagonism of the retrograde amnesic effect of either ECS or intracranial 5-HT. While this approach holds promise in relating possible changes at synaptic sites to cerebral protein synthesis and the implications that this holds for learning and memory processes, considerable additional data are required to relate transmitter interactions to the synthesis of specific proteins relevant to memory processes.

8. Concluding Comments

In 1929, Lashley wrote: "The whole theory of learning and of intelligence is in confusion. We know at present nothing of the organic basis of these functions and little enough of either the variety or uniformities of their expression in behavior." The situation appears to be little better at present. There have been important finds; there have been theories. They have all contributed to some of the confusion in the field, but little to the solution of problems.

Search and research over the past ten years had demonstrated that macromolecules in the brain show systematic changes, quantitative and qualitative, during the process of learning. Some of the changes are long-lasting, possibly as long as memory lasts. However, the presence of a correlation does not necessarily indicate a causal relationship. To demonstrate causality requires experimental manipulation of the chemical substances. A quantitative or qualitative change in a specific molecule must result in a change in behavior, i.e., facilitation of learning or disruption of memory. Yet, no one has found a method for facilitating the synthesis of RNA or proteins in the brain; no substance has been available to disrupt macromolecular synthesis without producing multiple effects. Thus, macromolecular theory of memory still remains untested. Search for other molecules has also been unsuccessful. It is quite obvious that some electrolytes and transmitter substances in the central nervous system are involved in learning: there is no behavior that does not involve these chemicals. What is required is the elucidation of mechanisms with which these chemicals contribute to a lasting change in behavior. The search for the engram has been assisted by methodological and conceptual maps, but the critical crossroads of sites and mechanisms remain to be ascertained and charted.

Preparation of this material was partially supported by National Research Council of Canada Grant AO233 (to S.N.).

REFERENCES

Adair, L. B., Wilson, J. E., Zemp, J. W., and Glassman, E. (1968a) Brain function and macromolecules. III. Uridine incorporation into polysomes of mouse brain during short term avoidance conditioning. *Proc. Nat. Acad. Sci.* **61**, 606-613.

Adair, L. B., Wilson, J. E., and Glassman, E. (1968b) Brain function and macromolecules. IV. Uridine incorporation into polysomes of mouse brain during different behavioral experiences. *Proc. Nat. Acad. Sci.* **61**, 917-922.

Adams, H. E., Hoblit, P. R., and Sutker, P. B. (1969) Electroconvulsive shock, brain acetylcholinesterase activity and memory. *Physiol. Behav.* **4**, 113-116.

Adey, W. R. (1961) Studies of hippocampal electrical activity during approach learning. In *Brain Mechanisms and Learning*, A. Fessard, R. W. Gerard, J. Konorski, and J. F. Delafresnaye, Eds., Blackwells, Oxford, pp. 577-588.

Agranoff, B. W. and Klinger, P. D. (1964) Puromycin effect on memory fixation in the goldfish. *Science* **146**, 952-953.

Agranoff, B. W., Davis, R. E. and Brink, J. J. (1965) Memory fixation in the goldfish. *Proc. Nat. Acad. Sci.* **54**, 788-793.

Agranoff, B. W., Davis, R. E., and Brink, J.J. (1966) Chemical studies on memory fuxation in goldfish. *Brain Res.* **1**, 303-309.

Agranoff, B. W., Davis, R. E., Casola, L., and Lim, R. (1967) Acetinomycin-D blocks formation of memory of shock-avoidance in goldfish. *Science* **158**, 1600-1601.

Albert, D. J. (1966) Memory in mammals: Evidence for a system involving nuclear ribonucleic adic. *Neuropsychologia* **4**, 79-92.

Altman, J. and Chorover, S. L. (1963) Autoradiographic investigation of the distribution and utilization of intraventricularly injected adenine-^{3}H, uracil-^{3}H, and thimidine-^{3}H in the brains of cats. *J. Physiol.* **169**, 770-779.

Altman, J. and Das, G. D. (1966a) Behavioral manipulations and protein metabolism of the brain: Effects of motor exercise on the utilization of leucine-H^3. *Physiol. Behav.* **1**, 105-108.

Altman, J., Das, G. D., and Chang, J. (1966b) Behavioral manipulations and protein metabolism of the brain: Effects of visual training on the utilization of leucine-H^3. *Physiol. Behav.* **1**, 111-115.

Andry, D. K. and Luttges, M. W. (1972) Memory traces: Experimental separation by cycloheximide and electroconvulsive shock. *Science* 1972, **178**, 518-520.

Appel, S. H. (1965) Effects of inhibition of RNA synthesis on neural information storage. *Nature* **207**, 1163-1166.

Astin, A. W. and Ross, S. (1960) Glutamic acid and human intelligence. *Psychol. Bull.* **57**, 429-434.

Babich, F. R., Jacobson, A. L., Bubash, S., and Jacobson, A. (1965a) Transfer of a response to naive rats by injection of ribonucleic acid extracted from trained rats. *Science* **149**, 656-657.

Babich, F. R., Jacobson, A. L., and Bubash, S. (1965b) Cross-species transfer of learning: Effect of ribonuleic acid from hamsters on rat behavior. *Proc. Nat. Acad. Sci.* **54**, 1299-1302.

Barondes, S. H. (1970) Cerebral protein synthesis inhibitors block long-term memory. *Internat. Rev. Neurobiol.* **12**, 177-205.

Barondes, S. H. and Cohen, H. D. (1968) Arousal and the conversion of "short-term" to "long-term" memory. *Proc. Nat. Acad. Sci.* **61**, 923-929.

Barondes, S. H. and Cohen, H. D. (1966) Puromycin effect on successive phase of memory storage. *Science* **151**, 594-595.

Barondes, S. H. and Cohen, H. D. Comparative effects of cycloheximide and puromycin on cerebral protein synthesis and consolidation of memory in mice. *Brain Res.* 4, 44-51.

Barondes, S. H. and Jarvik, M. E. (1964) The influence of actinomycin-D on brain RNA synthesis and on memory. *J. Neurochem.* , 187-195.

Beach, G., Emmens, M., Kimble, D. P., and Lickey, M. (1969) Autoradiographic demonstration of biochemical changes in the limbic system during avoidance training. *Proc. Nat. Acad. Sci.* 62, 692-696.

Bianchi, C. and Marazzi-Uberti, E. (1969) Acquisition and retention of a conditioned avoidance response in mice as influenced by pemoline, by some of its derivatives and by some CNS stimulants. *Psychopharmacologia* 15, 9-18.

Bohus, B. and de Wied, D. (1966) Inhibitory and facilitating effects of two related peptides on extinction of avoidance behavior. *Science* 153, 318-320.

Bogoch, S. (1968) *The Biochemistry of Memory*, Oxford University Press, New York.

Bohdanecka, M., Bohdanecky, Z., and Jarvik, M. E. (1967) Amnesic effects of small bilateral brain puncture in the mouse. *Science* 157, 334-336.

Bowman, R. E. and Strobel, D. A. (1969) Brain RNA metabolism in the rat during learning. *J. Compar. Physiol. Psychol.* 67, 448-456.

Briggs, M. H. and Kitto, G. B. (1962) The molecular basis of memory and learning. *Psychol. Rev.* 69, 537-541.

Brown, H. (1966) Effect of ribonucleic acid (RNA) on the rate of lever pressing in rats. *Psychol. Rec.* 16, 173-176.

Brush, F. R., Davenport, J. W., and Polidora, V. J. (1966) TCAP: Negative results in avoidance and water maze learning and retention. *Psychonomic Sci.* 4, 183-184.

Buckholtz, N. S. and Bowman, R. E. (1970) Retrograde amnesia and brain RNA content after TCAP. *Physiol. Behav.* 5, 911-914.

Byrne, W. L., Samuel, D., Bennett, E. L., Rosenzweig, M. R., Wasserman, E., Wagner, A. R. Gardner, F., Galambos, R., Berger, B. D., Margules, D. L., Fenichel, R. L., Stein, L., Corson, J. A., Enesco, H. E., Chorover, S. L., Holt, III, C. E., Schiller, P. H., Chiappetta, L., Jarvik, M. E., Leaf, R. C., Dutcher, J. D., Horovitz, Z. P., and Carlson, P. L. (1966) Memory transfer. *Science* 153, 658-659.

Cameron, D. E. and Solyom, L. (1961) Effects of ribonucleic acid on memory. *Geriatrics* 16, 74-81.

Carlton, P. (1963) Cholinergic mechanisms in the control of behavior by the brain. *Psychol. Rev.* 70, 19-39.

Cohen, H. D., Ervin, F., and Barondes, S. H. (1966) Puromycin and cycloheximide: Different effects on hippocampal electrical activity. *Science* 154, 1557-1558.

Cohen, H. D. and Barondes, S. H. (1967) Puromycin effect on memory may be due to occult seizure. *Science* 157, 333-334.

Cohen H. D. and Barondes, S. H. (1968a) Cycloheximide impairs memory of an appetitive task. *Commun, Behav. Biol.* A-1, 337-340.

Cohen, H. D. and Barondes, S. H. (1968b) Effect of acetoxycycloheximide on learning and memory of a light-dark discrimination. *Nature* 218, 271-273.

Coleman, M. S., Pfingst, B., Wilson, J. E., and Glassman, E. (1971) Brain function and mecromolecules, VIII. Uridine incorporation into brain polysomes of hypophysectomized rat and ovariectomized mice during avoidance conditioning. *Brain Res.* 26, 349-360.

Cook, L., Davidson, A. B., Davis, D. J., Green, H., and Fellows, E. J. (1963) Ribonucleic acid: Effect on conditioned behavior in the rats. *Science* 141, 268-269.

Cooper R. M. and Krass, M. (1963) Strychnine: Duration of effects on maze-learning. *Psychopharmacologia* 4, 472-475.

Corning, W. C. and John, E. R. (1961) Effect of ribonuclease on retention of conditioned response in regenerated planarians. *Science* 134, 1363-1365.

Corson, J. A. and Enesco, H. E. (1966) Some effects of injections of ribonucleic acid. *Psychonomic Sci.* 5, 217-218.

Cyert, L. A., Moyer, K. E., and Chapman, J. A. (1967) Effect of magnesium pemoline on learning and memory of a one-way avoidance response. *Psychonomic Sci.* 7, 9-10.

Daniels, D. (1971) Actinomycin-D: Effects on memory and brain RNA synthesis in an appetitive learning task. *Nature* 231, 395-397.

Das, G. D. and Altman, J. (1966) Behavioral manipulations and protein metabolism of the brain: Effects of restricted and enriched environments on the utilization of leucine-H³. *Physiol. Behav.* 1, 109-110.

Davis, R. E., Bright, P. J., and Agranoff, B. W. (1965) Effect of ECS and puromycin on memory in fish. *J. Compar. Physiol. Psychol.* 60, 162-166.

Deutsch, J. A. (1971) The cholinergic synapse and the site of memory. *Science* 174, 788-794.

Deutsch, J. A., Hamburg, M. D., and Dahl, H. (1966) Anticholinersterase-induced amnesia and its temporal aspects. *Science* 151, 221-223.

Deutsch, J. A. and Leibowitz, S. F. (1966) Amnesia or reversal of forgetting by anticholinesterase, depending simply on time of injection. *Science* 153, 1017-1018.

Dingman, W. and Sporn, M. B. (1961) The incorporation of 8-azaguanine into rat brain RNA and its effect on maze-learning by the rat. An inquiry into the biochemical bases of memory. 1, 1-11.

Dingman, W. and Sporn, M. (1964) Molecular theories of memory. *Science* 144, 26-29.

Doty, B. and Howard, S. (1968) Facilitative effects of post-trial magnesium pemoline on avoidance conditioning in relation to problem difficulty. *Life Sci.* 7, 591-597.

Douglas, R. J. (1967) The hippocampus and behavior. *Psychol. Bull.* 67, 416-442.

Egyházi, E. and Hydén, H. (1961) Experimentally induced changes in the base composition of the ribonucleic acids of isolated nerve cells and their origodendroglial cells. *J. Bioph. Biochem. Cytol.* 10, 403-410.

Ervin, F. R. and Anders, T. R. (1970) Normal and pathological memory: Data and a conceptual scheme. In *The Neurosciences: Second Study Program*, F. O. Schmitt, Ed., Rockefeller Univ. Press, New York, pp. 163-176.

Essman, W. B. (1966) Facilitation of memory consolidation by chemically induced acceleration of RNA synthesis. *Fed. Proc.* 25, 208.

Essman, W. B. (1968) Changes in ECS-induced retrograde amnesia with DBMC: Behavioral and biochemical correlates of brain serotonin antagonism. *Physiol. Behav.* 3, 527-532.

Essman, W. B. (1970) Some neurochemical correlates of altered memory consolidation. *Trans. N.Y. Acad. Sci.* 32, 948-973.

Essman, W. B. (1971) Drug effects and learning memory processes. In *Advances in Pharmacology and Chemotherapy*, Vol. 9, S. Garattini, A. Goldin, F. Hawkings, and I. J. Kobin, Eds., New York, Academic Press, pp. 241-330.

Essman, W. B. (1972) Neurochemical changes in ECS and ECT. *Seminars Psychiat* 4, 67-79.

Essman, W. B. (1973) *Neurochemistry of Cerebral Electroshock.* Spectrum Publ., New York, 1973.

Fessard, A., Gerard, R. W., Konorski, J., and Delafresnaye, J. F. (1961) *Brain Mechanisms and Learning: A Symposium,* Blackwell, Oxford.

Fjerdingstad, E. J., Nissen, T., and Roigaard-Petersen, H. H. (1965) Effect of ribonucleic acid (RNA) extracted from the brain of trained animals on learning in rats. *Scand. J. Psychol.* 6, 1-6.

Flexner, J. B., Flexner, L. B., and Stellar, E. (1963) Memory in mice as affected by intracerebral puromycin. *Science* 141, 57-59.

Flexner, L. B., Flexner, J. B., Roberts, R. B., and de la Haba, G. (1964) Loss of recent memory in mice as related to regional inhibition of cerebral protein synthesis. *Proc. Nat. Acad. Sci.* 52, 1165-1169.

Flexner, L. B., Flexner, J. B., de la Haba, G., and Roberts, R. B. (1965a) Loss of memory as related to inhibition of cerebral protein synthesis. *J. Neurochem.* 12, 535-542.

Flexner, L. B., Flexner, J. B., and Stellar, E. (1965b) Memory and cerebral protein synthesis in mice as affected by graded amounts of puromycin. *Exper. Neurol.* 13, 264-272.

Flexner, L. B. and Flexner, J. B. (1966) Effects of acetoxycycloheximide and of an acetoxycycloheximide-puromycin mixture on cerebral protein synthesis and memory in mice. *Proc. Nat. Acad. Sci.* 55, 369-374.

Flexner, J. B. and Flexner, L. B. (1971) Restoration of expression of memory lost after treatment with puromycin. *Proc. Nat. Acad. Sci.* 57, 1651-1654.

Flexner, L. B., Flexner, J. B., and Roberts, R. B. (1967) Memory in mice analyzed with antibiotics. *Science* 155, 1377-1383.

Flexner, L. B. and Flexner, J. B. (1968) Studies on memory: The long survival of peptidyl-puromycin in mouse brain. *Proc. Nat. Acad. Sci.* 60, 923-927.

Flood, J. F., Bennett, E. L., Rosenzweig, M. R. and Orme, A. E. (1972) Influence of training strength on amnesia induced by pretraining injections of cycloheximide. *Physiol. Behav.* 9, 589-600.

Francis, J. P., Zabarenko, L. M., and Patton, R. A. (1951) The role of amino acid supplementation and dietary protein level in several learning performance of rats. *J. Compar. Physiol. Psychol.* 44, 26-36.

Frey, P. W. and Polidora, V. J. (1967) Magnesium pemoline: Effect on avoidance conditioning in rats. *Science* 155, 1281-1282.

Gaito, J. (1961) A biochemical approach to learning and memory. *Psychol. Rev.* 68, 288-292.

Gaito, J. and Zavala, A. (1964) Neurochemistry and learning. *Psychol. Bull.* 61, 45-62.

Gaito, J., Davison, J. H., and Mottin, J. (1968a) Effects of magnesium pemoline on shock avoidance conditioning and on various chemical measures. *Psychonomic Sci.* 13, 257-258.

Gaito, J., Mottin, J., and Davison, J. H. (1968b) Chemical variation in brain loci during shock avoidance. *Psychonomic Sci.* 13, 41.

Gaito, J., Mottin, J., and Davison, J. H. (1968c) Chemical variation in the ventral hippocampus and other brain sites during conditioned avoidance. *Psychonomic Sci.* 13, 259-260.

Gaito, J., Davison, J. H., and Mottin, J. (1969) Chemical variation in brain loci during water maze performance. *Psychonomic Sci.* 14, 46-48.

Gardner, E. L., Glick, S. D., and Jarvik, M. E. (1972) ECS dissociation of learning and one-way cross-dissociation with physostigmine and scopolamine. *Physiol. Behav.* 8, 11-15.

Garg, M. and Holland, H. C. (1968a) Consolidation and maze learning: The effects of post-trial injections of a stimulant drug (Picrotoxin). *Psychopharmacologia* 12, 96-103.

Garg, M. and Holland, H. C. (1968b) Consolidation and maze learning: The effects of post-trial injection of a depressant drug (Pentobarbital sodium). *Psychopharmacologia* 12, 127-132.

Geller, A., Robustelli, F., Barondes, S. H., Cohen, H. D., and Jarvik, M. E. (1969) Impaired performance by post-trial injections of cycloheximide in a passive avoidance. *Psychopharmacologia* 14, 371-376.

Geller, A., Robustelli, F., and Jarvik, M. E. (1970) A parallel study of the amnesic effects of cycloheximide and ECS under different strengths of conditioning. *Psychopharmacologia* 16, 281-289.

Gerard, R. W. (1961) The fixation of experience. In *Brain Mechanisms and Learning*, A. Fessard, R. W. Gerard, J. Konorski, and J. F. Delafresnaye, Eds., Blackwells, Oxford, oo, 21-32.

Glasky, A. J. and Simon, L. N. (1966) Magnesium pemoline: Enhancement of brain RNA polymerase. *Science* 151, 702-703.

Glassman, E., Schlesinger, K., and Wilson, J. (1966) Increased synthesis of RNA in the brains of goldfish during short-term learning experience. *Fed. Proc.* 25, 713.

Glassman, E. (1970) The incorporation of uridine into brain RNA during short experiences. *Brain Res.* 21, 157-168.

Glickman, S. E. (1961) Perseverative neural processes and consolidation of the memory trace. *Psychol. Bull.* 58, 218-233.

Goldsmith, L. J. (1967) The effect of intracerebral actinomycin D and of electroconvulsive shock on passive avoidance. *J. Compar. Physiol. Psychol.* 63, 126-132.

Grafstein, B. (1956) Mechanism of spreading cortical depression. *J. Neurophysiol.* 19, 154-171.

Grastyán, E. (1961) The significance of the earliest manifestations of conditioning in the mechanism of learning. In *Brain Mechanisms and Learning*. A. Fessard, R. W. Gerard, J. Konorski, and J. F. Delafresnaye, Eds., Blackwells, Oxford, pp. 243-264.

Gross, C. G. and Carey, F. M. (1965) Transfer of learned response by RNA injection: Failure of attempt to replicate. *Science* 150, 1749.

Gurowitz, E. M., Lubar, J. F., Ain, B. R., and Gross, D. A. (1967) Disruption of passive avoidance learning by magnesium pemoline. *Psychonomic Sci.*, 8, 19-20.

Halas, E. S., James, R. L., and Knutson, C. S. (1962) An attempt at classical conditioning in the planarian. *J. Compar. Physiol. Psychol.* 55, 969-971.

Halstead, W. C. (1951) Brain and intelligence. In *Cerebral Mechanisms in Behavior: The Hixon Symposium*, L. A. Jeffress, Ed., Wiley, New York, p. 244-272.

Hamburg, M. D. (1967) Retrograde amnesia produced by intraperitoneal injection of physostigmine. *Science* 156, 973-974.

Hamilton, H. C. and Maher, E. B. (1947) The effects of glutamic acid on the behavior of the white rat. *J. Compar. Physiol. Psychol.* 40, 463-468.

Harlow, H. F. and Woolsey, C. N. (1958) *Biological and Biochemical Bases of Behavior.* Univ. of Wisconsin Press, Madison.

Hartry, A. L., Keith-Lee, P., and Morton, W. D. (1964) Planaria: Memory transfer through cannibalism reexamined. *Science* **146**, 274-275.

Hebb, C. (1970) C.N.S. at the cellular level: Identity of transmitter agents. *Annu. Rev. Physiol.* **32**, 165-192.

Hebb, D. O. (1949) *The Organization of Behavior,* Wiley, New York.

Hudspeth, W. J. (1964) Strychnine: Its facilitatory effect on the solution of a simple oddity problem by the rat. *Science* **145**, 1331-1333.

Hullett, J. W. and Homzie, M. J. (1966) Sensitization effect in the classical conditioning of *Dugesia Dorotocephala. J. Compar. physiol. Psychol.* **62**, 227-230.

Hydén, H. (1959) Quantitative assey of compounds in isolated, fresh nerve cells and glial cells from control and stimulated animals. *Nature* **184**, 433-435.

Hydén, H. (1961) Satellite cells in the nervous system. *Sci. Amer.* **205** (6), 62-70.

Hydén, H. and Egyházi, E. (1962) Nuclear RNA changes of nerve cells during a learning experiment in rats. *Proc. Nat. Acad. Sci.* **48**, 1366-1373.

Hydén, H. and Egyházi, E. (1963) Glial RNA changes during a learning experiment in rats. *Proc. Nat. Acad. Sci.* **49**, 618-624.

Hydén, H. and Egyházi, E. (1964) Changes in RNA content and base composition in cortical neurons of rats in a learning experiment involving transfer of handedness. *Proc. Nat. Acad. Sci.* **52**, 1030-1035.

Hydén, H. and Lange, P. W. (1965) A differentiation in RNA response in neurons early and late during learning. *Proc. Nat. Acad. Sci.* **53**, 946-952.

Hydén, H. and Lange, P. W. (1970) Protein synthesis in the hippocampal pyramidal cells of rats during a behavioral test. *Science*159, 1370-1373.

Hydén, H. and Lange, P. W. (1970) Brain cell protein synthesis specifically related to learning. *Proc. Nat. Acad. Sci.* **65**, 898-904.

Irwin, S. and Benuazizi, A. (1966) Pentylenetetrazol enhances memory function. *Science* **152**, 100-102.

Jacobson, A. L. Babich, F. R., Bubash, S., and Jacobson, A. (1965). Differential approach tendencies produced by injection of ribonucleic acid from trained rats. *Psychonom. Sci, 4,* 3-4.

Kahan, B., Krigman, M. R., Wilson, J. E., and Glassman, E. (1970) Brain function and macromolecules, VI. Autoradiographic analysis of the effect of a brief training experience on the incorporation of uridine into mouse brain. *Proc. Nat. Acad. Sci.* **65**, 300-303.

Kety, S. S. (1972) Biogenic amines of the central nervous system and their possible involvement in emotion and learning. In *Drugs, Development, and Cerebral Function,* W. L. Smith, Ed., C. Thomas, Springfield, Ill., p. 288-304.

Krech, D., Rosenzweig, M. R., Bennett, E. L., and Krueckel, B. (1954) Enzyme concentrations in the brain and adjustive behavior patterns. *Science* **120**, 994-996.

Krech, D., Rosenzweig, M. R., and Bennett, E. L. (1960) Effects of environmental complexity and training on brain chemistry. *J. Compar. Physiol. Psychol.,* **53**, 509-519.

Lashley, K. S. (1963) *Brain Mechanisms and Intelligence,* (University of Chicago Press, Chicago, 1929), Dover Publications, New York.

Lewis, D. J. and Bregman, N. J. (1972) The cholinergic system, amnesia, and memory. *Physiol. Behav.* **8**, 511-514.

Lorente de Nó, R. (1938) Analysis of the activity of the chains of internuncial neurons. *Neurophysiol.* **1**, 207-244.

Lubar, J. F., Boitano, J. J., Gurowitz, E. M., and Ain, B. R. (1967) Enhancement of performance in the Hebb-Williams maze by magnesium pemoline. *Psychonomic Sci.* **7**, 381-382.

Luttges, M., Johnson, T., Buck, C., Holland, H., and McGaugh, J. (1966) An examination of 'transfer of learning' by nucleic acid. *Science* **151**, 834-837.

Machlus, B. and Gaito, J. (1968a) Detection of RNA species unique to a behavioral task. *Psychonomic Sci.* **10**, 253-254.

Machlus, B. and Gaito, J. (1968b) Unique RNA species developed during a shock avoidance task. *Psychonomic Sci.* **12**, 111-112.

Machlus, B. and Gaito, J. (1969) The use of successive competition hybridization to detect RNA species in a shock avoidance task. *Nature* **222**, 573-574.

Marx, M. H. (1948) Effects of supernormal glutamic acid on maze learning. *J. Compar. Physiol. Psychol.* **41**, 82-92.

Marx, M. H. (1949) Relationship between supernormal glutamic acid and maze learning. *J. Compar. Physiol. Psychol.* **42**, 313-319.

Mayor, S. J. (1969) Memory in the Japanese quail: Effects of puromycin and acetoxycycloheximide. *Science* **166**, 1165-1167.

McConnell, J. V. (1962) Memory transfer through cannibalism in planaria. *J. Neuropsychiat.* **3**, (suppl.1), 42-48.

McGaugh, J. L. (1966) Time-dependent processes in memory storage. *Science* **153**, 1351-1358.

McGaugh, J. L. and Petrinovich, L. (1959) The effects of strychnine sulphate on maze learning. *Amer. J. Psychol.* **72**, 99-102.

McGaugh, J. L. and Thompson, C. W. (1962) Facilitation of simultaneous discrimination learning with strychnine sulphate. *Psychopharmacologia* **3**, 166-172.

McGaugh, J. L., Thompson, C. W., Westbrook, W. H., and Hudspeth, W. J. (1962) A further study of learning facilitation with strychnine sulphate. *Psychopharmacologia* **3**, 352-360.

McGaugh, J. L. and Petrinovich, L. F. (1965) Effects of drugs on learning and memory. *Internat. Rev. Neurobiol.* **8**, 139-196.

McGaugh, J. L. and Krivanek, J. A. (1970) Strychnine effects on discrimination learning in mice: Effects of dose and time of administration. *Physiol. Behav.* **5**, 1437-1442.

Morris, N. R. Aghajanian, G. K., and Bloom, F. E. (1967) Magnesium pemonline: Failure to affect in vivo synthesis of brain RNA. *Science* **155**, 1125-1126.

Nakajima, S. (1969) Interference with relearning in the rat after hippocampal injection of actinomycin D. *Compar. Physiol. Psychol.* **67**, 457-461.

Nakajima, S. (1972) Proactive effect of actinomycin D on maze performance in the rat. *Physiol. Behav.* **8**, 1063-1067.

Nasello, A. G. and Izquierdo, I. (1969) Effect of learning and of drugs on the ribonucleic acid concentration of brain structures of the rat. *Exper. Neurol.* **23**, 521-528.

Nissen, T., Roigaard-Petersen, H. H., and Fjerdingstad, E. J. (1965) Effect of rubonucleic acid extracted from the brain of trained animals on learning in rats, II. Dependence of the RNA effect on training condition prior to RNA extraction. *Scand. J. Psychol.* **6**, 265-270.

Oshima, K., Gorbman, A., and Shimada, H. (1969) Memory-blocking agents: Effects on olfactory discrimination in homing salmon. *Science* **165**, 86-88.

Overton, D. A. (1966) State-dependent learning produced by depressant and atropine-like drugs. *Psychopharmacologia* **10**, 6-31.

Paré, W. (1961) The effect of caffeine and seconal on a visual discrimination task. *J. Compar. Physiol. Psychol.* **54**, 506-509.

Plotnikoff, N. (1966) Magnesium pemoline: Enhancement of learning and memory of a conditioned avoidance response. *Science* **151**, 703-704.

Plotnikoff, N. (1969) Pemoline and magnesium hydroxide (PMH): Performance enhancement after ECS. *Psychonomic Sci.* **17**, 180.

Porter, P. B. and Griffin, A. C. (1950) Effects of glutamic acid on maze learning and recovery from electroconvulsive shocks in albino rats. *J. Compar. Physiol. Psychol.* **43**, 1-15.

Potts, A. and Bitterman, M. E. (1967) Puromycin and retention in the goldfish. *Science* **158**, 1594-1596.

Prien, R. F., Wagner, M. J., Jr., and Kahan, S. (1963) Lack of facilitation in maze learning by picrotoxin and strychnine sulfate. *Amer. J. Physiol.* **204**, 488-492.

Quartermain, D. and McEwen, B. S. (1970) Temporal characteristics of amnesia produced by protein synthesis inhibitor: Determination by shock level. *Nature* **228**, 677-678.

Quartermain, D., McEwen, B. S., and Azmitia, E., Jr. (1970) Amnesia produced by electroconvulsive shock or cycoheximide: Conditions for recovery. *Science* **169**, 683-686.

Quartermain, D. McEwen, B. S., and Azmitia, E. C., Jr. (1972) Recovery of memory following amnesia in the rat and mouse. *J. Compar. Physiol. Psychol.* **79**, 360-370.

Randt, C. T., McEwen, B. S., and Quartermain, D. (1971) Amnesic effects of cycloheximide on two strains of mice with different memory characteristics. *Exper. Neurol.* **30**, 467-474.

Reeves, C. (1966) Cholinergic synaptic transmission and its relationship to behavior. *Psychol. Bull.* **65**, 321-335.

Reynierse, J. H. (1967) Reactions to light in four species of planaria. *J. Compar. Physiol. Psychol.* **63**, 366-368.

Roberts, R. B., Flexner, J. B., and Flexner, L. B. (1970) Some evidence for the involvement of adrenergic sites in the memory trace. *Proc. Nat. Acad. Sci.* **66**, 310-313.

Røigaard-Petersen H. H., Nissen, Th., and Fjerdingstad, E. J. (1968) Effect of ribonucleic acid (RNA) extracted from the brain of trained animals on learning in rats III. Results obtained with an improved procedure. *Scandi. J. Psychol.* **9**, 1-16.

Rosenzweig, M. R., Krech, D., and Bennett, E. L. (1960) A search for relations between brain chemistry and behavior. *Psychol. Bull.* **57**, 476-492.

Rosenzweig, M. R., Krech, D., Bennett, E. L., and Diamond, M. C. (1962) Effects of environmental complexity and training on brain chemistry and anatomy: A replication and extention. *J. Compar. Physiol. Psychol.* **55**, 429-437.

Schneider, C. W. and Chenoweth, M. B. (1971) Effects of cycloheximide on unrestricted behavioral patterns of mice. *Brain Res.* **25**, 625-631.

Scoville, W. B. and Milner, B. (1957) Loss of recent memory after bilateral hippocampal lesions. *J. Neurol. Neurosurg. Psychiat.* **20**, 11-19.

Segal, D. S., Squire, L. R., and Barondes, S. H. (1971) Cycloheximide: Its effects on activity are dissociable from its effects on memory. *Science* **172**, 82-84.

Serota, R. G. (1971) Acetoxycycloheximide and transient amnesia in the rat. *Proc. Nat. Acad. Sci.* **68**, 1249-1250.

Serota, R. G., Roberts, R. B., and Flexner, L. B. (1972) Acetoxycycloheximide-induced amnesia: Protective effects of adrenergic stimulus. *Proc. Nat. Acad. Sci.* **69**, 340-342.

Siegel, R. K. (1967) Yeast ribonucleic acid: Effects on avoidance behavior of the neonate chick. *Psychopharmacologia* **12**, 68-77.

Siegel, R. K. (1968) Effects of ribonucleic acid (RNA) on interval scheduling in the domestic pigeon. *Psychonomic Sci.* **18**, 53-57.

Solyom, L., Beaulien, C., and Enesco, H. E. (1966) The effect of RNA on the operant behavior of white rats. *Psychonomic Sci.* **6**, 341-342.

Squire, L. R. and Barondes, S. H. (1970) Actinomycin-D: Effects on memory at different times after training. *Nature* **225**, 649-650.

Squire, L. R., Geller, A., and Jarvik, M. E. (1970) Habituation and activity as affected by cycloheximide. *Commun. Behav. Biol.* **5A**, 249-254.

Squire, L. R., Glick, S. D., and Goldfarb, J. (1971) Relearning at different times after training as affected by centrally and peripherally acting cholinergic drugs in the mouse. *J. Compar. Physiol. Psychol.* **74**, 41-45.

Stein, H. H., and Yellin, T. O. (1967) Pemoline and magnesium hydroxide: Lack of effect on RNA and protein synthesis. *Science* **157**, 96-97.

Stellar, E. and McElroy, W. D. (1948) Does glutamic acid have any effect on learning? *Science* **108**, 281-283.

Swanson, R., McGaugh, J. L., and Cotman, C. (1969) Acetoxycycloheximide effects on one-trial inhibitory avoidance learning. *Commun. Behav. Biol.* **4**, 239-245.

Ungar, G. and Oceguera-Navarro, C. (1965) Transfer of habituation by material transferred from brain. *Nature* **207**, 301-302.

Ungar, G., Gelson, L., and Clark, R. H. (1968) Chemical transfer of learned fear. *Nature* **217**, 1259-1261.

Uphouse, L. L., MacInnes, J. W., and Schlesinger, K. (1972a) Effects of conditioned avoidance training on polyribosomes of mouse brain. *Physiol. Behav.* **8**, 1013-1018.

Uphouse, L. L., MacInnes, J. W., and Schlesinger, K. (1972b) Uridine incorporation into polyribosomes of mouse brain after escape training in an electrified T-maze. *Physiol. Behav.* **8**, 1019-1023.

Vanderwolf, C. H. (1969) Hippocampal electrical activity and voluntary movement in the rat. *Electroenceph. Clin. Neurophysiol.* **26**, 407-418.

Wagner, A. R., Carder, J. B., and Beaty, W. W. (1966) Yeast ribonucleic acid: Effects on learned behavior in the rat. *Psychonomic Sci.* **4**, 33-34.

Weil-Malherbe, H. (1936) Studies on brain metabolism: Mechanism of glutamic acid in brain. *Biochem. J.* **30**, 665-676.

Weiner, N. and Deutsch, J. A. (1968) The temporal aspects of anticholinergic and anticholinersterase induced amnesia for an appetitive habit. *J. Compar. Physiol. Psychol.* **66**, 613-617.

Yanagiha, T. and Hyden, H. (1971) Protein synthesis in regions of rat hippocampus during learning. *Exper. Neurol.* **31**, 151-164.

Zabarenko, L. M., Pilgrim, F. J., and Patton, R. A. (1951) The effect of glutamic acid supplementation on problem solving of the instrumental conditioning type. *J. Compar. Physiol. Psychol.* **44**, 126-133.

Zelman, A., Kabat, L., Jacobson, R., and McConnell, J. V. (1963) Transfer of training through injection of "conditioned" RNA into untrained planarians. *Worm Runners Dig.* 5, 14-21.

Zemp, J. W., Wilson, J. E., Schlesinger, K., Boggan, W. O., and Glassman, E. (1966) Brain function and macromolecules I. Incorporation of uridine into RNA of mouse brain during short-term training experience. *Proc. Nat. Acad. Sci.* 55, 1423-1431.

Zemp, J. W., Glassman, E., and Wilson, J. E. (1967) Site of increased labeling of RNA in brains of mice during short-term learning. *Fed. Proc.* 26, 676.

Zimmerman, F. T. and Ross, S. (1944) Effect of glutamic acid and other amino acids on maze learning in the white rat. *Arch. Neurol. Psychiat.* 51, 446-451.

Zimmerman, F. T., Burgemeister, B. B., and Putnam, T. J. (1947) A group study of the effect of glutamic acid upon mental functioning in children and adolescents. *Psychosomatic Med.* 9, 175-183.

CHAPTER 2

Environmental Influences Upon Neurometabolic Processes in Learning and Memory

L. VALZELLI

1. INTRODUCTION

In recent years a number of studies have explored the influences of the environment on animal behavior and on physiological, pharmacological, and biochemical responses

A very important finding is that infantile experiences reflect upon adult learning abilities, as well as on many other biological parameters, as demonstrated by Denenberg and Karas (1960) and by Denenberg and Morton (1962). Early handling and gentling in laboratory rats for a few minutes daily, starting at weaning and continuing into adulthood, results in a more pronounced resistance to stress and mortality (Weininger, 1953,

1956) and to later deprivation; (Levine and Otis, 1958), as well as in faster growth (Weininger, 1956), more stable emotionality (Denenberg et al., 1964), better maze performance (Bernstein 1952), and in increased exploratory behavior (De Nelsky and Denenberg, 1967a, b).

Social interaction and mean level of environmental stimulation (Welch, 1964) appear, therefore, to be important factors in shaping later behavioral attitudes and responses of animals.

Moreover, enrichment of environmental experience profoundly modifies anatomical and biochemical features of the central nervous system, including an increase of brain weight (Rosenzweig, 1966; Rosenzweig et al., 1968; Ferchmin et al., 1970), of cortical depth and glial cell number (Diamond et al., 1964, 1966), of the brain total acetylcholinesterase and cholinesterase activity (Rosenzweig et al., 1969), and of brain RNA content (Ferchmin et al., 1970) in different animal species. It is interesting to note that such cerebral changes are accompanied by an enhancement of learning and problem-solving abilities (Rosenzweig, 1964; Krech et al., 1962; Forgays & Forgays, 1952; Hymovitch, 1952).

Conversely, it has been widely demonstrated that an impoverished environment and a low level of social interaction result in a reverse situation, both for brain anatomy and biochemistry as well as for behavioral patterns and facilities. (Krech et al., 1962; Denenberg et al., 1964; Rosenzweig, 1966; Rosenzweig et al., 1968; Bennett et al., 1964, 1966; Ferchmin et al., 1970).

2. THE "ISOLATION SYNDROME" IN MICE

a. Effects on Behavior

It is well known that a sharp decline in the level of enviromental stimulation during a prolonged period of isolation of a single animal from its normal social setting, induces a strong, repetitive and compulsive inter-or intraspecies and interanimal aggressive behavior (Allee, 1942; Scott, 1959; Seward, 1946; Valzelli, 1967a, Yen et al., 1959). This is particularly evident and easily obtained in male Albino mice (Valzelli, 1969a, 1971a). Such aggressive behavior, which is the most striking consequence of isolation, seems to be only the epiphenomenon of many other physiological, behavioral, and brain activity alterations (Table I), including higher nervous functions of animals. To these important brain activities Sokolov (1963) attributes the orienting reflex, one component of which, exploratory behavior, is severely impaired in isolated aggressive mice (Valzelli, 1969b, 1971b; Fig. 1).

Exploratory ability represents a very delicate behavioral parameter and

TABLE I

Physiological, Neurochemical, Pharmacological, and Behavioral Changes
Observed in Isolation-Housed Male Albino Mouse

Observations
Initial increase of locomotor activity
Increased general reactivity
Increased response to painful stimulation
Induction of gastric pathology
Hyperirritability
Increased vocalization
Tremor
Piloerection
Compulsive aggression
Decreased brain 5HIAA
Decreased brain 5HT turnover
Decreased 5HT turnover in diencephalon
Minor decrease in brain NE turnover
Increased DA turnover
Cerebellar neuronal RNA decrement with increased duration of isolation[a]
Cerebellar glial RNA increment with increased duration of isolation[a]
Decrease in brain N-acetyl-L-aspartic acid
Unchanged brain MAO activity
Unchanged brain choline acetylase activity
Increased AChE activity associated with external synaptic membrane of nerve endings from cerebral cortex[b]
Unchanged brain aspartic acid
Unchanged brain glutamic acid
Decreased exploratory behavior
Reduced avoidance response acquisition[c]

[a]From Essman (1971b).
[b]From Essman (1971d).
[c]From Essman (1970).

requires an extemely well balanced emotional baseline, so that every change of emotionality reflects upon exploration. Fiske and Maddi (1961) affirmed that, in the absence of specific tasks animal behavior is directed towards the maintenance of its normal inner activation level, so that the animals whose activation is higher than normal will not explore. In other words, socially deprived animals, like isolated aggressive mice, reach such an elevated level of inner tension that their exploratory abilities become greatly impaired.

Moreover, even some elementary but essential behavioral responses associated with basic drives are dramatically compromised by isolation. When mice are housed in groups of eight each in special Makralon cages, where the water supply is automatically supplied, requiring the animals to

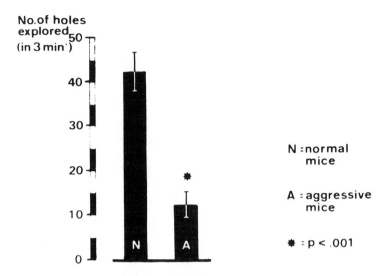

No.of holes
explored 50
(in 3 min.)

N = normal mice

A = aggressive mice

✻ = p < .001

Fig. 1. Exploratory behavior of normal (N) and aggressive (A) mice (hole-board test).

use their tongues to operate a small lever inserted in the water duct, they easily learn and perform this simple task. But over 30 per cent of those mice which have been isolated and that are without previous experience, do not learn to perform such a response for delivery of water and reduce their thirst; they die in five to ten days. In view of the imitative learning process in rodents, by which a naive animal can learn and perform specialized tasks from observing the behavioral performance of an experienced mate (Osgood, 1953; Miller & Dollard, 1941; Pallaud, 1968, 1969a, b), the mice were housed eight per cage for one week before being randomly housed in single cages for the isolation procedure. However, despite this expedient, while no mice died during the period of grouped housing, 18 percent of the same mice, their total inability when housed singly, died in the first week of isolation, as a result of their total inability to drink water (Table II). This striking result seems to indicate clearly that isolation disrupts a learned task which is especially important because it is directly linked to survival.

It is, therefore, not surprising that isolated-aggressive mice show less learning ability than normal ones, even with a simple task like the classic avoidance-conditioning shuttle-box task. In fact, in such an experimental situation, normal mice reach a hundred percent performance in seven sessions of 3 minutes each, while aggressive animals show only 65 percent acquisition under the same conditions (Fig. 2). However, it must be emphasised that the intensity of the shock is crucial to the improvement or worsening of the acquisition pattern of aggressive animals. They are

TABLE II

Lethality by Thirst on Grouped and Isolated Mice[a]

| Experimental Conditions | Lethality % by thirst after | | | Total |
	4 days	8 days	4 weeks	%
Grouped	0	0	0	0
Isolated without previous experiences	20	12	0	32
Isolated after 1 week of shaping	10	8	0	18

[a]See text for details.

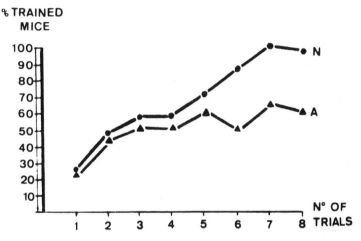

Fig. 2. Avodiance learning (shuttle box) in normal (N:●) and aggressive (A:▲) mice.

more reactive, more irritable and more sensitive to painful stimuli than their normal mates (Valzelli, 1969a), and their task performance can be disrupted by shock intensity usually employed for the training of normal mice.

These results, inspite of some differences due to experimental conditions and/or training situations, agree with those described by Essman (1970, 1971a) in isolated-aggressive mice tested by another avoidance technique, and further support the hypothesis of the profound negative influence of isolation on learning and memory processes.

b. Effects on Brain Chemistry

The manifold expressions of animal behavior resulting from the activation and reciprocal integration of several brain circuits and specialized areas lead to a hierarchy of responses to a given stimulus. The more complex these areas are the more precise the response. The activity of such circuits depends upon the presence of neurochemical transmitters in brain as well as on the availability of these substances at the receptor sites. It therefore seems reasonable to attribute different acquired behavioral response dispositions to different biochemical aspects of brain function.

In 1938, Kohler affirmed that the prime effect of a nerve impulse is a series of biochemical events taking place in the nervous tissue and, as far back as 1915, Cannon suggested that rage and fear reactions are sustained by a release of epinephrine.

More recently, several authors have demonstrated the influence of environmental complexity and stimulation on animal behavior, brain anatomy and chemistry (Krech et al. 1960, 1962, 1966; Diamond et al., 1964; Rosenzweig, 1966; Rosenzweig et al., 1962, 1968, 1969; Ferchmin et al., 1970).

This leads to the concept of the biochemical and anatomical plasticity of the brain (Bennett et al., 1964), mainly as a function of previous life experiences and environment requirements (Rosenzweig, 1966; Welch, 1964).

Prolonged isolation of male mice results not only in the above-mentioned behavioral alterations, but also induces several modifications of brain neurochemistry, including a variety of enzymatic differences in the cerebral cortex and subcortical areas; these have been particularly relevant for cholinergic transmission and energy metabolism (Bennett et al., 1970), as well as for changes in biogenic amines (Valzelli, 1967a,b, 1971a; Essman, 1969, 1971b; Garattini et al., 1969; Welch & Welch, 1971), glial and neuronal RNA levels (Essman, 1971b), microsomal activity (Essman et al., 1972) and N-acetyl-L-aspartic acid levels (Marcucci et al., 1968).

As far as neurotransmitters are concerned, the absolute levels of these substances in brain are not significantly changed by isolation (Table III), while their dynamic features, as determined by turnover measurements estimated according to the method of Tozer et al. (1966), differs from that of control animals living together under normal conditions (Table IV).

TABLE III

Serotonin (5HT), Norepinephrine (NE), and Dopamine (DA) Levels in the Whole Brain of Normal (N) and Aggressive (A) mice[a]

Tissue	Weight %	5HT		N E		D A	
		N	A	N	A	N	A
Whole brain	100	0.65 ±0.03	0.65 ±0.03	0.45 ±0.02	0.42 ±0.03	1.09 ±0.05	1.04 ±0.04

[a]Each figure corresponds to 8 determinations ± standard error.

TABLE IV

Brain Serotonin (5HT), Norepinephrine (NE), and Dopamine (DA) Turnover
in Normal and Aggressive by Isolation Mice[a]

Type of Mice	5 HT Turnover		NE Turnover		DA Turnover	
	Rate (γ/g/hr)	Time (hr)	Rate (γ/g/hr)	Time (hr)	Rate (γ/g/hr)	Time (hr)
Normal	0.46±0.01	1.10'	0.05	8.32'	0.08	6.10'
Aggressive	0.26±0.01[b]	2.20'	0.03[b]	10.15'	0.13[b]	3.54'

[a] Each figure corresponds to 8 determinations ± standard error.
[b] $p < 0.01$.

The decrease in brain serotonin (5-HT) turnover, which is the most typical biochemical change in isolated animals, affects mainly the diencephalic area and the corpora quadrigemina, which are associated with the limbic system and the expression of emotional behavior (Garattini et al., 1969).

It has been suggested that the level of brain 5-HT plays a critical role in learning and memory. An increase of this neurochemical tansmitter results in a decreased learning ability, while a reduced brain 5-HT level causes an increased rate of learning (Woolley, 1965; Tenen, 1967; Essman, 1971a). Conversely, the depletion of brain catecholamines consistently impairs acquisition (Kety, 1970; Essman, 1971a). In view of this, it seems important to emphasize that amine turnover represents a dynamic measure quite different from that of absolute levels. An increased turnover is not comparable to experimental situations in which an increase of the brain amine content is present, and a decreased turnover does not correspond to a decrease of such levels (Valzelli, 1973).

Further, the role of absolute levels of brain 5-HT and catecholamines in relation to learning and memory processes, derives from observation of normal mice after administration of drugs capable of blocking the synthesis or causing the inactivation of a single neurotransmitter. Such an experimental approach is comparable with the central neurochemical changes which occur in isolated aggressive mice, in which modifications of brain amine turnover are contiguous and may reciprocally interact, in various ways, to sustain the disturbed learning of such animals.

However, p-chlorophenylanaline (PCAPA), an extensively studied inhibitor of brain 5-HT synthesis evidently improves the learning performance of aggressive mice, while impairing that of normal animals (Fig. 3). This reverse effect on behavior also reflects upon the activity of the drug on brain 5-HT content in both types of mice (Table V).

The interactions of 5-HT with nucleic acids in brain (Essman & Essman,

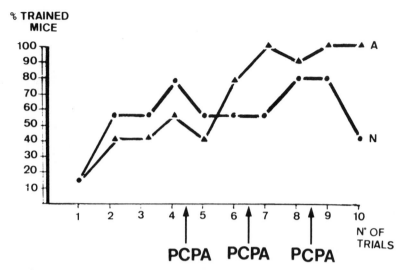

Fig. 3. Effect of p-chlorophenylalanine (PCPA = 150 mg/kg i.p. daily for 3 days) on avoidance learning (shuttle box) in normal (N:•) and aggressive (A:▲) mice.

TABLE V

Effect of p-Chlorophenylalanine (PCPA) Administration
(150 mg/kg i.p. daily for 3 days) on Brain 5HT and 5HIAA Levels
in Normal (N) and Aggressive (A) Mice (4 hr after the last administration)

| | | | | | Brain Contents (γg/g) | | | |
| | | N | | | | A | | |
Treatment	5HT	% var.	5HIAA	% var.	5HT	% var.	5HIAA	% var.
Saline	0.68±0.02	–	0.51±0.03	–	0.66±0.02	–	0.42±0.02	–
PCPA	0.42±0.02	−39	0.21±0.02	−59	0.46±0.02	−30	0.25±0.03	−42

1969; Bittman & Essman, 1970) are also interesting particularly regarding the increase in glial RNA and the simultaneous decrease in neuronal RNA content in mice subjected to prolonged isolation. (Essman, 1971b). This could be related to the disruption of learning and memory traces induced by the administration of drugs wich impair or inhibit RNA and/or protein synthesis in brain (Flexner et al., 1963, 1971).

Furthermore, several studies have advocated a role for cholinergic transmission in the modulation of learning and memory processes (Russell et al., 1961; Bohdanecky & Jarvik, 1967; Leaf & Muller, 1966; Deutsh & Lutzky, 1967; Essman & Essman, 1971). It is interesting to observe that nicotine, which is presumed to act through a release of brain acetylcholine

(Armitage & Hall, 1967; Essman, 1971c), facilitates the acquisition of shuttle-box avoidance in those animals that show an initial poor avoidance performance (Bovet et al., 1963; Bovet and Bovet-Nitti, 1965); while it impairs the avoidance learning in those mice that are genetically characterized by a high level of avoidance performance (Bovet et al., 1966). Recently this dual effect of nicotine has also been demonstrated to be present in isolated and in normally grouped mice; in this latter situation, nicotine did not affect the avoidance acquisition rate, while this drug is evidently able to improve the performance of mice kept in isolation (Essman, 1971d).

However, it seems useful to point out that neurotransmitters by definition, allow the transmission of the nerve impulse from one neuron to other neuronal elements within the context of a series of neuronal webs which, in turn, relate to several anatomical circuits and systems modulating different and highly specialized behaviors that are activated by both internal and external stimuli. In this way variations in brain neurotransmitter level, or turnover, may serve as an index of potential change in the activity of such circuits and systems.

Within this context, attention might be shifted from an emphasis upon the relationships between altered behavior and localization of involved brain sites.

c. Neuroanatomical Correlates

It has long been recognized that the limbic system of the brain is intimately involved with basic drives, chiefly concerned with emotional behavior. Many studies have demonstrated that altered emotional states can affect the level of brain excitability (Adler, 1971). Moreover, as reviewed elsewhere (Valzelli, 1967a, 1971a), numerous experiments showed involvement of the central pathways, nuclei, and structures which are important in sustaining aggressive behavior.

Among such structures, are the olfactory bulbs, olfactory bandelets, praepyriform cortex, lateral hypothalamus, amygdala, uncus, dorsal hippocampus, cingulate gyrus, central gray matter, medial thalamus, superior quadrigeminal bodies, tip of the temporal lobes and frontal cortex; all of these are involved in the modulation of aggression (Anand & Dua, 1955; Karli & Vergnes, 1963; Vergnes & Karli, 1963, 1969; Fonberg, 1965; Egger & Flynn, 1967, 1969; Moyer, 1968; Blanchard & Blanchard, 1968; Gumulka et al., 1970), and the importance of many of them has also been demonstrated for learning and memory mechanisms. In fact, frontal and temporal cortex, thalamus, cingulate gyrus, hippocampus, and amygdala (Horvath, 1963; Robinson, 1963; Ojemann, 1966; Buffery, 1967) represent the main stations of the anatomical web involved in discrimination, internal inhibition, learning and memory consolidation processes. It is obvious that any emotional alteration can profoundly affect both behavior and memory functions.

In this context, the relationship between amygdala and hippocampus may represent one transitional point between aggressive behavior and disturbed learning present in isolated mice. Some studies have shown that protein synthesis in the hippocampus and other limbic areas is increased during the learning phase (Zemp et al., 1967; Hyden & Lange, 1968; Beach et al., 1969). Moreover, the limbic system is diffusely innervated by monaminergic neuronal projections (Dahlström & Fuxe, 1964a, b; Fuxe, 1964); this observation could account to some extent, for the brain amine changes that occur in such animals.

3. EFFECTS OF BENZODIAZEPINES ON THE "ISOLATION SYNDROME"

Several previous studies have concerned themselves with the effect of psychotropic drugs on isolated mice, mainly in terms of their possible antiaggressive activity (Yen et al., 1959; Valzelli, 1967a; Valzelli, 1967a, 1971; Sofia, 1969; Christmas & Maxwell, 1970), their dual action on exploratory behavior of normal and aggressive mice (Valzelli, 1969b, 1971b), and of their differing effects in countering aggression in rats or mice (Valzelli & Bernasconi, 1971).

Among the large family of psychoactive drugs, the benzodiazepine derivates, and chlordiazepoxide and medazepam in particular, seem to exert the most interesting activity in mice, both in controlling aggressive behavior and in improving exploratory performance (Valzelli, 1969b, 1971b; Valzelli & Bernasconi, 1971; Valzelli et al., 1971). This is consistent with the above suggestions regarding the role of the amygdala and hippocampus in disturbed behavior. Benzodiazepines are known to exert their activity on the limbic system and have been shown to act principally on amygdalo-hippocampal complex (Olds & Olds, 1969; Jalfre et al., 1971). Moreover, some benzodiazepines were recently shown to decrease both norepinephrine and dopamine turnover in specific areas of the rat brain (Taylor & Laverty, 1969) and also to modify the brain content of several neurotransmitters, including 5-HT and its main metabolite, the 5-hydroxyindolacetic acid (5HIAA) in normal mice (Fennessy & Lee, 1972). Chlordiazepoxide is capable of decreasing brain 5-HT turnover only in normal mice, while medazepam decreases 5-HT turnover in the brain of normal animals and increases turnover in isolated aggressive mice almost to the level characteristic of their group mates (Table VI). Moreover, chlordiazepoxide increases the brain level of N-acetyl-L-aspartic acid which, as previously reported, is decreased in mice, as a result of isolation while medazepam is not effective in modifying this biochemical parameter (Table VII).

The poor learning ability of isolated-aggressive mice in the shuttle-avoidance situation (see Fig. 3) is not changed by the administration of chlordiazepoxide which impairs the avoidance performances of normal mice (Fig. 4). This has also been reported in rabbits (Chisholm & Moore, 1970a, b). Medazapam consistently improves the avoidance behavior of aggressive mice without any negative effects on the learning ability of their normal group-housed litter. (Fig. 5).

Very few and experimental data have been reported in the literature concerning the effect of benzodiazepines on avoidance behavior of laboratory animals and no information is available on the effect of these substances on learning in normal and aggressive mice. It seems, therefore,

TABLE VI

Effect of Chlordiazepoxide (CDO = 7.5 mg/kg i.p.)
and of Medazepam (MDZ = 10 mg/kg i.p.) on Brain 5HT Turnover
(1 hr after administration) of Normal (N) and Isolated-Aggressive
Albino Swiss Male Mice (A)

| | Brain 5HT Turnover | | | |
| | N | | A | |
Treatment	Rate $(\gamma/g/hr)$	Time (hr)	Rate $(\gamma/g/hr)$	Time (hr)
Saline	0.41±0.01	1.14'	0.28±0.01	1.58'
CDO	0.27±0.02[a]	2.10'	0.27±0.02	2.08'
MDZ	0.50±0.02[a]	55'	0.37±0.01[a]	1.30'

[a] $p < 0.01$ in respect to saline-treated animals.

TABLE VII

Effect of Chlordiazepoxide (CDO = 15 mg/kg i.p.)
and of Medazepam (MDZ = 15 mg/kg i.p.) on normal (N) and aggressive (A) mice
on brain N-acetyl-L- Aspartic Acid (NAA) 2 hr after Drug Administration

| | Brain NAA content mg/kg ± standard error | | |
Treatment	N	A	% Variation
Controls	1.085±0.022	0.940±0.008[a]	–
CDO	1.058±0.016	1.179±0.002[b]	+11.4
MDZ	1.091±0.035	0.926±0.013	−1.5

[a] $p < 0.01$ in respect to N.
[b] $p < 0.01$ in respect to A.

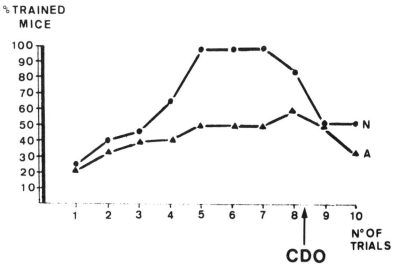

Fig. 4. Effect of chlordiazepoxide (CDO = 7.5 mg/kg i.p.) on avoidance learning
(shuttle box) in normal (N:•) and aggressive (A:▲) mice.

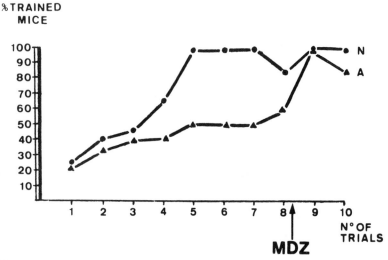

Fig. 5. Effect of medazepam (MDZ = 10 mg/kg i.p.) on avoidance learning (shuttle
box) in normal (N:•) and aggressive (A:▲) mice.

important to emphasize once more that, as reported elsewhere (Valzelli &
Bernasconi, 1971), the effect of many psychoactive drugs, administered at
the same dosage and with the same experimental schedule can exert
different effects depending upon the emotional baseline upon which they
are superimposed.

4. CONCLUSIONS

The expression of the isolation syndrome, as initially proposed in this paper, seems to encompass more of the manifold alterations induced by prolonged isolation in rodents than previous limitations confined to "aggressiveness by isolation"; thus, attention is focused primarily upon the most evident symptom evolving from isolated mice. In fact, both studies summarized in this paper demonstrate that isolation results in profound disruption of normal animal behavior including compulsive and repetitive outbursts, hyperreactivity to stimuli, alterations of learning and memory processes, impairment of higher nervous functions, changes of brain protein synthesis, the turnover of neurochemical transmitters, variations of microsomal activity, and a series of autonomic symptoms.

Such modifications can be attributed to a change of the functional status of the limbic system and perhaps of some of its highly specialized structures such as the amygdala, and hippocampal complex, which are known to govern many peripheral functions, behavioral capacity and learning ability.

It remains necessary to find some clear-cut evidence indicating the primary pre-eminent or direct casual relationships for neurochemical principles as determinants of the isolation syndrome. It seems likely that a series of complex interactions occurring among numerous aspects of brain neurochemical alterations may sustain the disturbed behavior brought about by prolonged isolation.

It seems obvious, that, for the present, any beneficial effects of psychoactive drugs upon those behaviors characterizing the isolation syndrome still remain to be further examined for a clarification of mechanisms through which such relationships are mediated.

However, the experimental technique of isolation in rodents seems to represent a very useful tool for exploration of the complexity of brain function and, at the same time, a method for a better understanding of certain aspects of disturbed behavior in man.

5. SUMMARY

A disruption of normal environmental conditions for mice, as represented by prolonged isolation, induces aggressiveness and a series of behavioral alterations, such as changes in the higher nervous functions, as shown when exploratory behavior is investigated.

Moreover, aggressive mice are less able to learn simple tasks, such as avoidance behavior, and respond differently from normal animals to psychoactive drugs. The effect of centrally acting drugs both on avoidance behavior and on brain serotonin chemistry has been compared in aggressive and normal mice.

42   VALZELLI

REFERENCES

Adler, M. W. (1971) Limbic lesion-induced changes in cerebral excitability. In *Drugs Development and Cerebral Functions,* W. L. Smith, Ed., C. C. Thomas, Springfield, Ill., pp. 167-176.

Allee, W. C. (1942) Group organization among vertebrates. *Science* 95: 289-293.

Anand, B. K. and Dua, S. (1955) Stimulation of limbic system of brain in waking animals. *Science* 122: 1139.

Armitage, A. K. and Hall, G. H. (1967) Further evidence relating to the mode of action of nicotine in the central nervous system. *Nature (London)* 214: 977-979.

Beach, G., Emmens, M., Kimble, D. P. and Lickey, M. (1969) Autoradiographic demonstration of biochemical changes in the limbic system during avoidance training. *Proc. Nat. Acad. Sci.* 62: 691-696.

Bennett, E. L., Diamond, M. C., Krech, D. and Rosenzweig, M. R. (1964) Chemical and anatomical plasticity of brain. *Science* 146: 610-619.

Bennett, E. L. Rosenzweig, M. R. and Diamond, M. C. (1966) Rat brain: effects of environmental enrichment on wet and dry weights. *Science* 163: 825-826.

Bennett, E. L., Rosenzweig, M. R. and Diamond, M. C. (1970) Time courses of effects of differential experience Ed., Academic Press, New York, pp. 55-89.

Bernstein, L. (1952) A note on Christie's "Experimental naiveté and experiential naiveté". *Psychol. Bull.* 49: 38-40.

Bittman, R. and Essman, W. B. (1970) Abstr. papers, 3rd. Annu. Winter Conf. on Brain Res., Snowmass-at-Aspen, Colo.

Blanchard, R. J. and Blanchard, D. C. (1968) Limbic lesions and reflexive fighting. *Compar. Physiol. Psychol.* 66: 603-605.

Bohdanecky, Z. and Jarvik, M. E. (1967) Impairment of one-trail passive avodiance learning in mice by scopolamine, scopolamine methylbromide and physostigmine. *Internat. Jo. Neuropharmacol.* 6: 217-222.

Bovet, D., Bignami, G. and Robustelli, F. (1963) Action de la nicotine sur le conditionnement à la reaction d'eritement chez le rat. *C. R. Acad. Sci.* 256: 778-780.

Bovet, D. and Bovet-Nitti, F. (1965) Action of nicotine U.S. Von Euler, Ed., on conditioned behavior on naive and pretrained rats. *Tobacco Alkaloids and Related Compounds,* Pergamon Press, Oxford, pp. 125-142.

Bovet, D., Bovet-Nitti, F. and Oliverio, A. (1966) Effects of nicotine on avoidance conditioning of inbred strains of mice. *Psychopharmacologia* 10, 1-5.

Brodie, B. B., Costa, E., Dlabac, A., Neff, N. H. and Smookler, H. H. (1966) Application of steady state kinetics to the estimation of synthesis rate and turnover time of tissue catecholamines. *Pharmacol. Exper. Therap.* 154, 493-498.

Buffery, A. W. H. (1967) Learning and memory in baboons with bilateral lesions of frontal or inferotemporal cortex. *Nature (London)* 214, 1054-1056.

Cannon, W. B. (1915) *Bodily Changes in Pain, Hunger, Fear and Rage,* Appleton Publ., New York.

Chisholm, D. C. and Moore, J. W. (1970a) Effect of chlordiazepoxide on the acquisition of shuttle avoidance in the rabbit. *Psychonomic Sci.* 19, 21-22.

Chisholm, D. C. and Moore, J. W. (1970b) Effects of chlordiazepoxide on discrimination fear conditioning and shuttle avoidance performance in the rabbit. *Psychopharmacologia* 18, 162-171.

Christmas, A. J. and Maxwell, D. R. (1970) A comparison of the effects of some banzodiazepines and other drugs on aggressive and exploratory behavior in mice and rats. *Neuropharmacology* 9, 17-29.

Dahlström, A. and Fuxe, K. (1964a) Evidence for the existence of monoamine containing neurons in the central nervous system. I. Demonstration of mono-amines in the cell bodies of brain stem neurons. *Acta Physiol. Scand.* **62**, (suppl. 232), 1-55.

Dahlström, A. and Fuxe, K. (1964b) Evidence for the existence of monoamine neurons in the central nervous system. II. Experimentally induced changes in the intraneuronal amine levels of bulbospinal neuron systems. *Acta Physiol. Scand.* **64** (suppl. 247), 1-36.

Delgado, J. M. R. (1969) Offensive-defensive behaviour in free monkeys and chimpazees induced by radio stimulation of the brain. In *Aggressive Behaviour* S. Garattini and E. B. Sigg, Eds., Excerpta Medica Foundation, Amsterdam, pp. 109-119.

De Nelsky, G. Y. and Denenberg, V. H. (1967a) Infantile stimulation and adult exploratory behavior: effects of handling upon tactual variation seeking. *Compar. Physiol. Psychol.* **63**, 309-312.

De Nelsky, G. Y. and Denenberg, V. H. (1967b) Infantile stimulation and adult exploratory behaviour in the rat: Effects of handling upon visual variation-seeking. *Animal Behav.* **15**, 568-573.

Denenberg, V. H. and Karas, G. G. (1960) Interactive effects of age and duration of infantile experience on adult learning. *Psychol. Rep.* **5**: 357-364.

Denenberg, V. H. and Morton, J. R. C. (1962) Effects of pre-weaning and post-weaning manipulations upon problem-solving behavior. *Physiol. Psychol.* **55**, 1096-1098

Denenberg, V. H., Morton, J. R. and Haltmeyer, G. C. (1964) Effect of social grouping upon emotional behaviour. *Animal Behav.* **12**, 205-208.

Deutsch, J. A. and Lutzky, H. (1967) Memory enhancement by antichilinesterase as a function of initial learning. *Nature (London)* **213**, 742.

Diamond, M. C., Krech, D. and Rosenzweig, M. R. (1964) The effects of an enriched environment on the histology of the rat cerebral cortex. *Jo. Compar. Neurol.* , **111-120.**

Diamond, M. C., Law, F., Rhodes, H., Lindner, B., Rosenzweig, M. R., Krech, D. and Bennett, E. L. (1966) Increases in cortical depth and glia numbers in rats subjected to enriched environment. *Jo. Compar. Neurol.* **128**, 117- 126.

Egger, M. D. and Flynn, J. P. (1967) Further studies on the effects of amygdaloid stimulation and ablation on hypothalamically elicited attack behavior in cats. In *Progress in Brain Research* vo. 27, *Structure and Function of the Limbic System,* Elsevier Publ., W. R. Adey and T. Tokizane, Eds., Amsterdam, pp. 165-182.

Essman, W. B., (1969) "Free" and motivated and amine metabolism in isolated mice. In *Aggressive Behaviour,* S. Garattini and E. B. Sigg, Eds., Excerpta Medica Foundation, Amsterdam, pp. 203-208.

Essman, W. B. (1970) Some neurochemical correlates of altered memory consolidation. *Trans. N. Y. Acad. Sci.* **32**, 948-973.

Essman, W. B. (1971a) Drug effects and learning and memory processes. *Advan. Pharmacol. Chemother.* **9**, 241-330.

Essman, W. B. (1971b) Neurochemical changes associated with isolation and environmental stimulation. *Biol. Psychiat.* **3**, 141-147.

Essman, W. B. (1971c) Metabolic and behavioral consequences of nicotine. In *Drugs, Development and Cerebral Functions,* W. L. Smith, Ed., C. C. Thomas, Springfield, Ill.

Essman, W. B. (1971d) Changes in cholinergic activity and avoidance behavior by nicotine in differentially housed mice. *Internat. Jo. Neurosci.* **2**, 199-206.

Essman, W. B. and Essman, S. G. (1969) Enchanced memory consolidation with drug-induced regional changes in brain RNA and serotonin metabolism. *Pharmako-Psychiat. Neuropsychopharmacol.,* **2**, 28-34.

Essman, W. B. and Essman, S. G. (1971) Cholinergic mechanisms and avoidance behavior acquisition: Effects of nicotine in mice. *Psychol. Rep.* **29**, 987-993.

Essman, W. B., Heldman, E., Barker, L. A. and Valzelli, L. (1972) Development of microsomal changes in liver and brain of differentially housed mice. *Fed. Proc.* **31**, 121.

Fennessy, M. R. and Lee, J. R. (1972) The effect of benzodiazepines on brain amines of the mouse. *Arch. Internat. Pharmacodyn. Thèrap.* **197**, 37-44.

Ferchmin, P. A., Eterovic, V. A. and Caputto, R. (1970) Studies on brain weight and RNA content after short periods of exposure to environmental complexity. *Brain Res.* **20**, 49-57.

Fiske, D. W. and Maddi, S. R. (1961) *Functions of Varied Experience*, Dorsey, Homewood, Ill.

Flexner, J. B., Flexner, L. B. and Stellar, E. (1963) Memory in mice as affected by intracerebral puromycin. *Science* **141**, 57-59.

Flexner, L. B., Gambetti, P., Flexner, J. B. and Roberts, R. B. (1971) Studies on memory: Distribution of peptidyl-puromycin in subcellular fractions of mouse brain. *Proce. Nati. Acad. Sci.* **68**, 26-28.

Fonberg, E. (1965) Effect of partial destruction of the amygdaloid complex on the emotional-defensive behavior of dogs. *Bull. Acad. Polon. Sci.* **13**, 429-432.

Forgays, D. G. and Forgays, J. W. (1952) The nature of the effect of free-environmental experience in the rat. *Compara. Physiol. Psychol.* **45**, 322-328.

Fuxe, K. (1964) Distribution of monoamine nerve terminals in the central nervous system. *Acta Physiol. Scand.* **64** (suppl. 247), 37-86.

Garattini, S., Giacalone, E. and Valzelli, L. (1969) Biochemical changes during isolation-induced aggressiveness in mice. In *Aggressive Behaviour*, S. Garattini and E. B. Sigg, Eds., Excerpta Medica Foundation, Amsterdam, pp. 179-187.

Gumulka, W., Samanin, R. and Valzelli, L., (1970) Effect of chlorpromazine on 5-hydroxytryptamine metabolism in hippocampal stimulated rats. *Europ. Jo. Pharmacol.* **12**, 276-279.

Horvath, F. E. (1963) Effects of basolateral amygdalectomy on three types of avoidance behavior in cats. *Jo. Compar. Physiol. Psychol.* **56**, 380-389.

Hydén, H. and Lange, P. W. (1968) Protein synthesis in the hippocampal pyramidal cells of rats during a behavioral test. *Science* **159**, 1370-1373.

Hymovitch, B. (1952) The effects of environmental variations on problem solving in the rat. *Jo. Compara. Physiol. Psychol.* **45**, 313-321.

Jalfre, M., Monachon, M. A. and Haefely, W. (1971) Effects on the amygdalo-hippocampal evoked potential in the cat of four benzodiazepines and some other psychotropic drugs. *Naunyh-Schmiedelebergs Arch. Pharmakol.* **270**, 180-191.

Karli, P. and Vergnes, M. (1963) Déclenchement du comportement d'agression interspécifique rat-souris par des lésions expérimentales de la bandelette olfactive latérale et du cortex prépyriforme. Séances *Soc. Biol.* **157**, 372-374.

Kety, S. S. (1970) The biogenic amines in emotion and arousal. In *The Neurosciences: Second Study Program*, F. O. Schmitt, Ed., Rockfeller Univ. Press, New York. pp. 324-336.

Köhler, W. (1938) *The Place of Value in a World of Facts*, New York: Liveright Publ., 1938.

Krech, D., Rosenzweig, M. R. and Bennett, E. L. (1960) Effects of environmental complexity and training on brain chemistry. *Jo. Compara. Physiol. Psychol.* **53**, 509-519.

Krech, D., Rosenzweig, M. R. and Bennett, E. L. (1962) Relations between brain chemistry and problem-solving among rats raised in enriched and impoverished environments. *Jo. Compar. Physiol. Psychol.* **55**, 801-807.

Krech, D., Rosenzweig, M. R. and Bennett, E. L. (1966) Environmental impoverishment, social isolation and changes in brain chemistry and anatomy. *Physiol. Behav.* 1, 99-104.

Leaf, R. C. and Muller, S. A. (1966) Effect of scopolamine on operant avoidance acquisition and retention. *Psychopharmacologia* 9, 10-11.

Levine, S. and Otis, L. S. (1958) The effects of handling before and after weaning on the resistance of albino rats to later deprivation. *Can. Jo. Psychol.* 12, 103-108.

Marcucci, F., Mussini, E., Valzelli, L. and Garattini, S. (1968) Decrease in N-acetyl-L-aspartic acid in brain of aggressive mice. *Jo. Neurochem.* 15, 53-54.

Miller, N. E. and Dollard, (1941) *Social Learning and Imitation,* Yale Univ. Press, New Haven.

Moyer, K. E. (1968) Kinds of aggression and their physiological basis. *Commun. Behav. Biol.* 2, (pt.A); 65-87.

Ojemann, R. G. (1966) Correlations between specific human brain lesions and memory changes. *Neurosci. Res. Prog. Bull.* 4, (suppl.); 1-70.

Olds, M. E. and Olds, J. (1969) Effects of anxiety-relieving drugs on unit discharges in hippocampus, reticular midbrain, and pre-optic area in the freely moving rat. *Internat. J. Neuropharmacol.* 8: 87-103.

Osgood, C. E. (1953) *Method and Theory in Experimental Psychology,* New York Univ. Press, New York.

Pallaud, B. (1968) Mise en evidence d'un comportament d'imitation chez la souris. *Rév. Comport. Animal.*

Pallaud, B. (1969a) Influence d'un congénére sur l'apprentissage chez la souris. *Co. Re Acad. Sci.* 268: 118-120.

Pallaud, B. (1969b) Infleuce d'un congénére sur la performance chez la souris. *C Acad Sci.* 269: 1101-1104.

Robinson, E. (1963) Effect of amygdalectomy on fear-motivated behavior in rats. *Jo. Compar. Physiol. Psychol.* 56: 814-820.

Rosenzweig, M. R. (1964) Effects of heredity and environment on brain chemistry, brain anatomy and learning ability in the rat. *Sympo. Physiol. Determinates Behav.: Implications Mental Retardation* (Kansas Study Education) 14: 3-34.

Rosenzweig, M. R. (1966) Environmental complexity, cerebral change, and behavior. *Amer. Psychologist* 21: 321-332.

Rosenzweig, M. R., Krech, D., Bennett, E. L. and Diamond, M. C. (1962) Effects of environmental complexity and training on brain chemistry and anatomy: a replication and extension. *Jo. Compar. Physiol. Psychol.* 55: 429-437.

Rosenzweig, M. R., Love, W. and Bennett, E. L. (1968) Effects of a few hours a day of enriched experience on brain chemistry and brain weights. *Physiol. Behav.* 3: 819-825.

Rosenzweig, M. R., Bennett, E. L., Diamond, M. C. Wu, S., Slagle, R. W. and Saffran, E. (1969) Influences of environmental complexity and visual stimulation on development of occipital cortex in rat. *Brain Res.* 14: 427-445.

Russell, R. W., Watson, R. H. J. and Frankenaeuser, M. (1961) Effects of chronic reductions in brain cholinesterase activity on acquisition and extinction of a conditioned avoidance respones. *Scand. J. Psychol.* 2: 21-29.

Scott, J. P. (1959) *Aggression.* Univ. of Chicago Press, Chicago, Ill.

Seward, J. P. (1946) Aggressive behavior in the rat. IV. Submission as determined by conditioning, extinction, and disease. *J. Compar. Psychol.* 39: 51-75.

Sofia, R. D. (1969) Effects of centrally active drugs on four models of experimentally-induced aggression in rodents. *Life Sci.* 8 (pt.I): 705-716.

Sokolov, E. N. (1963) Higher nervous functions; the orienting reflex. *Annu. Rev. Physiol.* 25: 545-580.

Taylor, K. M. and Laverty, R. (1969) The effect of chlordiazepoxide, diazepam and nitrazepam on catecholamine metabolism in regions of the rat brain. *Europ. J. Pharmacol.* 8: 296-301.

Tenen, S. S. (1967) The effects of p-chlorophenylalanine, a serotonin depletor, on avoidance acquisition, pain sensitivity and related behavior in the rat. *Psychopharmacologia* 10: 204-219.

Tozer, T. N., Neff, N. H. and Brodie, B. B. (1966) Application of steady state kinetics to the synthesis rate and turnover time of serotonin in the brain of normal and reserpine treated rats. *J. Pharmacol. Exper. Therap.* 153: 177-182.

Valzelli, L. (1967a) Drugs and aggressiveness. *Advan. Pharmacol.* 5: 79-108.

Valzelli, L. (1967b) Biological and pharmacological aspects of aggressiveness in mice. In *Neuropsycho pharmacology* (Proc. 5th Int. CINP Congress, Washington, D.C., 1966) pp.28-31. H. Brill, Ed., Excerpta Medica Foundation, Amsterdam, pp. 28-31.

Valzelli, L. (1969a) Aggressive behaviour induced by isolation. In *Aggressive Behaviour*, S. Garattini and E. B. Sigg, (Eds.), Excerpta Medica Foundation, Amsterdam, pp. 70-76.

Valzelli, L. (1969b) The exploratory behaviour in normal and aggressive mice. *Psychopharmacologia* 15: 232-235.

Valzelli, L. (1971a) Agressivité chez le rat et la souris: aspects comportementaux et biochimiques. *Actual. Pharmacol.* 24: 133-152.

Valzelli, L. (1971b) Further aspects of the exploratory behavior in aggressive mice. *Psychopharmacologia* 19: 91-94.

Valzelli, L. (1972) *Principi di Psicofisiologia e Neurochimica* Manfredi Editore, Milano.

Valzelli, L. (1973) *Psychopharmacology: an Introduction to Experimental and Clinical Principles,* W. B. Essman, Ed., Spectrum Press, New York.

Valzelli, L., Giacalone, E. and Garattini, S. (1971) Pharmacological control of aggressive behavior in mice. *Europ. J. Pharmacol.* 2: 144-146.

Valzelli, L. and Bernasconi, S. (1971) Differential activity of some psychotropic drugs as a function of emotional level in animals. *Psychopharmacologia* 20: 91-96.

Valzelli, L., Ghezzi, D. and Bernasconi, S. (1971) Benzodiazepine activity on some aspect of behavior. *Totus Homo.* 3: 73-79.

Vergnes, M. and Karli, P. (1963) Effets de lésions expérimentales du néocortex frontal et du noyan caudé sur l'agressivité interspécifique rat-souris. *C. Séances Soc. Biol.* 157: 176-178.

Vergnes, M. and Karli, P. (1969) Effets de la stimulation de l'hypothalamus latéral de l'amygdale et de l'hippocampe sur le comportement d'agression interspécifique rat-souris. *Physiol. Behav.* 4: 889-894.

Weininger, O. (1953) Mortality of albino rats under stress as a function of early handling. *Can. J. Psychol.* 7: 111-114.

Weininger, O. (1956) The effects of early experience on behavior and growth characteristics. *J. Compar. Physiol. Psychol.* 49: 1-9.

Welch, B. L. (1964) Psychophysiological response to the mean level of environmental stimulation: A theory of environmental integration. In *Symposium of the Medical Aspects of Stress in the Military Climate,* D. McK. Rioch, Ed., U.S. Government Printing Office, Washington, D.C.

Welch, A. S. and Welch, B. L. (1971) Isolation, reactivity and aggression: evidence for an involvement of brain catecholamines and serotonin. In *The Physiology of Aggression and Defeat* B. E. Eleftheriou and J. P. Scott, (Eds.), Plenum Press, New York.

Woolley, D. W. (1965) A method for demonstration of the effects of serotonin on learning ability. In *Pharmacology of Conditioning, Learning and Retention,* M. Ya. Mikhel'son and V. G. Longo, Eds., Pergamon Press, Oxford, pp. 231-236

Yen, C. Y., Stanger, L. and Millman, N. (1959) Ataractic suppression of isolation-induced aggressive behavior. *Arch. Internat. Pharmacodyna. Thérap.* **123**, 179-185.

Zemp, J. W., Wilson, J. E. and Glassman, E. (1967) Brain function and macromolecules. II. Site of increased labeling of RNA in brains of mice during a short-term training experience. *Proc. Nat. Acad. Sci.* **58**, 1120-1125.

CHAPTER 3

Hippocampal Function and Learning Capacity

IVAN IZQUIERDO

1. INTRODUCTION

The present article reviews some recent evidence from our laboratory relating hippocampal function to learning, with special reference to observations made in rats with a genetically low learning capacity. The correlation implied by the title of this chapter must be viewed as an open question rather than as an established fact; it is hoped that the present discussion will contribute towards an answer to that question.

49

The first three sections of this review are, in many respects, introductory, and have been included in order to illuminate the experimental data discussed in the last three sections. Further information on general electrical, biochemical, and pharmacological properties of the hippocampus can be found elsewhere (Green, 1964; Izquierdo, 1971a, b, 1972; Izquierdo & Nasello, 1972; Izquierdo et al., 1971). Many studies by us, as well as by others, are ignored here for the sake of brevity and, in order to avoid lengthy bibliographic lists, review articles by the appropriate authors, in which they comment on their own work, have been cited.

2. ROLE OF THE HIPPOCAMPUS IN LEARNING

In 1937, Klüver and Bucy published the first report of their series on behavioral effects of temporal lobe lesions and from then on it became increasingly clear that one of the fundamental symptoms was the loss of recent memory (Klüver & Bucy, 1937, 1938, 1939). By then, the psychiatric entity called "Korsakoff syndrome" was well known: it features memory loss and hippocampal and mamillary lesions. In 1957, on the basis of data from human surgery, Scoville and Milner concluded that the loss of recent memory, which Klüver and Bucy associated with temporal lobe injury, was in fact the result of hippocampal damage.

Since that time, the role of the hippocampus in learning and memory has been accepted, and it was strengthened notably by the outstanding observation of Penfield that electrical stimulation of the temporal lobe induced vivid recollections of past experience in humans (Penfield, 1958; Penfield & Pérot, 1963). Discussing these observations, and others on hippocampal ablation, Penfield (1958) concluded that "without the hippocampus and the hippocampal gyrus, the recording of current experience is impossible". The hippocampus was recognized as a crucial component of neural circuits involved in learning.

Subsequent studies on hippocampal lesions in experimental animals, however, produced results much less dramatic than those observed in humans. Some early papers even surprisingly reported what might be termed an "increase of learning efficiency" (Green, 1964), with enhanced resistance to extinction (Isaacson et al., 1961). Most of the work on hippocampal lesions in animals, however, seemed to point to a loss of the capacity to inhibit repetitive, additional or otherwise irrelevant responses, and a concept was developed of the hippocampus as an inhibitory center, crucial to the performance of correct learned responses, but not necessarily related to the actual storage of acquired information (Kimble, 1968). In fact, the idea that memory traces actually lie stored within the hippocampus gradually lost acceptance, and it left Green (1964) "unimpressed"; he was "more inclined to think that the amnesia after hippocampal . . . lesions in man can best be interpreted as due to the disturbance of incoming or of outgoing paths (i.e., transactional mechanisms) and/or to side effects of seizure discharges".

In fact, lesions might be regarded as a method generally too crude and inadequate for the study of brain function (Izquierdo, 1972; Izquierdo & Izquierdo, 1970). It was the only available method for many years; however, since the advent of increasingly refined recording techniques and, particularly, since the introduction of the spreading depression procedures (Leao, 1944), which allows temporary suppressions of the electrical activity of a restricted zone, lesions have become obsolete. Spreading depression is reversible, and it does not cause either gliosis or irritation, nor does it induce functioning of vicarious circuits, by virtue of the short duration of its effect. (Izquierdo, 1972).

Hippocampal spreading depression does interfere with acquisition of a learned response (Bures, 1964). This is clearly compatible with the observations of Scoville and Milner (1957) and Penfield (1958) on human surgery.

It is interesting to note that both in rats (Olds & Olds, 1961) and in humans (Bickford et al., 1958), strong direct electrical stimulation of the hippocampus has similar effects to those of spreading depression. It seems likely that such direct pulses may act not by actual stimulation, but by inducing seizure discharges, which are usually followed by spreading depression. The hippocampus has the lowest seizure threshold among brain structures (Green, 1964; Izquierdo, 1971a, 1972; Izquierdo & Nasello, 1972), and it is exquisitely sensitive to direct electrical stimulation, and even to the slightest mechanical irritation (Green, 1964; Izquierdo & Vásquez, 1968). Electrical pulses applied directly to the hippocampus will interfere with its electrical activity, and therefore with whatever sort of information processing taking place in relation to learning (Izquierdo, 1972).

A major advance occurred with the introduction of recording techniques. Grastyán et al. (1959) reported that theta rhythm, which had previously become attenuated in the course of habituation, reappeared prominently on the first few associations of the conditioned stimulus with an unconditioned one. Since during both habituation and conditioning, theta rhythm appeared to be associated with inhibition of the orienting response, they concluded that it was an expression of the inhibitory role of the hippocampus. Adey and his group, in a series of remarkable papers which have appeared since 1960 (see Adey, 1961, 1966), also noted the peculiar prominence and continuity of theta rhythm during training; but they also observed that typical phase relations occurred between simultaneously recorded hippocampal and entorhinal theta rhythm depending on whether the animal was about to perform a correct or an incorrect response. Since theta waves anteceded actual behavioral responses, these could be predicted by examination of the phase relations of the electrographic records. Adey concluded that the hippocampus participated in the learning process in the role of a decision-maker, the decision being based in phase comparison of theta waves. He and his colleagues have thoroughly explored this matter in diverse learning situations, with refined auto- and cross-correlation techniques, and have gathered some pharmacological data to support their contentions (Adey, 1961, 1966).

The so-called "Adey versus Grastyán controversy" has been re-examined recently by Bennett (1971). On the basis of Adey and Grastyán's published data, and of some of his own, Bennett arrived at the conclusion that "the current evidence best supports a view relating the occurrence of theta to orienting and attention". This is quite remarkable, since ten years earlier Adey specifically stated that his "records show no evidence of this . . . activity at times when the animal's head and trunk were undergoing turning from side to side in a fashion reminiscent of classical pavlovian orientation, although such activity" (the theta waves) "was present during locomotion to a goal immediately preceding and following periods of orientation" (Adey, 1961), and Grastyán and his group (1959) clearly correlated hippocampal theta with inhibition and not with performance of the orienting response.

We actually see no reason why the notion that the hippocampus stores information (Penfield, 1958), possibly for further analysis upon each presentation of the conditioned signals (Adey, 1961, 1966), must necessarily be considered as opposite to the idea that the hippocampus serves an inhibitory role (Kimble, 1968; Grastyán et al., 1959), In fact, in order to decide whether the animal will perform a correct learned response or not, the hippocampus must recognize signals and compare them with information either stored in it or somewhere else in the brain; furthermore, the decision to perform a given response implies the inhibition of all other behavior which is not strictly relevant (Izquierdo, 1972).

To summarize, it may be concluded that there is much evidence relating the hippocampus to learning. Some of the evidence suggests that it is either a site, or part of a circuit, involved in the storage of memory traces; other data suggest that it serves an inhibitory role. Both lines of evidence are not mutually exclusive, but may even be complementary.

3. HIPPOCAMPAL CORRELATES OF LEARNING

a. Electrical Activity

On the basis of the data of Adey, Grastyán, Bennett, and others, showing that the occurrence of long trains of theta waves in the hippocampus correlate with the acquisition and performance of learned responses, Grastyán and his group (1959) remarked that theta waves "represent a conditioned reflex manifestation". This correlation is independent of the eventual role of the theta waves in inhibition or in decision-making.

Hippocampal theta waves originate between the basal and the apical dendrites of pyramidal cells (Green et al., 1960), and may be visualized as a series of evoked responses to trains of spikes originating in the medial septal nucleus and arriving at the hippocampus through the dorsal fornix (Stumpf, 1965). It is interesting to note here that septal and hippocampal lesions have very similar effects on learned behavior (Fried, 1969).

Before its relation to learning had been established, hippocampal theta rhythm was considered to be a correlate of attention, or the hippocampal equivalent of neocortical desynchronization to novel stimuli (Green and Arduini, 1954). Later studies, however, showed that the first presentation of a given stimulus causes hippocampal desynchronization, and that theta waves occur, rather, on repetition of the stimulus, thus being "a conditioned . . . manifestation" and a correlate of inhibition of orienting responses. (Grastyán et al., 1959). The question arises whether hippocampal theta rhythm may not be a more general correlate of the processing of previously stored information, and not just of learning. The phase comarator role proposed by Adey (1961, 1966) might partly imply this. During the phase of sleep in which dreams are believed to occur, the hippocampus also features a long-lasting, stable theta activity (Jouvet, 1965). It is obvious that during dreaming, the brain handles data previously acquired and somehow stored in it by a memory mechanism (Izquierdo, 1972). No doubt, some association and perception is possible during the dreaming phase of sleep (paradoxical sleep); animals may be aroused from it by stimuli with a learned significance (Izquierdo et al., 1965). However, the possibility that new images, not based on memory, are actually created during dreams is doubtful, with the possible exception of the man described by Coleridge, who dreamed that he received a flower in Paradise, and then woke up with the flower in his hand (Borges, 1968).

b. Biochemical Activity

Memory storage is believed to involve the transduction of electrophysiological information into more stable, presumably self-regenerative chemical events (Kandel & Spencer, 1968). There have been long discussions and many speculations on the nature of these chemical events. Some have proposed changes in desoxyribonucleic acids (DNA and RNA); others have postulated changes in protein synthesis, related to the production of new branchings of nerve cells, or to the enlargement of synaptic surfaces, or to transmitter metabolism; others have proposed changes in the macromolecules which occupy the extracellular space (see Adey, 1969; Izquierdo, 1972; Kandel & Spencer, 1968, for references). Whatever the chemical changes underlying memory are, it seems obvious nowadays, on the basis of current biochemical knowledge, that these changes must be initiated by the production of RNA, and subsequently of proteins, presumably enzymatic (Izquierdo, 1972). So, the minimum requirement of a proposition that a given brain region is involved in memory, is that a demonstrable enhanced RNA and protein production can be found in it as a result of learning.

This minimum requirement has been fulfilled for the hippocampus. The first suspicion that learning could cause an increased RNA synthesis in the hippocampus evolved from a paper by Zemp et al. (1967), who reported an increased incorporation of ^{3}H-uridine into RNA in brain sections, which included a large part of the hippocampus, from trained animals. In 1969, Bowman and Strobel carried out a similar study, by examining anatomically defined areas of the brain; they found a more marked RNA labeling in the hippocampus than elsewhere. Simultaneously with this paper, Nasello and I (1969) published a report on the effect of acute and "chronic" learning, and of drugs known to affect learning, on the total RNA concentration of hippocampus, neocortex, and other areas. We observed that a 25-min session of active avoidance in a shuttle box caused an increase of both neocortical and hippocampal RNA; a 6-day training schedule using the same procedure caused a RNA increase only in the hippocampus; a 25-min session of pseudoconditioning, using the same type and number of stimuli as were used for learning, had no effect. Single intraperitoneal injections of amphetamine or nicotine, in doses known to favor learning, increased hippocampal RNA; 10-day treatments caused a decrease. (Nasello and Izquierdo, 1969). Such treatments, however, have been recently found to deteriorate, rather than enhance, learning (Montini et al., 1970). The increase of hippocampal RNA found after single doses of amphetamine and nicotine was confirmed later by Daroqui and Orsingher (1972), who observed, in addition, that eserine, another learning-enhancing agent, shared the same effect.

An important point with regard to hippocampal RNA, is that the actual correlate of learning appears to be increased concentration, and not just increased synthesis. Gattoni and I (1971) observed that the incorporation of ^{3}H-uridine into nuclear and cytoplasmic hippocampal and neocortical RNA was much more increased after pseudoconditioning than after true conditioning; the former, however, was accompanied either by no change (Nasello & Izquierdo, 1969) or by a fall (Gattoni & Izquierdo, 1971) of RNA concentration, whereas the second was accompanied by a definite increase. An explanation of this finding is provided by some as yet unpublished results of Gattoni and I; after pseudoconditioning there is a marked increase of both neocortical and hippocampal acid ribonuclease activity, which does not occur upon conditioning. No change was detected after either behavioral procedure in alkaline ribonuclease activity.

If even a 25-min training procedure is capable of raising hippocampal RNA, the question must be posed of how long this rise will last. One would expect it to be not too long, since otherwise hippocampal RNA would grow indefinitely during the life span of an animal. An early observation of Zemp et al. (1966) on whole brain homogenates showed that the increased ^{3}H-uridine uptake by RNA caused by training occurred only during the fist 15 min after it. Of course, it may be argued that since this observation was on the whole brain, a change specific to the hippocampus might have gone undetected (Izquierdo, 1972). Gattoni and I, however, observed in 1971 that the increased hippocampal RNA concentration detected in rats after training was no longer visible 15 min after it, which agrees with the 1966 data of Zemp et al. on whole brain.

Another question arises as to whether there is any evidence that training causes the synthesis of a given specific type of RNA, or if all hippocampal RNA species increase at the same time. In studies on whole brain, some have claimed that a unique RNA type may be formed during training (Machlus and Gaito, 1968); there are, however, many reservations to be made regarding this experiment about the specificity of this change to learning. Some of these reservations were raised by the authors themselves. In their 1966 paper on whole brain homogenates, Zemp et al. found that the ^{3}H-uridine incorporation into RNA was heterogeneous as to RNA types separated by ultracentrifugation, and in this sense neither specific to learning nor to cerebral tissue. In fact, an increased and indiscriminate synthesis of RNA leading to increased concentration is typical of any organ submitted to moderate physiological stimulation: liver, thyroid gland, adrenals, pancreas (see references in Nasello & Izquierdo, 1969), cerebral tissue (Itoh & Quastel, 1969), autonomic ganglia and other nervous tissues (Glassman, 1969). The once popular concept that RNA molecules carry coded information relevant to learning (Hydén, 1959) is now outmoded (Kandel & Spencer, 1968); perhaps with justice, in view of the recent data that synaptic stimulation of nerve cells (apparently of the most diverse type of nerve cell) increases their RNA synthesis (Berry, 1969; Izquierdo et al., 1969; Kernell & Peterson, 1970; Marichich & Izquierdo, 1970; Peterson & Kernell, 1970; Gisiger, 1971).

In consequence, the question of whether learning involves the synthesis of specific RNA types in the brain or in the hippocampus is not yet answered, and available data tends to suggest that the eventual answer might be negative.

Protein synthesis has also been observed in the hippocampus during learning; there is, unfortunately, no clear indication of the function of these proteins. Beach et al. (1969) reported that a greater uptake of ^{3}H-leucine may be seen in autoradiographs of the hippocampus of trained rats than in other structures or in untrained animals. Hydén and Lange (1968, 1970) observed an increase of the synthesis of certain acidic proteins in the hippocampus of trained animals. They made no comparisons with other areas, however, and thus were unable to conclude whether this change is specific to the hippocampus or not. At any rate, the proteins that Hydén and Lange studied might be related to the origin of the RNA increase, and not necessarily be a result of it; these acidic proteins are apparently nuclear, and might actually be DNA derepressor molecules (Hydén and Lange, 1968). An interesting alternative to the function of these acidic proteins is posed by the experiments of Calissano and Bangham (1971), who observed that they exert a Ca^{++} regulated effect on the permeability to K^+ of artificial lipid membranes. The potential importance of this observation is speculative, and may be related to our own results to be found below in Sections 4, 5, and 6 of this review.

During electroshock convulsions, the rate of brain protein synthesis falls (Cotman et al., 1971). These seizures are known to interfere with the setting down of memory traces (McGaugh, 1966), and start with hippocampal involvement (Barcik, 1970). It is not surprising that seizures depress protein synthesis, since they are known to transitorily lower RNA in the brain as well (Chitre et al., 1964). Interference with drugs of brain, and particularly hippocampal, protein or RNA synthesis usually impairs learning (see the chapter by Nakajima in this volume).

4. HIPPOCAMPAL MODELS OF LEARNING

Models are not to be confused with correlates (Kandel & Spencer, 1968). Theta rhythm, and increased RNA concentration and protein synthesis, are hippocampal correlates of learning: they occur during it, and, if interfered with, result in learning impairment. The events to be discussed in the present section are simply paradigms; they may or may not eventually be found to be correlates.

a. Enduring Changes in Electrical Activity

Hippocampal pyramidal cells respond differentially to all sorts of internal or external sensory stimuli (Green & Machne, 1955; Green, 1964; Yokota et al., 1967). In fact, even if all sensory stimuli eventually cause excitatory postsynaptic potentials at these cells, probably because they all arrive by two or three common final, excitatory pathways (Green, 1964; Yokota et al., 1967), they are not all equally capable of inducing pyramidal firing (Yokota et al., 1967). There are several possible reasons for this: relative temporal or spatial dispersion at early stations such as the mesencephalic tegmentum or others, preferential arrival through one or other of the final common pathways—fornix, temporo-ammonic tract, commisural fibers, etc. (Yokota et al., 1967; Izquierdo, 1972). It is evident, then, that by presenting two different sensory stimuli in pairs, one might affect the response to the second stimulus by the first, just by simple temporal summation (Yokota et al., 1967).

Repeated paired sensory stimulation induces long-lasting changes (minutes, hours) both of the unitary (Olds & Olds, 1961) and of field (Brazier, 1961) responses to one or both members of the pair. Obviously, these enduring changes can not be explained by temporal summation alone, which brings us back to the possibility of chemical changes and to the corresponding uncertainties. One alternative possibility is the deformation of synaptic membranes by synaptic currents proposed by Elul (1966); such deformations may, in theory, outlive the actual causative factor for many minutes or hours. They have, however, been so far noticed only in tissue cultures.

b. Heterosynaptic Facilitation and Posttetanic Potentiation

When two stimuli are given to hippocampal afferent pathways in close succession, the field response to the second may be enhanced by the first. If both pulses are to the same pathway, the phenomenon is called *homosynaptic facilitation*; if each pulse is to a different pathway, the phenomenon is called *heterosynaptic facilitation*. The facilitatory effect of single volleys starts at about 40 msec and lasts up to about 600 msec from the peak of the first evoked response of the pair (Vásquez et al., 1969); maximum facilitation occurs at 80 msec, which then could be called the "optimum" interstimulus interval (Izquierdo & Nasello, 1970).

When an afferent pathway is stimulated repetitively, successive responses to single shocks delivered to that same pathway, or to other pathways, are also enhanced. In the former case we are in the presence of *homosynaptic posttetanic potentiation*; in the latter, the event is *heterosynaptic*. Both types of posttetanic potentiation occur in the hippocampus; in fact, it appears to be the only nervous structure so far where heterosynaptic posttetanic potentiation of monosynaptic responses has been described (Izquierdo & Vásquez, 1968). Homo- or heterosynaptic posttetanic potentiation lasts several seconds or even minutes (Izquierdo & Vásquez, 1968; Nasello et al., 1969).

Heterosynaptic facilitation and posttetanic potentiation are rather obvious paradigms of learning (one reflex is modified by association with another reflex) (Kandel & Spencer, 1968). These phenomena correspond quite closely to the so-called "principle of contiguous excitation" believed to be historically the basis of the modern hypotheses on the mechanism of conditioning, and described by William James (1890): "when two elementary brain processes have been active together or in immediate succession, one of them, on re-occurring, tends to propagate its excitement to the other" (Kimble, 1961).

Hippocampal facilitation and posttetanic potentiation are closely interrelated, and the latter may be viewed as a special case of the former. This becomes especially clear when one analyzes hippocampal field responses during faradic stimulation. The first few evoked responses of the train build up rapidly, as a result of successive facilitation of each by the preceding one. Once the build-up has become established, a sudden switch to a single shock mode will reveal heightened responses, which return to normal gradually: this is posttetanic potentiation (Green & Adey, 1956; Izquierdo & Nasello, 1970).

Heterosynaptic potentiation of hippocampal evoked responses may also be brought about pharmacologically. Amphetamine nicotine and eserine induce firing in bursts by medial septal cells, an effect which can be blocked by atropine and which causes hippocampal theta or faster rhythms (Stumpf, 1965; Izquierdo et al., 1971; Izquierdo, 1972). The bursts originating in medial septal cells travel to the hippocampus by the dorsal formix (Stumpf, 1965; see section 3b), and, thus, may be considered as a tetanic stimulation of the former. After the systemic injection of amphetamine, eserine or nicotine, or after their intraseptal administration, hippocampal field responses to subicular or commisural stimulation become enhanced (Izquierdo et al., 1968). This effect can only be explained by heterosynaptic potentiation, via the firing of fornical afferents; neither subicular nor commisural fibers pass through or relay on the medial septum, on one hand, and, on the other, the direct topical application of amphetamine, eserine or nicotine on the hippocampus is without any effect on evoked responses. Intraperitoneal or intraseptal atropine blocks the effect of the other three agents (Izquierdo et al., 1968).

It is interesting to recall here that, as has been noted before (section 3b), amphetamine, nicotine and eserine are drugs which favor memory consolidation (Izquierdo et al., 1971; Izquierdo, 1972) and that they cause both theta rhythm and an increase of hippocampal RNA (Nasello & Izquierdo, 1969; Daroqui & Orsingher, 1972).

The mechanism of hippocampal facilitation and posttetanic potentiation has been studied extensively in our laboratory. Both seem to be due to the transitory elevation of extracellular potassium $(K^+)_o$ caused by the release of this ion by stimulation, from nerve cells or fibers into the restricted local extracellular space. For a theoretical account of how stimulation builds $(K^+)_o$ up for periods of milliseconds up to minutes, see Lebovitz (1970). For evidence that hippocampal facilitation and posttetanic potentiation are due to a $(K^+)_o$ build-up, see Izquierdo (1967,

1971a,b, 1972), Izquierdo and Nasello (1970), Izquierdo et al. (1970, 1971), and Nasello et al. (1969). This evidence derives from three main sources: a) the effect of veratrine, tetraethylammonium and diphenyl-hidantoin, drugs which affect K^+ release and, in consequence, its extracellular accumulation, on facilitation, posttetanic potentiation and seizures; b) the effect of perfusing higher than normal K^+ concentrations through the hippocampus; c) measurements of the actual release of K^+ from the hippocampus upon physiologic and epileptogenic afferent stimulation.

It is interesting to point out here that too intense or too prolonged repetitive stimulation of afferent pathways causes hippocampal seizures (Green, 1964). These are triggered when $(K^+)_o$ rises up to a certain "critical" level (Izquierdo, 1967; Izquierdo & Nasello, 1970), about three times as high as that thought to be associated with, say, theta rhythm (Izquierdo et al., 1970, 1971; Izquierdo, 1971a, b; 1972; Izquierdo & Nasello, 1972; Marichich & Izquierdo, 1972). Thus, in the hippocampus, seizures may be considered as the result of an exaggeration of the mecha-nism which, in normal conditions, permits enhanced synaptic activity lead-ing to facilitation and potentiation. Seizures such as those of electroshock (Barcik, 1970), which are initiated in the hippocampus, hinder learning.

In 1963, Sachs (cited by John, 1965) observed that injection of a moderate amount of KCl into the lateral ventricles of cats, improved their rate of acquisition of a learned response, whereas a higher amount of KCl caused seizures and impaired learning. Since intraventricular injections reach, of course, the hippocampus immediately, it is certainly tempting to imagine that the results of Sachs may be related to the induction of synaptic potentiation and seizures in this structure, at the two KCl dose levels he used (Izquierdo, 1972).

One point is of importance regarding hippocampal physiology. When $(K^+)_o$ is very high, a single volley delivered to any hippocampal afferent pathway will cause a seizure (Izquierdo et al., 1970; Izquierdo, 1971b); when $(K^+)_o$ is moderately high, a single afferent volley will induce facilitation of ensuing responses to other volleys (Vásquez et al., 1969; Izquierdo & Nasello, 1970). Thus, the outcome of a single stimulus will differ markedly depending on the level of hippocampal $(K^+)_o$ (Izquierdo, 1972), and, of course, this will have important implications for the nature of the corresponding information emitted at the hippocampal output (the afferent fibers of the fornix; see Vásquez et al., 1969) and transmitted to those structures to which the hippocampus projects.

5. STIMULUS RECOGNITION IN THE HIPPOCAMPUS AND LEARNING

As pointed out in Section 1, whatever the role of the hippocampus in learning may be, in order to have any it must feature a means to recognize signals with reference to previous experience: recent experience, if the role is related to acquisition or to memory consolidation; not necessarily recent, if it participates in retrieval.

As mentioned in Section 3, pyramidal cells respond differentially to the diverse sensory stimuli, and paired stimulation could lead to interaction. facilitation and posttetanic potentiation (see 3.b), particularly in their heterosynaptic varieties, clearly increase very markedly the range of possibilities of interaction; especially so, when one considers the fact that the facilitating power of a given afferent stimulus depends greatly on the nature of the stimulus with which it is associated. Thus, pulses delivered to the fornix facilitate more often (and up to a greater degree) responses to further pulses to the fornix than to commisural stimuli; and only in a small percentage of cases, responses to subicular stimuli, etc. (Vásquez et al., 1969; Izquierdo & Nasello, 1970).

Since facilitation and posttetanic potentiation apparently are constant phenomena, at least in normal rats (see Izquierdo et al., 1972); and since apparently all types of sensory modalities converge on pyramidal cells (see Section 3.a.), it seems likely that facilitation and/or potentiation actually occur in the hippocampus during learning. Certainly, stimulus association is the basis of conditioning, and is probably also inherent to other forms of learning.

The occurrence of theta rhythm could cause differential facilitation of hippocampal responses to diverse afferent stimuli. The repeated bombardment of pyramidal cells by the trains of pulses which come by the fornix probably occurs mainly at the basal dendrites, where these fibers seem to terminate (Petsche et al., 1966). Since there is evidence that the incidence of faciliation depends on the vicinity of the terminals of the fibers to which both pulses of a pair are given (Vásquez et al., 1969), it seems likely that signals arriving either by the fornix, or by commisural fibers (Green, 1964; Izquierdo et al., 1971; Izquierdo, 1972), will have their responses more enhanced by theta rhythm than others. There is indirect evidence that during theta rhythm, hippocampal $(K^+)_o$ rises up to 11 mq/liter (Marichich & Izquierdo, 1970, 1972; Isquierdo et al., 1971), which is the optimum $(K^+)_o$ level for synaptic function (Izquierdo et al., 1970, 1971; Izquierdo, 1971b, 1972).

The occurrence of hippocampal facilitation, let alone its participation, in learning, are, however, as yet mere theoretical postulations. No one has so far observed them during a training procedure; but, on the other hand, nobody has looked for them with adequate averaging techniques. In fact, both heterosynaptic facilitation and depression might be expected, which would increase the range of interaction possibilities; excessive $(K^+)_o$ elevations may actually depress evoked responses (Izquierdo & Vásquez, 1968; Izquierdo, 1972).

The synthesis of RNA by nerve cells is regulated by synaptic currents, as mentioned in Section 3.b.; since hippocampal evoked responses are a function of synaptic currents (Green & Petsche, 1961; Izquierdo & Vásquez, 1968), hippocampal RNA synthesis should be sensitive to their facilitation (Izquierdo, 1972). Thus, it seems reasonable to think that stimulus recognition by the hippocampus could be closely linked to an immediately dependent chemical process, initiated by RNA synthesis. This implies a hypothesis on how the hippocampus participates in learning (Izquierdo, 1969, 1972).

As was mentioned in Section 3.b, hippocampal facilitation and posttetanic potentiation are phenomena dependent on the release of K^+ by stimulated fibers or cells, and on the subsequent accumulation of $(K^+)_o$. The hippocampal RNA increase seen after learning (Nasello & Izquierdo, 1969) or after afferent stimulation (Marichich & Izquierdo, 1970) also seems to depend on $(K^+)_o$. For one thing, it can also be caused in the hippocampus by high-K^+ perfusion (Izquierdo et al., 1969), as happens in isolated neocortical slabs when the K^+ in the bath is raised (Itoh & Quastel, 1969). For another, afferent stimulation such as was found to increase hippocampal RNA (Marichich & Izquierdo, 1970), also released hippocampal K^+ (Marichich & Izquierdo, 1972), and causes its external accumulation (Izquierdo et al., 1970).

Therefore, if K^+ release, $(K^+)_o$ accumulation, facilitation and the RNA increase are events related to the role of the hippocampus in learning, one should be able to detect some deficiency in one of them in rats who feature a low inborn learning capacity. The investigation of this problem is the subject of the following sections.

6. HIPPOCAMPAL K^+ RELEASE

a. Stimulation in Poor Learners

Bignami and Bovet (1965) inbred rats which showed a poor performance of active avoidance responses in a shuttle box; after several generations, they were able to obtain a fairly homogeneous rat population, most of which were poor learners in this test. Levin and Orsingher (1970) repeated this selection procedure in our laboratory and observed that, at least from the 5th generation on, these rats, which had been genetically selected for their poor performance in a shuttle box, resulted also in poor learners in a Lashley III maze, where they ran for food. Since both training processes involved essentially different procedures and motivation, Levin and Orsingher concluded that these rats had a genetically determined general inability to learn. The criterion established by Levin and Orsingher to consider a rat as a "poor-learner" in the shuttle box was the performance of less than 15% conditioned responses over 50 trials (using buzzes as conditioned stimuli, shocks to a floor grid as unconditioned stimuli, barrier-crossing responses as conditioned responses, and one trial every 30 sec). Over 70% of the rats in the general stock of our vivarium perform well above this criterion (Izquierdo et al., 1972).

The release of hippocampal K^+ caused by afferent stimulation was investigated in poor learners of the 5th generation, and compared with that of "normal" animals (i.e., those from the general stock which made 40% or more conditioned responses in the shuttle box test). All animals were anesthetized with urethane (1.5 g/kg, intraperitoneally) and placed in a stereotaxic machine, where their dorsal hippocampus was exposed bilaterally by suction. Technical details were as given elsewhere (Izquierdo, 1967; Izquierdo et al., 1970, 1972; Izquierdo & Orsingher, 1972). The rats were subdivided in pairs. One member of each pair was left unstimulated for 35 min after surgery; the other, after 10 min of rest following the operation, received 10/sec pulses to the fornix during 25 min; hippocampal electrical activity was monitored in a storage oscilloscope, and stimulation parameters were continuously adjusted so as to obtain a constant 0.6 mV surface negative evoked response throughout. Both members of each pair (one stimulated, the other unstimulated) were processed consecutively. At the end of the 35 min of rest, or of the 25 min of stimulation, the hippocampus from the recording side was quickly removed, homogenized and processed for electrolyte assay in a flame photometer, as described elsewhere (Izquierdo et al., 1970; Izquierdo & Orsingher, 1972; Izquierdo et al., 1972; Marichich & Izquierdo, 1972). The difference in hippocampal K^+ content between the unstimulated and the stimulated rat of each pair was considered a measure of the K^+ release caused by stimulation (Keesey et al., 1965; Marichich & Izquierdo, 1972; Nasello et al., 1972). It was observed that the release of K^+ by stimulation was lower in the pairs of poor-learner rats (2.1 ± 1.2 meq/kg fresh tissue, n = 11) than in normal animals (5.4 ± 1.0 meq/kg, n = 10); the difference was significant in a "t" test below the p = 0.02 level (Izquierdo & Orsingher, 1972).

This lower release of hippocampal K^+ upon stimulation of the poor-learner rats was not due to a more rapid reuptake by membrane ATPase. For one thing, the difference in K^+ release between normal rats and poor learners was maintained in rats in which the above experiment was repeated under hippocampal perfusion with $10^{-5}M$ ouabain (Izquierdo & Orsingher, 1972), which is a potent inhibitor of membrane ATPase (Skou, 1965). For another, determinations of Na-K-Mg-ATPase and activity performed by us in homogenates of hippocampal and neocortical tissue, gave very similar values in both types of rat (Izquierdo & Orsingher, 1972).

b. Stimulation in Random Rats

In a later experiment, we decided to find out whether the release of K^+ caused by stimulation in the hippocampus of rats could be a function of their performance of conditioned avoidance responses in a shuttle box in animals not selected genetically.

For this experiment, 84 animals of 80 to 200 days of age, and 160 to 350 g of body weight were trained to learn the barrier-crossing response in the shuttle box as indicated in the preceding section. Once their performance had been recorded, they were distributed in pairs. Both members of each pair were of the same sex, of similar weight and age, and had featured a similar performance in the shuttle box (plus or minus 10% conditioned responses over 50 trials). All rats were then anesthetized, submitted to surgery, and processed as in the preceding section; one member of each pair received no stimulation during 35 min after surgery while the other received 10 min of rest followed by 25 min of 10/sec fornical stimulation. The K^+ content of the hippocampus of all rats was determined, and the difference between the stimulated and the unstimulated member of each pair was considered a measure of the K^+ release caused by stimulation in that pair (see above). A linear correlation ($r = 0.65$) was observed between the log of the K^+ release of each pair and its average previous performance in the shuttle box (Izquierdo et al., 1972).

Of course it would be rash to conclude from this experiment that there is a correlation between hippocampal K^+ release by stimulation and learning capacity; after all, only performance in a shuttle box was measured as an eventual parameter of the latter (Izquierdo et al., 1972). However, there seems to be a relation between performance in a shuttle box and maze running for food, at least in rats genetically selected (Levin & Orsingher, 1970), and so these results may be considered as a tenative approach to answering this question. At any rate, clearly these data on K^+ release from the hippocampus of rats from the general stock, are consistent with the previous observations made on genetically selected poor learners, commented on in the preceding section.

c. Physiological Consequences of Low K^+ Release

As mentioned in Section 3.b. and d., hippocampal facilitation, posttetanic potentiation, seizures, and RNA buildup in response to stimulation, are all events apparently caused by the release and subsequent external accumulation of K^+, caused by afferent pulses (Izquierdo, 1972; Izquierdo et al. 1970, 1972.) In consequence, since poor-learner rats have a deficient capacity to release hippocampal K^+, upon stimulation, one would expect also some deficit in these hippocampal properties (see Section 4).

The first phenomenon to be investigated was the relation between the number of afferent pulses needed to cause a seizure and hippocampal $(K^+)_o$. Previously, it had been observed that, at a fixed rate of stimulation (10/sec), this relation is linear (Izquierdo et al. 1970). In poor-learner rats of the 5th generation, it was found that this linearity was preserved, but that at each $(K^+)_o$ concentration, more stimuli were needed than in normal rats in order to obtain a full-fledged hippocampal discharge. This was not due to a lower sensitivity to $(K^+)_o$, since a perfusion of 39 meq/liter of K^+ readily caused seizures both in normal and in poor-learner rat hippocampus. In consequence, the higher number of stimuli that were needed in the latter in order to elicit a seizure could be viewed as the result of their lower capacity to release intracellular K^+ upon each pulse (Izquierdo & Orsingher, 1972).

The incidence of hippocampal facilitation was studied in poor-learner rats of the 7th generation, and compared with that in "high-performance" animals (i.e., rats from the general stock who made 70% or more conditioned responses in the shuttle box over 50 trials). Homosynaptic facilitation could be observed in all of the 18 cases examined in the high-performers, and heterosynaptic facilitation (between fornix—and commisural—evoked potentials) in every case but one. By contrast, in the poor learners, homosynaptic facilitation could be detected in only 8 out of 16 observations, and heterosynaptic facilitation only once. Since a wide range of stimulus parameters and of evoked response amplitudes (from 0.4 to over 3mV) were examined in this study (Izquierdo et al. 1972), the results cannot be attributed to chance, or to a different threshold in the two types of rat. In fact, the latter possibility had been ruled out previously, since we had observed that the stimulus threshold for obtaining a given hippocampal-evoked response was quite similar in normal rats and in poor learners (Izquierdo and Orsingher, 1972).

Posttetanic potentiation is the result of repetitive pulses, and so it should be accompanied (and caused) by a higher and longer-lasting $(K^+)_o$ buildup than facilitation (Lebovitz, 1970). There were, however, a few failures to detect heterosynaptic posttetanic potentiation in the hippocampus of poor learner rats, whereas both homo- and heterosynaptic posttetanic potentiation were found in all of the high-performers (Izquierdo et al. 1972).

The relatively low incidence of posttetanic potentiation and homosynaptic facilitation, and the practical absence of heterosynaptic facilitation in rats with a genetically determined low learning ability, is also clearly attributable to their low capacity to release hippocampal K^+ upon stimulation.

With regard to the RNA increase caused by afferent stimulation in the hippocampus (Marichich & Izquierdo, 1970), which had also been attributed to K^+ release and $(K^+)_o$ accumulation (see Section 4), it could not be detected in poor-learner rats of the 7th generation; of course, it was clearly seen in their high-performance controls (Izquierdo, Orsingher and Ogura, 1972).

These results fit in with the prediction formulated at the end of Section 4, that if the hypothesis that K^+ release, $(K^+)_o$ accumulation, facilitation (and/or potentiation), and the RNA increase, play a role in learning, one should be able to detect a deficit in one or more of them in rats with a poor learning capacity. In fact, all of these events were deficient in these animals.

d. Differences Between K^+ Release

The crucial defect in the hippocampus of the poor learners, which explains all the others we observed, is, obviously, their low release of K^+ upon stimulation. What is the cause of this lower K^+ release?

One possibility is that the number of synapses activated by a given afferent pulse, in order to elicit a given postsynaptic field response, is lower in the hippocampus of poor learners. In fact, there are some claims in the literature that learning capacity may be correlated with the number of synaptic branchings, or that learning occurs through the growth of new synapses, or the enlargement of those already present (see Kandel & Spencer, 1968). We have no direct evidence either in favor or against this possibility, but there is one indirect observation which makes it very unlikely: the stimulation parameters needed to evoke a given hippocampal surface response were very similar in poor learners and in normal rats (see Section 6.b: Izquierdo & Orsingher, 1972). Unless one imagines an extremely precise compensation in terms of more quanta of transmitter released, for a lower number of synapses, this possibility should be ruled out. On the other hand, if the evoked response caused by a given afferent pulse is the same in both types of rat, it would not really be important if one has more synaptic knobs than the other, for the efficiency of that connection would be the same in both.

The possibility that K^+ release was similar in both types of rat, but that in poor learners it was more rapidly recaptured by the membrane ATPase of cells so it could not accumulate, was also ruled out by us (see Section 6.a.; Izquierdo & Orsingher, 1972).

This leaves us with the alternative that either the afferent fibers and their terminals, or pyramidal cells, or both, effectively let less K^+ flow through their membranes when these are stimulated in poor-learner rats, than in normal ones. It is not yet possible to decide whether the reduced K^+ efflux occurs in pre- or in postsynaptic elements (Izquierdo, et al.

1970); available technical procedures do not permit such a discrimination. However, independent of the neural elements in which the lower K^+ release occurs, there are again two possibilities to account for it.

One is that there may be a lower K^+ gradient across hippocampas cell membranes in the poor learners. This possibility was made unlikely by the finding that both K^+ and Na^+ concentrations were closely similar in hippocampal and neocortical homogenates, and in cerebrospinal fluid samples of poor-learner and of normal rats (Izquierdo & Orsingher, 1972). Since the total volume occupied by the extracellular space is much smaller, and contains much less K^+ than the intracellular compartment, at least for this ion it may be said that a determination in a whole tissue homogenate will give values reflecting quite closely those of the intracellular compartment (Izquierdo et al. 1970; Marichich & Izquierdo, 1972). With regard to the cerebrospinal fluid, since it is not possible to measure $(K^+)_o$ directly in the extracellular clefts, one may consider its values as the closest possible measure of those in the actual extracellular fluid (Cohen, et al. 1968). However, both our determinations of ionic contents in tissue homogenates and in cerebrospinal fluid may be considered as merely a crude approximation of whether the K^+ gradient across neural membranes is lower in the poor learners. For one thing, electrolyte measurements in whole tissue ignore differences that may exist between glial and neuronal cells; glia probably constitutes a large percentage of the weight of the tissue sample under analysis. Unfortunately, current techniques for separation of neuronal and glial cells are unsuitable for electrolyte assays. Further, an important gradient may exist between the ionic composition of the fluid immediately outside hippocampal nerve cells, and the cerebrospinal fluid; intercellular clefts are rich in mucopolysaccharides and other polyanionic macromolecules, which may "trap" the K^+ which flows out of cells and cause large local accumulations of it, with consequent localized reductions of the $(K^+)_i/(K^+)_o$ gradient (Adey, 1969).

The other possibility to explain the lower K^+ release from the hippocampus of poor-learner rats is that its neural membranes have a biochemical defect by which they are less able to increase their K^+ conductance when stimulated than those of normal animals (Izquierdo & Orsingher, 1972). Unfortunately, too little is know about what components of neural membranes are involved in K^+ currents. The experiments by Calissano and Bangham (1971) mentioned in Section 1.b., on an increase of K^+ permeability of artificial lipid membranes when brain-specific acid proteins are added to them, seem to open up a possibility worth further exploration. In preliminary experiments performed in this laboratory, however, Orsingher, Ogura and Patrito have been unable to detect any quantitative difference between the acidic protein content of hippocampus homogenates from normal and poor-learner rats. Instead they found a lower amount of certain basic proteins which run close to the beta-globulin fraction in polyacrylamide gel disc electrophoresis. It is, however, certainly premature to link this finding with those on K^+ release. At any rate, the biochemical analysis of presumable membrane constituents offers a promising approach resolving this question.

7. CLOSING COMMENT

From the literature survey of Sections 2. and 3., it may be concluded that the hippocampus apparently has a role in learning, and that several aspects of its activity actually correlate with learning, and that several aspects of its *subserve* an inhibitory role, or acts as a decision-maker; it seems possible that it carries out both functions. In Section 4 some models were introduced which suggest possible ways in which the hippocampus may recognize stimuli, and develop a chemical activity linked to this recognition; Section 5. outlines a hypothesis of the role of the hippocampus in learning based on facilitation and RNA synthesis. Facilitation and the RNA increase are phenomena dependent upon the release of K^+ from cells during stimulation, and subsequent extracellular accumulation. In Section 6., a deficit in K^+ release, leading to defective facilitation and to a lack of the RNA response, is described in rats with a low learning capacity.

It is hoped that the data discussed here serve to stimulate further research both on the role of K^+ in hippocampal physiology and of hippocampal function in learning.

The author wishes to thank Prof. Otto A. Orsingher for his valuable comments and criticism while preparing this manuscript.

8. REFERENCES

Adey, W. R. (1961) Brain mechanisms and the learning process. *Fed. Proc.* **20**, 617-627.

Adey, W. R. (1966) Neurophysiological correlates of information transaction and storage in brain tissue. In Progress in Psychological Psychology. Vol. 1. E. Stellar and J. M. Sprague, Eds., Academic Press, pp. 1-43.

Adey, W. R., Ed., (1969) Slow electrical phenomena in the central nervous system. *Neurosci. Res. Prog. Bull* **7**, 75-180.

Barcik, J. D. (1970) Hippocampal afterdischarge and conditioned emotional response. *Psychonomic Sci.* **10**, 297-298.

Beach, G., Emmans, M., Kimble, D. P. and Lickey, M. (1969) Autoradiographic demonstration of biochemical changes in the limbic system during avoidance training. *Proc. Nat. Acad. Sci.* **62**, 692-697.

Bennett, T. L. (1971) Hippocampal theta activity and behavior–A review. *Commun. Behav. Biol.* **6**, 37-48.

Berry, R. W. (1969) Ribonucleic acid metabolism of a single neuron: Correlation with electrical activity. *Science* 166, 1021-1023.

Bickford, R. G., Mudder, D. W., Dodge, Jr., H. W., Svien, H. J., and Rome, H. P. (1958) Changes in memory function produced by electrical stimulation of the temporal lobe in man. *Res. Publi. Assoc. Res. Nervous Dis.* 36, 227-243.

Bignami, G. and Bovet, D. (1965) Expérience de séléction par rapport à une réaction conditionné d'évitement chez le rat. *C. R. Acad. Sci. (Paris)* 260, 1239-1244.

Borges, J. L. (1968) *Otras in Quisiciones.* Emecé, Buenos Aires, pp. 25-30.

Bowman, R. E. and Strobel, D. A. (1969) Brain RNA metabolism in the rat during learning. *J. Compar. Physiol. Psychol.* 67, 448-456.

Brazier, M. A. B. (1961) Paired sensory modality stimulation studied by computer analysis. *Anna. N.Y. Acad. Sci.* 91, 1054-1063.

Bures, J. (1964) Spreading depression. In *Animal Behaviour and Drug Action,* H. Steinberg, A. V. S. DeReuch and J. Knight, Eds., Churchill, London, pp. 373-377.

Calissano, P. and Bangham, A. D. (1971) Effect of two specific brain proteins (S-100 and 14.3.2.) on cation diffusion across artifcial lipid membranes. *Biochemi. Biophys. Res. Communi.* 43, 504-507.

Chitre, V. S., Chopra, S. P., and Talwar, G. P. (1964). Changes in the ribonucleic acid content of the brain during experimentally induced convulsions. *J. Neurochemi.* 11, 439-448.

Cohen, M. W., Gerschenfeld, H. M., and Kuffler, S. W. (1968) Ionic environment of neurones and glial cells in the brain of an amphibian. *J. Physiol.* 197, 363-380.

Cotman, C. W., Banker, G., Zornetzer, S. F., and McGaugh, J. L. (1971) Electroshock effects on brain protein synthesis: Relation to brain seizures and retrograde amnesia. *Science* 173, 454-456.

Daroqui, M. R. and Orsingher, O. A. (1972, in press) Effect of alpha-methyl-tyrosine pretreatment on the drug-induced increase of hippocampal RNA. *Pharmacology.*

Elul, R. (1966) Dependence of synaptic transmission on protein metabolism of nerve cells: A possible electrokinetic mechanism of learning; *Nature* 210, 1127-1131.

Fried, P. A. (1969) Effects of septal lesions on conflict resolution in rats. *J. Compar. Physiol. Psychol.,* 69 , 375-380.

Gattoni, R. C. and Izquierdo, I. (1971) Condicionamiento y pseudocondicionamiento: Efectos sobre concentración y síntesis de RNA en hipocampo y neocorteza de rata. *Proc. IV Annu. Meeting,* Sociedad Argentina de Farmacología Experimental, p. 75.

Gisiger, V. (1971) Triggering of RNA synthesis by acetylcholine stimulation of the post-synaptic membrane in a mammalian ganglion. *Brain Res.* 33, 139-147.

Glassman, E. (1969) The biochemistry of learning: An evaluation of the role of RNA and protein. *Annu. Rev. Biochem.* 38, 605-646.

Grastyán, E., Lissák, K., Madarász, I., and Donhoffer, H. (1959) Hippocampal electrical activity during the development of conditioned reflexes. *Electroenceph. Clin. Neurophys. J.* 11, 409-430.

Green, J. D. (1964) The hippocampus. *Physiol. Rev.* 44, 561-608.

Green, J. D. and Arduini, A. (1954) Hippocampal electrical activity in arousal. *J. Neurophysiol.* 17, 533-557.

Green, J. D. and Machne, X. (1955) Unit activity of rabbit hippocampus. *Amer. J. Physiol.* 181, 219-224.

Green, J. D. and Adey, W. R. (1956) Electrophysiological studies of hippocampal connections and excitability. *Electroencepha. Clin. Neuro-physiol. J.* 8, 245-262.

Green, J. D., Maxwell, D. S., Schindler, W., and Stumpf, C. (1960) Rabbit EEC "theta" rhythm: Its anatomical source and relation to activity in single neurons. *J. Neurophysiol.* 23, 403-420.

Green, J. D. and Petsche, H. (1961) Hippocampal electrical activity. IV. Abnormal electrical activity. *Electroenceph. Clin. Neurophysiol. J.* **13**, 868-879.

Hydén, H. (1959) Biochemical changes in glial cells and nerve cells at varying activity. In *Proceedings of the IV International Congress of Biochemistry*, Vol. 3 Pergamon Press, London, pp. 64-89.

Hydén, H. and Lange, P. W. (1968) Protein synthesis in the hippocampal pyramidal cells of rats during a behavioral test. *Science* **159**, 1370-1373.

Hydén, H. and Lange, P. W. (1970) Protein changes in nerve cells related to learning and conditioning. In *The Neurosciences Second Study Program*, F. O. Schmitt, Ed., Rockefeller Univ. Press, New York, pp. 278-289.

Isaacson, R. O., Douglas, R. J., and Moore, R. Y. (1961) The effect of radical hippocampal ablation on acquisition of avoidance responses. *J. Compara. Physiol. Psychol.* **54**, 625-628.

Itoh, T. and Quastel, J. H. (1969) Ribonucleic acid biosynthesis in adult and infant rat brain in vitro. *Science* **164**, 79-80.

Izquierdo, I. (1967) Effect of drugs on the spike complication of hippocampal field responses. *Exper. Neurol.* **19**, 1-10.

Izquierdo, I. (1969) Eletrofisiologia e síntese de RNA no hippocampo: Possível participacao no mecanismo central da aprendizagem. *Cien. e Cultura (Sao Paulo)* **21**, 549.

Izquierdo, I. (1971a) The mechanism of hippocampal seizures. *Cien. Cultura (Sao Paulo)* **23**, 487-491.

Izquierdo, I. (1971b) Efectos del potasio sobre el asta de Amón. In *Recientes Progreses en Biología*, J. A. Moguilevsky and R. H. Mejía, Eds. Bona, Buenos Aires, pp. 371-378.

Izquierdo, I. (1972, in press) Hippocampal physiology: Experiments on regulation of its electrical activity, on the mechanism of seizures, and on a hypothesis of learning. *Behav. Biol.* **7**.

Izquierdo, I., Wyrwicka, W., Sierra, G., and Segundo, J. P. (1965) Establissement d'un réflexe de trace pendant le sommeil naturel chez le chat. *Actualités Neurophysiol.* **6**, 277-296.

Izquierdo, I. and Vásquez, B. J. (1968) Field potentials in rat hippocampus: Monosynaptic nature and heterosynaptic post-tetanic potentiation. *Exper. Neurol.* **21**, 133-146.

Izquierdo, I., Vásquez, B. J. and Nasello, A. G. (1968) Indirect effect of drugs on hippocampal field responses to commissural and to subicular stimulation. *Pharmacology* **1**, 178-182.

Izquierdo, I., Marichich, E. S., and Nasello, A. G. (1969) Effect of potassium on hippocampal ribonucleic acid concentration. *Exper. Neurol.* **25**, 626-631.

Izquierdo, I. and Nasello, A. G. (1970) Pharmacological evidence that hippocampal facilitation, posttetanic potentiation and seizures may be due to a common mechanism. *Exper. Neurol.* **27**, 399-409.

Izquierdo, I., Nasello, A. G., and Marichich, E. S. (1970) Effects of potassium on rat hippocampus: The dependence of hippocampal evoked and seizure activity on extracellular potassium levels. *Arch. Intérnat. Pharmacodyn. Thérap.* **187**, 318-328.

Izquierdo, I. and Izquierdo, J. A. (1970) Effects of drugs on deep brain centers. *Annu. Rev. Pharmacol.* **11**, 189-208.

Izquierdo, I., Nasello, A. G., and Marichich, E. S. (1971) The dependence of hippocampal function on extracellular potassium levels. *Currents Mod. Biol.* **4**, 35-46.

Izquierdo, I. and Nasello, A. G. (1972, in press) Pharmacology of the brain: The hippocampus, learning and seizures. In Progress in Drug Research, Vol. 16, E. Jucker, Ed., Birkäuser Verlag, Basel.

Izquierdo, I. and Orsingher, O. A. (1972) A physiological difference in the hippocampus of rats with a low inborn learning ability. *Psychopharmacologia* 12, 386-396.

Izquierdo, I., Orsingher, O. A., and Levin, L. E. (1972a, in press) Hippocampal potassium release upon stimulation and learning capacity of rats. *Behav. Biol.* 7.

Izquierdo, I., Orsingher, O. A., and Ogura, A. (1972b, in press) Hippocampal racilitation and RNA build-up in response to stimulation in rats with a low inborn learning capacity. *Behav. Biol.* 7.

James, W. (1890) *Principles of Psychology*. Holt, New York, p. 566.

John, E. R. In *The Anatomy of Memory*, (1970) D. P. Kimble, Ed., Science and Behavior Books, Palo Alto, pp. 273-275.

Jouvet, M. (1965) Paradoxical sleep- a study of its nature and mechanisms. *Prog. Brain Res.* 18, 20-57.

Kandel, E. R. and Spencer, W. A. (1968) Cellular neurophysiological approaches in the study of learning. *Physiol. Rev.* 48, 65-134.

Keesey, J. C., Wallgren, H., and McIlwain, H. (1965) The sodium, potassium and chloride of cerebral tissues: Maintenance, change on stimulation and subsequent recovery. *Biochem. J.* 95, 289-300.

Kernell, D. and Peterson, R. P. (1970) The effect of spike activity versus synaptic activation on the metabolism of ribonucleic acid in molluscan giant neurone. *J. Neurochem.* 17, 1087-1094.

Kimble, D. P. (1968) Hippocampus and internal inhibition. *Psychol. Bull.* 70, 285-295.

Kimble, G. A. (1961) *Hilgard and Marquis' Conditioning and Learning*, Appleton Century Crafts, New York.

Klüver, H. and Bucy, P. C. (1937) "Psychic blindness" and other symptoms following bilateral temporal lobectomy in Rhesus monkeys. *Amer. J. Physiol.* 119, 352-353.

Klüver, H. and Bucy, P. C. (1938) An analysis of certain effects of bilateral temporal lobectomy in monkeys with special reference to psychic blindness. *J. Compara. Psychol.* 5, 33-34.

Klüver, H. and Bucy, P. C. (1939) Preliminary analysis of functions of the temporal lobe of monkeys. *Arch. Neurol. Psychiat.* 42, 979-1000.

Leao, A. A. P. (1944) Spreading depression of activity in cerebral cortex. *J. Neurophysiol.* 7, 359-390.

Lebovitz, R. M. (1970) A theoretical examination of ionic interactions between neural and nonneural membranes. *Biophys. J.* 10, 423-444.

Levin, L. E. and Orsingher, O. A. (1970) Selección de ratas de bajo nivel de aprendizaje en base a la performance en una "shuttle-box". *Proceedings of the III Annual Meeting* Sociedad Argentina de Farmacología Experimental, p. 18.

Machlus, B. and Gaito, J. (1968) Unique RNA species developed during a shock avoidance task. *Psychonomic Sci.* 12, 111-112.

Marichich, E. S. and Izquierdo, I. (1970) The dependence of hippocampal RNA levels on the frequency of afferent stimulation. *Naturwissenschaften* 57, 254.

Marichich, E. S. and Izquierdo, I. (1972) Potassium loss from rat hippocampus during electrical activity. *Arch. Intérnat. Pharmacodyn. Thérap.* 196, 353-356.

McGaugh, J. L. (1966) Time-dependent processes in memory storage. *Science* 153, 1351-1358.

Montini, E. E., Gattoni, R. C., and Izquierdo, I. (1970) Efectos sobre el aprendizaje del tratamiento cronico con inyecciones "post-trial" de anfetamina, nicotina y salina. *Proceedings of the III Annual Meeting*, Sociedad Argentina de Farmacología Experimental, pp. 20-21.

Nakajima, S. Biochemical disruption of memory: reexamination. this volume p. -

Nasello. A. G. and Izquierdo, I. (1969) Effect of learning and of drugs on the ribonucleic acid concentration of brain structures of the rat. *Exper. Neurol.* 23, 521-528.

Nasello, A. G., Marichich, E. S., and Izquierdo, I. (1969) Effect of veratrine and tetraethylamminium on hippocampal homosynaptic and heterosynaptic posttetanic potentiation. *Exper. Neurol.* 22, 516-520.

Nasello, A. G., Montini, E. E. and Astrada, C. A. (1972, in press) Effects of veratrine, tetraethylamminium and diphenylhidantoin on potassium release by rat hippocampus. *Pharmacology*.

Olds, J. and Olds, M. E. (1961) Interference in learning in paleocortical systems. In *Brain Mechanisms and Learning* A. Fessard, R. W. Gerard, J. Konorski, and J. F. Delafresnaye, Eds., Blackwells, Oxford, pp. 153-187.

Penfield, W. (1958) Functional localization in temporal and deep Sylvian areas. *Res. Publi. Assoc. Res. Nervous Ment. Dis.* 36, 210-226.

Penfield, W. and Pérot, P. (1963) The brain's record of auditory and visual experience—A final summary and discussion. *Brain,* 86, 595-696.

Peterson, R. P. and Kernell, D. (1970) Effects of nerve stimulation on the metabolism of ribonucleic acid in a molloscan giant neurone. *J. Neurochem.* 17, 1075-1085.

Petsche, H., Gogolák, G., and Stumpf, C. (1966) Die Projektion des Zellen des Schrittmachers für den Thetarhythmus auf dem Kaninchem Hippocampus. *J. Hirnforsch.* 8, 129-136.

Scoville, W. B. and Milner, B. (1957) Loss of recent memory after bilateral hippocampal lesions. *J. Neurol. Neurosurg. Psychiat.* 20, 11-21.

Skou, J. C. (1965) Enzymatic basis for active transport of Na^+ and K^+ across cell membranes. *Physiol. Rev.* 45, 596-617.

Stumpf, C. (1965) Drug action on the electrical activity of the hippocampus. *Internat. Rev. Neurobiol.* 8, 77-132.

Vásquez, B. J., Nasello, A. G., and Izquierdo, I. (1969) Hippocampal field potentials: Their interaction and their relation to hippocampal output. *Exper. Neurol.* 23, 435-444.

Yokota, T., Reeves, A. G., and Maclean, P. D. (1967) Intracellular olfactory response of hippocampal neurons in awake, sitting squirrel monkeys. *Science* 157, 1072-1074.

Zemp, J. W., Wilson, J. E., Schlesinger, K., Boggan, W. O., and Glassman, E. (1966) Brain function and macromolecules. I. Incorporation of uridine into RNA of mouse brain during short-term training experience. *Proc. Nat. Acad. Sci.* 55, 1423-1431.

Zemp, J. W., Wilson, J. E., and Glassman, E. (1967) Brain function and macromolecules. II. Site of increased labeling of RNA in brains of mice during a short term training experience. *Proc. Nat. Acad. Sci.* 58, 1120-1125.

CHAPTER 4

Transfer of Learning
in Rodents and Fish

E. J. FJERDINGSTAD

1. INTRODUCTION

The concept of "chemical transfer of learned information", i.e., the proposition that aspects of learned behavior may be induced in naive "recipient" animals by the injection of certain types of brain extract from trained "donor" animals, can be traced to a paper by J. V. McConnell (1962). He showed that naive planarian flatworms acquired a classical conditioning type of training significantly faster when receiving homo-genate of fellow planarians trained on the same paradigm. Although confirmed by several other reports (Jacobson, 1971) the phenomenon was widely doubted and often rejected, because it was considered unlikely that planarians were able to learn at all. However, this question, as well as that of the reality of the planarian transfer effect itself, would now seem to have been settled in the affirmative (Corning & Riccio, 1970; Jacobson, 1971).

Most of the authors of the original four reports of transfer effects in vertebrates acknowledge the impetus received from the work on planarians (Byrne, 1970). However, they were also greatly influenced by the more indirect evidence pointing to a close connection between memory and biochemical processes that had at that time (1965) been accumulated. This evidence may be divided into two types according to the approach employed: 1) Studies utilizing treatments that interfere with memory, 2) studies of chemical changes in the central nervous system caused by learning or other experience.

In studies of the first type it has been very consistently found that memory cannot be interfered with successfully (except by destroying the organism) unless this is done within a short time (hours) after training; this may be accomplished with any treatment that interferes with normal electrical activity, i.e., electroconvulsive shock (Jarvik, 1970) deep anesthesia, hypoxia, and hypothermia (Booth, 1967). Other agents that show a similar effect on memory are inhibitors of the synthesis of ribonucleic acid (RNA) (e.g., 8-azaguanine, actinomycin D) or of protein (puromycin, acetoxycycloheximide) (Deutsch, 1969). When these compounds are given before, during, or within a few hours after training, complete amnesia will result on a test after 24 hr, although the compounds do not interfere with performance or immediate memory of the task. These findings have led to the current biphasic model of memory in which an initial "short-term memory" consisting of specific electrical activities gradually leads to the formation of the permanent "long-term" memory through the process called consolidation, during which macromolecular synthesis necessary for permanent memory is supposed to take place (Byrne, 1970).

The fact that synthesis of new macromolecules does take place as a consequence of training or experience has been reported by several authors. Such changes were found both for RNA, where changes in amount and base ratio were seen (e.g., Hydén, 1967; Shashoua, 1968; Bateson et al., 1972) and, more recently also for protein (Hydén, 1972; Glassman, 1972).

The findings in these two fields are open to at least two different interpretations, the most radical being that the newly synthesized macromolecules carry a type of chemical code that is essential for the storage of the new information. The more conservative interpretation would be that the macromolecular synthesis is simply needed for growth phenomena, such as the formation of new neuronal connections (Agranoff, 1967; Cohen, 1970). Which is correct and, indeed, how important such biochemical changes are for the actual storage of memory cannot, of course, be answered by indirect methods, but only through the direct bioassay technique of transferring brain material from trained animals to naive recipients.

2. RESEARCH WITH RODENTS

a. Early Experiments

Our group at the University of Copenhagen started transfer work with mammals in 1964 (Fjerdingstad et al., 1965), influenced by the direct and indirect evidence for a chemical basis of memory described above. The rat rather than the planarian was chosen as experimental subject, both in order to avoid any discussion of whether our experimental subjects were able to learn, but also because it was thought that its wider range of behavior would prove valuable in further investigating the nature of the effect, if any was found.

The behavioral task used was a discriminative instrumental conditioning situation, a two-alley runway in which the subjects (male Wistar rats of 200 g were used throughout) were required to press a response platform in the lighted alley in order to obtain reinforcement. The latter was 0.1 ml of water per correct choice, and the rats were deprived for 24 hr before the start of training, which was continued until a criterion of less than 10% errors (of reinforcements) was reached, after 10-14 days of 60 reinforcements each (the rats were run to a fixed number of reinforcements every day to keep the level of deprivation constant). Training of donors and testing of recipients in these experiments were carried out in the same manner, i.e., testing was reinforced (a "savings" procedure). Twenty-four hours after reaching criterion, donors were sacrificed by removal of the brain under ether anesthesia, and pooled brains were used for preparation of an RNA extract by the cold phenol method of Laskov et al. (1959). This was subsequently injected intracisternally, under ether anesthesia, into naive recipient rats of the experimental group. A control recipient group received the same type of extract from naive donors, and a third group of rats were not injected, but were anesthetized in the same way as the two other groups. On training these three groups, significant differences were observed from the first day. The experimental group made fewer errors (Table I). This result, which has been obtained repeatedly (Røigaard-Petersen et al., 1968) is clearly consistent with a transfer of information via the injected brain extract. It has been argued that in reinforced testing in transfer work, what is observed may simply be facilitation of learning caused by some stimulating component in the trained extract rather than transfer of information. This is not likely, however, because the experimental recipients, although they showed fewer errors from the start of testing, actually learned more slowly than the two other groups, thus taking about the same number of trials to reach criterion level. A stimulating effect would have been expected to result in a steeper learning curve, starting from about the same level as the other

TABLE I

Mean % Errors in the Test Sessions of a Two-Alley Runway
Transfer Experiment in Rats

Recipient Group:	1 Trained extract	2 Naive extract	3 No Injection	p[b] (1 vs. 2)
Session				
I[a]	37.8	54.8	66.4	.17
II[a]	36.3	68.0	54.8	.014
1	39.3	61.3	101.0	.17
2	21.0	45.3	51.0	.057
3	23.0	40.0	36.4	.057
4	23.3	39.8	35.4	.17
5	9.8	31.8	23.0	.029
6	16.3	12.0	14.4	>.50
7	16.3	10.3	13.4	>.50

[a] Short sessions with 12 hr interval, the first of which was 12 hr after injection; the following sessions were run with an interval of 24 hr.
[b] Mann-Whitney U-test, one-tailed.

groups, but reaching criterion earlier. However, there are other ways to control for this possibility that will be discussed below.

Although we were all working completely independently, three other groups were pursuing similar lines of thought at the same time, so that within a few months in 1965 four reports of the transfer effect in mammals appeared. Babich et al. (1965) reported the transfer of a simple sound approach training by the intraperitoneal injection of RNA extract. A rather similar task was transferred by Reinis (1965) using intraperitoneal injection of a crude brain homogenate; and Ungar and Oceguera-Navarro (1965) used sound habituation as the behavioral task, also injecting homogenate intraperitoneally. Thus from the beginning of these investigations it was established that transfer effects could be obtained with several types of extract and routes of administration, and was not limited to any single type of behavioral situation.

These results, though quite clear-cut in themselves, aroused considerably more controversy than the planarian studies. A primary criticism was that they did not fit in with, or at least were not needed for, the commonly accepted ideas of how the brain stores information (Quarton, 1967; Barondes, 1972). In the discussions three questions emerged as being of paramount importance (Fjerdingstad, 1971a). 1) Was the effect a statistically reliable phenomenon? 2) Did it show task specificity or could it be explained as simply a general enhancement of learning? 3) Granted that the answer to the two first questions were positive, what was the nature of the active component?

b. Investigation of Specificity

While it is obviously beyond the capability of a single laboratory to convincingly answer question 1), the problem of specificity seemed the next in the rank of importance.

In two experiments we tried to investigate this by working with two different groups of trained donor rats, one being trained to go to the lighted alley, the other to go to the dark alley. Perhaps because we used differentially reinforced testing (in one case reinforcing for going to the dark, in another for going to the lighted alley), the results were not very clear-cut although indicating some degree of difference between the trained extracts (Nissen et al., 1965).

Better indication of specificity was found in some experiments with Skinner boxes by Dr. W. L. Byrne and the present author (Fjerdingstad et al., 1970). Here symmetrical two-bar Skinner boxes were used to train two groups of donor rats (200 g male Holtzmann rats), one of which was reinforced (with food pellets) only for pressing the right bar, and the other for pressing the left bar. In order to attain very high bar pressing rates on the correct bar, the training was done on an FR schedule, which was increased every day, so as to require ten presses per reinforcement on the 10th and final day of training.

Two to four hours after the end of training, donors were sacrificed and the brains removed for the preparation of "right-trained extract" and "left-trained extract." In a first experiment this was a crude supernatant of a homogenate in Truis-HCl buffer (0.01M Tris, pH = 7.5, containing 0.9% NaCl), given in doses of one and two brain equivalents per recipient, by intraperitoneal injection. In a second experiment cold phenol RNA extract (Røigaard-Petersen et al., 1968) was injected intracisternally in the amount of 1 mg RNA (about 2/3 brain equivalent) per recipient. Testing in both experiments was done by giving two unreinforced 10 min sessions 15 and 21 hr after injection, followed by daily 20 min test sessions where both bars were constantly reinforcing for every press. In this way the recipients were kept responding at a steady rate, without being influenced in their choice of bar. Therefore any preference shown could not be caused simply by an enhancement of learning. No differences were seen during the unreinforced test sessions, but during the reinforced testing in the 2 brain equivalent recipients of experiment I and the recipients of experiment II there was a significant tendency to press progressively more on the bar corresponding to the one reinforcing during donor training (Table II). These results might be interpreted as demonstrating transfer of specific information within a single stimulus dimension, considered by Dyal (1971) to be the ultimate test of behavioral specificity, and are in agreement with the results described by Rosenblatt and others (Rosenblatt & Rosen, 1971; Herblin, 1971) working with right-left discrimination in an only slightly different procedure. It is interesting that the effects of the two types of

TABLE II

Results of Two Experiments on Transfer of Right-Left Discrimination[a]

Recipients	Experiments: (one-tailed U-test)			
	I^b		II	
	$p = 0.002$		$p = 0.05$	
	L	R	L	R
	+3	+59	+58	+53
	−1	+51	−1	+26
	−18	+30	−9	+24
	−19	+21	−12	+7
	−40	+13	−20	+2
	−50	−10	−21	−12
			−28	−13
			−36	−13
			−49	

[a]Values are changes in the percentage of the total presses that were on the right bar from the first to the second reinforced session.
[b]Recipients of two brain equivalents of extract.

extract do not appear equally strong, left-trained extract apparently being more potent than right-trained extract. This may be due to interference from innate preferences, a problem which can lead to quite complex results (Rosenblatt & Rosen, 1971) in such symmetrical two-choice situations.

Evidence for specificity was also found in a series of experiments on the transfer of alternation between bars in a Skinner box (Fjerdingstad, 1969a). Here one group of donors, 200 g male Sprague-Dawley rats were reinforced (water was used as reinforcement) for alternation presses only, this being defined as pressing one bar following a press on the opposite bar. In this way a level of about 75% alternation could be reached in three weeks, indicating that it was a fairly difficult task for the rats. Another group of donors were reinforced for pressing either bar, but on a VR-3 schedule which served to keep the duration of the sessions approximately equal. These rats rapidly developed very strong preferences, in the majority of the cases for the left bar, even though there was no differential reinforcement. This may be the explanation of the apparently greater potency of the left-trained extract found in the earlier experiments. Either the extracts work better because of an underlying tendency in the majority of the recipients to go to the left anyway, or the left-trained extract contains components representing both the training and the (innate?) preference.

Recipients in these experiments were 20 g Swiss male mice which in three experiments received crude extract of 1.35 g brain each (supernatant of brains homogenized in distilled water as described by Ungar et al., 1968); in two following experiments the RNA extract described above was used. Both types of extract were given intraperitoneally and both were found to be active. Testing of recipients was again carried out with both bars constantly reinforcing, so that there would be nothing that could cause one group to alternate more than the other. Table III shows the result of recipient testing as pooled data of five experiments. It will be seen that recipients of alternation extract alternated significantly more than recipients of control extracts. This again is consistent with a transfer of task specific information, and probably represents a somewhat more advanced stage than the right-left discrimination studies, both because the task is more difficult, and because the transfer must involve the bar pressing schedule as such, and thus cannot be explained in terms of spatial preference.

c. Chemical Nature of the Active Component of Brain Extracts

Because of the large number of data connecting RNA changes and learning (see Introduction) our group, as well as that of Jacobson (Babich et al., 1965), had started with the assumption that RNA extracts would be most likely to yield transfer effects. Reinis (1965) and Ungar and Oceguera-Navarro (1965), however, began their work using crude homogenates of brain in physiological saline and distilled water, respectively. Ungar and co-workers then proceeded to identify and characterize the active component from different training situations through partioning and chromatography methods and found that it went to the phenol phase in a phenol-water system, that it could be destroyed by proteolytic enzymes, was dialyzable, and behaved like a molecule of molecular weight about 1500 on the Sephadex column (Ungar et al., 1968; Ungar, 1971). This evidence indicated a small peptide as the active agent. Similarly Rosenblatt (1969) working with right-left discrimination found evidence that the transfer effect was caused by an oligopeptide.

These results, together with the difficulties experienced in attempts to replicate some of the early work with RNA extracts (Gross and Carey, 1965; Luttges et al., 1966) led to some doubts about the reported transfer effects with RNA extracts. As mentioned above, we had found in experiments on transfer of right-left discrimination and alternation that RNA extracts were as effective as crude homogenates. After the present author joined Dr. Georges Ungar in his laboratory at Baylor College of Medicine in Houston, we carried out some collaborative work designed to answer these questions (Ungar & Fjerdingstad, 1971).

Dr. Ungar had been working for some time with a behavioral situation introduced into the transfer field by Gay and Raphelson (1967). The

TABLE III

Total Number of Alternations During Six Sessions in Recipient
Groups of Five Experiments on Transfer of Alternation[a]

Experimental group n = 27	Control group n = 28
	101
74	
68	
	64
59	
55	
	51
50	
47	
45	
44	44
43	
43	
42	
	41
40	
	39
38	
	37
35	
	34
33	
31	31
29	
	28
27	27
	26
25	25
23	
21	
	21
21	
	21
21	
	20
	18
	18
17	17
15	15
	13
	9
	6
5	5
	4
	4
	3
	3
1	
Mean 35.26	25.89

[a] P = 0.01 (one-tailed U-test).

apparatus consists of three boxes connected with short tunnels. From the center box, the start box (SB), one tunnel gives access to a dark box with a grid floor (DB) and the other to a box with white walls and a clear Plexiglas top (WB). The majority of most populations of rodents will, if placed in the center box move to the DB and show a strong preference (often called "innate") for staying there. If the entrance is closed and the animal is shocked through the grid floor, it will learn to avoid DB. This is essentially a one-trial learning situation. However, both in the work of Gay and Raphelson (1967) and of Ungar et al. (1968) this procedure is repeated many times (five times a day for one week or so) in training donor animals. Rats or, in Ungar's work, mice injected with brain extracts from such donors showed a strong tendency to avoid the dark box as compared to recipients of untrained extract. This was measured as the time out of a 3 min trial that was spent in the dark box (DBT), which would typically decrease from about 120 sec to 60 sec or less.

At the time the present author joined Dr. Ungar, the factor responsible for transferring dark avoidance in the described set-up had been isolated as a single peptide as shown by a single spot in thin-layer chromatography. We carried out a comparison of this preparation and the RNA extract by preparing both from a common pool of trained rat brains, injecting into recipients and testing them at the same time. Some groups were also given RNA extract treated with various enzymes. Table IV shows the DBT in groups of male 20 g Swiss mice injected with these preparations. It is obvious that RNA extract was at least as active as peptide. This was so even when the RNA was treated with chymotrypsin and with RNAse. Treatment with trypsin did, however, abolish the effect, thereby indicating that the activity resided not with the RNA itself, but with some peptide-like contaminant. Later it was found that the active component could be liberated from the RNA by dialysis in acid fluid (Ungar & Fjerdingstad, 1971), and the RNA extraction method we had developed in

TABLE IV

Comparison of the Effects of Peptide and RNA Preparations From Dark Avoidance Trained Donors on Time Out of 3 min Spent in the Dark by Recipients

	DBT[a]	± SD
Peptide	76	26
RNA	67	21
RNA and trypsin	109	29
RNA and chymotrypsin	68	34
RNA and ribonuclease	72	30
Control	121	25

[a]Means of 12 animals tested 24 to 48 hr after intraperitoneal injection of extracts.

Copenhagen was used as a convenient first stage in preparation of large amounts of the peptide called scotophobin, for subsequent determination of its sequence (Ungar, 1971; Ungar et al., 1971). Thus at least for this one behavioral situation it seems well established that the active component is of peptide nature (see also discussion on p. 94).

d. Experiments with One-Trial Learning Situations

One-trial learning situations have proven very useful in other areas of the study of memory, i.e., the field of consolidation, because the time of the learning experience can be so precisely defined (Cherkin and Lee-Teng, 1965). By its nature the dark avoidance situation employed by Ungar is a one-trial learning situation. However, it is claimed that transfer results can only be obtained if a relatively enormous amount of overtraining is given (Ungar, 1971). This is supposedly because of the necessity to build up very high concentrations of the transfer factor before any effect will be seen in recipients (Ungar, 1970), perhaps because uptake and/or utilization of the factor is very inefficient. Even though this may be true, it remains a rather unsatisfactory fact that an amount of experience clearly enough to deeply modify the behavior of the donor should not be sufficient to affect recipients, especially since one-trial learning situations would have obvious advantages for any type of time-course study.

In two different series of experiments evidence was found that one-trial learning situations may be transferable. The first of these was a replication of some studies of LeVan and his group (LeVan et al., 1969) on the transfer of radiation induced avoidance, the second utilized a quite novel behavioral approach, the "acoustic priming for audiogenic seizure" discovered by Henry (1967).

Radiation induced avoidance (Garcia et al., 1955) is seen in rodents who are exposed to high doses of ionizing radiation shortly after having consumed some substance with a characteristic taste that would ordinarily be preferred, such as sacharin, a solution of which is preferred over plain water. Following irradiation, however, the animals will strongly avoid consuming the compound in question. Preparing brain extracts from donors so treated, and injecting them into recipients which were subsequently tested for saccharin consumption without any previous irradiation, LeVan and co-workers (LeVan et al., 1969; Moos et al., 1969; LeVan et al., 1970) were able to transfer radiation-induced avoidance, i.e., a successful instance of transfer of one-trial learning. Similar, but less striking results have been obtained by others investigating the transferability of this type of learning (Revusky & DeVenuto, 1967; Martin, 1967 (personal communication).

Following the procedure of Moos et al. (1969), donor mice (50 days old male Cf-1 mice) were kept in individual cages with a choice between water and saccharin solution (in the first experiment 1% in tapwater, later changed to 1/10%), for 10 days, after which they were deprived of water for 24 hr, allowed a bottle of saccharin solution only for 20 min and irradiated (250 kV x-ray unit with 0.5 mm Cu-filter, 400 R at 60 R/min). Thirty minutes after irradiation the donor brains were removed after decapitation of donors, and a homogenate in ice-cold Ringer was prepared. Thirty microliters of this was injected 1/8 into the right posterior quadrant of the brain of naive recipient mice under light ether anesthesia. A control group received extract prepared from naive donors. During testing, recipients were simply given the choice of bottles with water and saccharin solution and consumptions recorded every 24 hours for periods of up to two weeks. As may be seen from Table V, in all three experiments experimental recipients consumed less saccharin solution than control recipients, which reached significance on two to several days of testing. Thus it seems that these results support the claim of LeVan et al. that radiation-induced avoidance can be transferred. Since critics of the transfer field often claim that there are very few replications outside of a group working with a specific paradigm this in itself is an important observation. However, the results are certainly less striking than the original work. It should be noted that in contrast to the findings of Moos et al. (1969), it

TABLE V

Mean % Saccharin Consumed in Recipient Groups of Three Experiments
on Transfer of Radiation-Induced Avoidance

Day	Experiment I (1% saccharin)		Experiment II (0.1% saccharin)		Experiment III (0.1% saccharin)	
	Experimentals $n = 13$	Controls $n = 11$	Experimentals $n = 15$	Controls $n = 15$	Experimentals $n = 15$	Controls $n = 15$
1	24.3	40.6	65.7[b]	74.9	71.1	66.3
2	32.7	28.7	53.6	69.4	67.6	66.6
3	30.1	23.3	73.5	78.6	84.3	81.7
4	29.6	41.7	60.4[b]	76.1	76.7	80.9
5	31.3	45.4	62.4	76.1	83.4[c]	93.5
6	31.9	39.4	64.0	71.4	80.9[b]	92.2
7	28.0[d]	40.8	60.6	86.1		
8	34.5	39.6	60.3	85.4		
9	35.8	43.5	66.1	80.1		
10	45.5	44.7	64.4	77.6		
11	28.9[a]	43.8	70.5	82.0		
12	35.6[b]	51.7	73.6	89.9		
13	33.8[c]	51.8	76.2	89.6		
14	36.9	47.8	63.9	81.9		

[a]$p = 0.05$; [b]$p < 0.025$; [c]$p < 0.01$; [d]$p < 0.005$ (one-tailed U-test).

appeared that none of the mice showed any preference for 1% saccharin over water, although a transfer effect could still be demonstrated as a further decrease in saccharin consumption of experimental recipients (experiment I). Only with 0.1% saccharin solution was any true preference seen; however, this did not increase the magnitude of the transfer effect. The low dose of brain extract used in these experiments (less than 1% of a brain equivalent) remains an interesting feature. This could possibly be due to the use of intracerebral injections, as much higher doses are necessary when employing other routes of administration (Moos et al., 1969). This might indicate that in the latter case at least 99% of the active component is lost after injection.

Another example of the transfer of one-trial learning is some recent work we have done on the transferability of acoustic priming for audiogenic seizure. This is quite preliminary, but of sufficient interest to warrant a short discussion.

Audiogenic seizures are convulsions that may be induced in rodents by exposure to a loud noise, for instance a powerful electric bell. These seizures may be divided into four different stages, the last of which is death (Table VI). Until quite recently only a few mouse strains were thought to be susceptible, possibly because of a genetic defect (Huff &

TABLE VI

Stages of Audiogenic Seizures in the Mouse According to Henry (1967).

Stage	Response of mouse
I	Wild running
II	Clonic seizures
III	Tonic seizures
IV	Death

Huff, 1962; Collins & Fuller, 1968). In 1967, however, Henry reported that even mice of the most resistant strain C57BL/6J could be made to seize if they were primed by one 30 sec sound exposure at 16 days of age, the time when they begin to hear. Although there was no obviously noticeable response to this first exposure to the stimulus, the mice would on a second exposure five days later show a high incidence of seizures, the majority of them dying (Henry, 1967).

There is some analogy between this phenomenon and the well known imprinting in newly hatched birds, i.e., in both cases there is a short sensitive period immediately after the relevant receptors begin to function. It is possible therefore that "priming" may be a type of learning. As such it would be an extreme example of one-trial learning, deeply affecting the subsequent behavior of the animal. For theoretical reasons, as well as for the evident practical advantages of such short training and testing sessions, it therefore seems worthwhile to investigate the possibility of transferring the priming effect by means of brain extract from primed donors injected into unprimed recipients.

So far two experiments on transfer of the priming effect have been carried out. In both experiments donors, 16 days old C57BL/6J mice of both sexes, were primed, one at a time, by a 30 sec exposure to an Edwards Electric bell (cat. no. 340-62), which was mounted on the lower surface of a wooden lid closing a cylindrical chromatography jar, 30 cm wide and 45 cm high. No obvious reaction to the sound was seen except for a slight startle at the onset. On day 19, the donors were sacrificed by decapitation and the brains homogenized in 3.5 ml ice-cold Ringer per brain. The recipients, naive littermates of the donors, were then injected intracerebrally as described for the studies on radiation-induced avoidance. On day 21, i.e., two days after injection, the recipients were then tested by a 30 sec exposure to the bell.

In the first of the experiments no control group was used, since it had been very well established (Henry, 1967; Henry & Bowman, 1969) that C57BL/6J mice do not seize without previous priming, and we only wanted to investigate whether there would be any observable effect at all. On testing, 3 out of 8 recipients seized (Table VII), going to stages 1, 3, and 4, respectively. With the above considerations in mind, this was

TABLE VII

Responses of Recipients to a 30 sec Sound Exposure in Two Experiments
on Transfer of Acoustic Priming for Audiogenic Seizure

Experiment	Group	Number of mice responding	Number of mice not responding
I	Experimental	3	5
II	Control	0	5
	Experimental	6[a]	4

[a]P = 0.05 (Fisher test)

sufficiently encouraging to call for a second experiment; although the possibility remained that the effect was due to a sensitizing action of the intercerebral injection procedure itself, independent of the type of extract. In the second experiment this possibility was controlled for by including a control group, injected at the same time as the experimental recipients, but with extract of naive donors (littermates of the primed donors). On testing 6 animals out of 10 in the experimental group were found to respond, while none of the control group showed any reaction. This was statistically significant as calculated by the Fisher test (Table VII).

We are proceeding with experiments of this type and, if confirmed, the results seem to indicate that even an experience as short as the 30 sec duration of the priming stimulus may give rise to sufficient chemical change in the brain to be detectable by the bioassay method.

It is interesting to note that experiments with priming through one ear only (the other being blocked with glycerol) and testing with the same or the contralateral ear have shown that only in the first case do seizures result. This indicates that the site of action of the priming stimulus must be at a level receiving only input from one side (Fuller & Collins, 1968; Henry, 1967). This is in agreement with the findings of Ward (1971), using a lesioning technique, that the effect must be restricted to regions of the auditory pathway at the level of or peripheral to the inferior colliculus. This information should make it relatively easy to localize the region of optimal concentration of the active factor.

3. RESEARCH WITH FISH

Although there is an extensive literature on learning in fish (Ingle, 1968) and they are known to learn and remember surprisingly well, no attempt to obtain transfer effects in fish was made until recently. However, goldfish had been used quite extensively in the inhibitor studies of Agranoff et al. (Agranoff, 1967); and Shashoua (1968) had found changes in neuronal RNA following learning in these fish. It seemed quite likely, therefore, that it would be possible to obtain transfer effects in fish too. Since goldfish have several advantages compared to rodents, being inexpensive to buy and keep and having an excellent color vision (Yager, 1969), this seems to be worth investigating.. (A further impetus was received from an allergy that the author developed to rodent hair.) At the same time Zippel and Domagk were also starting transfer work in fish, and the two independent reports were published nearly simultaneously (Zippel & Domagk, 1969; Fjerdingstad, 1969c).

In our work with fish we chose a behavioral technique which was already well established, the shuttle box of Agranoff and his group (Agranoff, 1967), with only slight modifications. The box itself was made from a clear plastic mousecage, 12.5 × 27.5 × 12.5 cm (length, width, height) tapering towards the bottom so as to be 4 cm narrower and shorter there. A black Plexiglas barrier divided it into two equally large compartments, leaving just enough space (2.8 cm) for the fish to shuttle under; such shuttles were monitored by a pair of infrared photocells. Shock (a pulsed dc current of 22.5 mA in 50 msec pulses with a frequency of 1 Hz) could be delivered through stainless steel mesh electrodes completely covering the two sides of each compartment. Two watt stimulus lights were mounted on both ends of the box to serve as CS. The box was completely automated and was controlled by electromechanical programming equipment.

In donor training the CS went on one a minute, always in the compartment where the fish was staying. After an interval, varied from 5 sec to 20 sec in difficult experiments, shock was presented on the same side for a further 20 sec Learning to escape almost immediately, the fish soon began to avoid, and within 10-12 days reached a group mean of 70% avoidance. This was also the case during the summer in spite of Agranoff's (1967) claims to the contrary (Fig. 1).

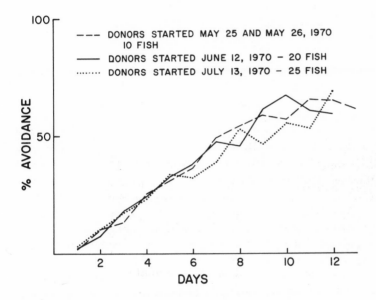

Fig. 1. Learning curves of three groups of donor goldfish trained in the shuttle box with a delay of 5 sec from the onset of stimulus lights to the onset of shock.

Twenty-four hours after the last training session donor goldfish were sacrificed, the brains removed, and the RNA extract described earlier was prepared. This was injected intracranially following the procedure used in Agranoff's laboratory (Davis, 1968) into naive recipients in an amount of 25 µg per recipient. Control recipients were similarly injected with an extract derived from naive donors. Subsequently both groups were exposed to a number of daily sessions of 10 unreinforced light presentations each, the first of these being given 24 hr after injection. Although never having experienced shock, recipients of the trained extract were found to avoid significantly more often than control recipients

(Table VIII). Several such studies were run with slightly varying procedures, all of which gave indications of transfer (Fjerdingstad, 1971b).

In order to overcome the main drawback of this procedure, i.e., the long time consumed by training one fish at a time for many days, a massed training situation was designed with Mr. Rodney C. Bryant at the

TABLE VIII

Mean Number of Avoidances in Recipients of a Shuttle Box
Avoidance Transfer Experiment in Fish

Recipient Group	Experimental $n = 10$	Control $n = 9$
Session		
1	3.40	1.78
2	8.40[a]	5.67

[a]$P = 0.025$ (Fisher test).

University of Tennessee. This was, essentially, an enlarged shuttle box with space for 12 fish at a time. However, in order to be certain that all the fish would be present in the same compartment at the beginning of a trial, it was found necessary to keep the shock on in one compartment until the onset of the stimulus light in the opposite compartment. Also it was, of course, no longer possible to record performance automatically by means of photocells, and visual inspection had to be substituted. Except for these changes, however, the schedule was the same and learning proceeded at approximately the same rate.

With the availability of larger numbers of trained donors it was decided to run an experiment with two different doses of brain extract, 30 and 60 μg per recipient. Surprisingly, significant intergroup differences were only seen in the group receiving the lower dose; however, there was a trend in the predicted direction in the 60 μg recipients, and the pooled data remained significant (Table IX). The reason for this decline of effect with

TABLE IX

Mean Number of Avoidances in Second Test Session of an Experiment
Using Mass Trained Donor Fish

Group	Trained 30 μg $n = 15$	Naive 30 μg $n = 15$	Trained 60 μg $n = 15$	Naive 60 μg $n = 14$	Trained pooled $n = 30$	Naive pooled $n = 29$
	3.53[a]	1.86	2.62	2.53	3.07[b]	2.18

[a]$p < 0.025$; [b]$p = 0.016$ (one-tailed U-tests).

increasing dose remains obscure, however, it has been reported by others that there are optimal doses above which a decrease (Ungar, 1971) or even a complete reversal (Rosenblatt, 1969) will result. In any case it is clear from the data that the phenomenon is not simply caused by an increased level of responding in controls.

Bryant (1971) has extended the use of this type of apparatus to massed testing of recipients and has been able to replicate and confirm the results obtained with individual testing. Massed training and testing procedures would, therefore, seem advantageous for further work requiring large numbers of donors and recipients, i.e., purification and isolation of further transfer factors.

Another possible use of the shuttle box, which we have recently begun to explore, is to use several different colors of stimulus lights, and train several different donor groups, reinforcing a different color for each group. The resulting extracts might then be tested by random, unreinforced presentation of all the colors, which should give a good indication of the specificity of the effect. Earlier work with transfer of color discrimination in fish has been carried out, but has been concerned with the shift of preference from one color to another as resulting from positive reinforcement (Domagk & Zippel, 1971).

Transfer effects in goldfish were also seen in a completely different type of experimental procedure that might be labeled "oxygen reinforced approach training". In this situation, advantage was taken of the readily observable strong tendency in goldfish to surface to take in air if the oxygen content of the water is lowered. By providing an oxygen-free atmosphere on top of oxygen-deprived water, with oxygen being available only from a small surface near the bottom, this behavior could be reversed, so that the fish would go to the bottom when oxygen deprived (Fig. 2). Perhpas becuase of the strongly reinforcing effect of oxygen under such conditions, this task was learned very rapidly (Fig. 3). When naive recipients were injected with RNA extracts from the brains of donors trained in this way, they were found to surface significantly less often than control recipients injected with extract from naive animals, even though testing was carried out with nitrogen over both upper and lower surfaces, i.e., testing was unreinforced (Fig. 4).

4. DISCUSSION

In this chapter transfer effects which were obtained with a variety of experimental approaches have been described. These are summarized in Table X. It will be seen that transfer effects are not limited to any single type of learning, extract, route of administration or experimental subject. Operant conditioning (1, 2, 3, 4, 8), classical conditioning (5, 7) as well as a situation with doubtful "learning status" (6) were found to be

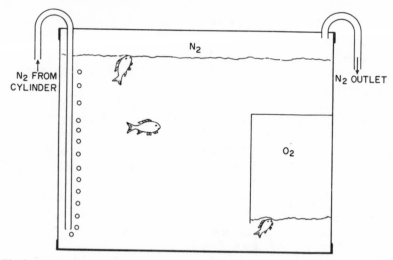

Fig. 2. Apparatus for oxygen-reinforced training of goldfish. Oxygen is washed out of the water by a stream of nitrogen, leaving a nitrogen atmosphere over the surface. After a period of trying in vain to get oxygen from the upper surface, the fish will learn to obtain it from the beaker near the bottom.

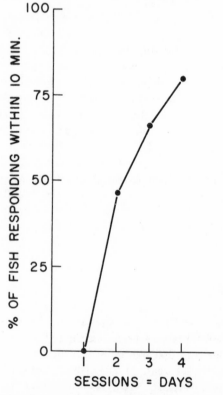

Fig. 3. Learning curve of a group of donor fish trained in the set-up shown in Fig. 2. A response was an approach to the beaker in order to take up oxygen.

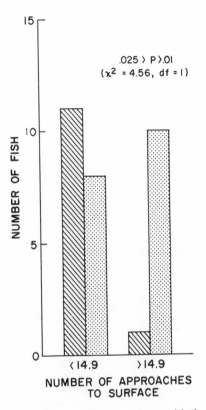

Fig. 4. Recipient performance in a transfer experiment with the set-up shown in Fig. 2. , ▨▨▨▨ Recipients of "trained extract." ▨▨▨▨ Recipients of naive extract.

transferable; positive (1, 2, 3, 4, 8) and negative (5, 7) reinforcement situations were equally effective. Homogenates (5, 6), crude supernatants (2, 3, 4) and partly purified RNA (1, 2, 3, 7, 8) extracts all had an effect, and the site of injection, whether intraperitoneal (2, 3, 4), intracisternal (1, 2), subdural (7, 8) or intracerebral (5, 6) did not appear crucial except insofar as intracerebral injections required lower doses. The effect was found in two classes of vertebrates, and transfer was also found between two closely related species. This is all in agreement with the findings of other authors (Dyal, 1971).

We may now consider the extent to which these results, and those of other investigators in the field, have answered the questions considered the most crucial at the present stage of transfer research (see page 76).

Question 1), whether the effect is statistically reliable, was widely discussed at the time of the original four reports and again when some early attempts to "replicate" the Babich et al. (1965) studies failed (Byrne

TABLE X

List of Experimental Approaches with which
Transfer Effects Were Obtained

Behavioral technique	Subjects	Extract and injection[a]	Reference
1) Light-dark discrimination in two-alley runway	Rats	"RNA" IC	Fjerdingstad et al., 1965; Nissen et al., 1965; Rigaard–Petersen et al., 1968
2) Right-left discrimination in Skinner box	Rats	"RNA" IC supernatant IP	Fjerdingstad et al., 1970
3) Alternation in Skinner box	Rats to mice	"RNA" IP supernatant IP	Fjerdingstad, 1969a
4) Approach training	Rats to mice	supernatant IP	Fjerdingstad, 1969b
5) Radiation induced avoidance	mice	Homogenate in Ringer I Cer.	Fjerdingstad, in press (replication of Moos et al., 1969)
6) Acoustic priming for audiogenic seizure	mice	Homogenate in Ringer I Cer.	Not published before
7) Avoidance in shuttle box	goldfish	"RNA" subd.	Fjerdingstad, 1969c
8) "Oxygen reinforced approach training"	goldfish	"RNA" subd.	Not published before

[a]I.C. = intracisternally; I.P. = intraperitoneally; I Cer. = intracerebrally; subd. = subdurally.

et al., 1966; Gross & Carey, 1965; Luttges et al., 1966). Following this, however, there has been a steady growth in the number of positive reports from an increasing number of laboratories, although there is also a fair number of negative reports. Thus, in 1971 Dyal could report that so far 133 experiments had shown positive results (i.e., with intergroup differences in the predicted direction reaching the $P = 0.05$ level by two-tailed tests), 115 negative results, and 15 were equivocal. Taking into account that in any new and difficult field problems in replicating are apt to appear, and also that for purely statistical reasons a positive result cannot be considered disproved by a negative, he concluded that the evidence heavily favored the reality of the phenomenon. The present data taken alone seems to lead to the same conclusion, in that some degree of transfer was found with each of the approaches listed in Table X. Whether or not one draws such a conclusion will of course depend to some extent on subjective factors or personal bias (Barondes, 1972). It is also fair to point out that some of the reported failures to obtain transfer effects may be due to modifications, although seemingly trivial, of original procedures (Luttges et al., 1966; Smits & Takemori, 1968). In one large, negative report (Frank et al., 1970) the main conclusion (that untrained extracts had as much effect on behavior as trained) was, in fact, based on an elementary error in statistical calculation.

The second question, whether the effect showed task specificity, was dealt with in the work with Skinner boxes (2, 3) in which an indication was found that specific bar pressing schedules could be transferred. This is in agreement with other findings of specificity in right-left discrimination situation (Golub & McConnell, 1971; Rosenblatt & Rosen, 1971; Weiss, 1971), color and taste discrimination in goldfish (Domagk & Zippel, 1971) as well as the weaker evidence provided by the reports that there is no cross-transfer between widely different situations (Dyal, 1971; Ungar, 1971; Rosenblatt & Rosen, 1971). The question of specificity is a difficult one, however, and should in reality be considered a question of type and degree rather than either/or (Dyal, 1971). In any case the puzzling "reversed effects" sometimes found when testing for specificity, especially in symmetrical two-choice situations should be taken into account (Nissen et al., 1965; Rosenblatt, 1969; Rucker, 1971) when evaluating the data. Rucker has argued that this may simply be a close dependent phenomenon that mimics the "overtraining reversal effect" well known from other learning studies, but too little is known yet to decide this question. It would appear that the best way to attack the problem would be the use of a behavioral approach similar to the shuttle box with multiple stimulus lights described above.

The question of the chemical nature of transfer factors appears to have been settled with the isolation, amino acid sequence determination, and synthesis of the transfer factor for dark avoidance, a peptide called scotophobin, by Ungar and co-workers (Ungar, 1971; Ungar et al., 1971). This factor, originally derived from rats trained according to he Gay and Raphelson (1967) procedure described earlier, was found to be a pentadecapeptide with a high content of basic amino acids. The synthetic material, which can easily be produced in larger amounts than could be obtained from any reasonable number of donor animals, has been made available to other researchers for testing. At a recent symposium on "Memory and Transfer of Information" in Göttingen, Germany (to be published), some of these researchers reported complete success in replicating the original findings that the material induces dark avoidance in rodents and even in fish (Guttman, 1972; McConnell, 1972). Others (Byrne, 1972) were not able to obtain any effects with the unreinforced testing used in the original work, but found a facilitating effect on *learning* of dark avoidance and a corresponding inhibitory effect on learning of light avoidance in the goldfish. Still others (Domagk & Thines, 1972; De Wied, 1972) were unable to replicate the original findings, and the latter concluded that the compound was unlikely to have any specific effect on behavior.

It is uncertain what could have caused this divergence of results. Instability of the material is apparently one possibility; probably another is that the behavioral task if not really a very suitable one for this kind of work. Although often called "innate", the degree of preference of rodents for the dark is not very constant, depending on illumination levels in animal rooms and laboratory and other factors that are either not controllable or not controlled by the experimenter. It is therefore likely to fluctuate strongly not only between laboratories, but also within animals. Obviously this makes interlaboratory replication difficult. It is the opinion of the present author that the "change of innate preference" type of behavioral task is in general less useful for transfer purposes, because it is usually not either known or investigated whether in fact the behavior is innate. The experimenter finds himself trying to change (extinguish) a behavior acquired in a manner which he does not know and cannot control. In contrast to this, methods employing a stimulus to which the donors are at first indifferent, and to which they then elaborate a clear-cut response during training (e.g., the shuttle box or priming procedures) appear more promising.

The mechanism of action of these peptides is still unknown. Reinis (1971) has reported a number of experiments with transfer and simultaneous use of metabolic inhibitors which he interprets as showing that transfer factors act by *depressing* hitherto inactive DNA cistrons. The conclusion that normal learning should then also involve derepression was supported by experiments which showed learning to be inhibited by the mutagen hydroxylamine. Ungar (1970, 1971) thinks that transfer peptides may arise by combination of smaller peptides, each characterizing one of two neurons between which a new synapse is formed. This may be catalyzed by transpeptidases (Ungar, 1972). The new combination would then somehow be able to open similar synapses in recipient brains. Further research will be needed, however, to decide which of these hypotheses most closely portrays what happens in the brain during learning.

In conclusion, then, it may be stated that the reality of the transfer effect appears well established, that there is good evidence for task specificity, and that the effect is probably caused by peptides.

5. REFERENCES

Agranoff B. W. (1967) Agents that block memory. In *The Neurosciences, A Study Program*, G. C. Quarton, T. Melnechuk and F. O. Schmitt, Eds., Rockefeller Univ. Press, New York, 756-764.

Babich, F. R., Jacobson, A. L., Bubash, S., and Jacobson, A. (1965) Transfer of a response to naive rats by injection of ribonucleic acid extracted from trained rats. *Science* 149, 656-657.

Barondes, S. H. (1972) Memory transfer. *Science* 176, 631-632.

Bateson, P. P. G., Horn, G., and Rose, S. P. R. (1972) Effects of early experience on regional incorporation of precursors into RNA and protein in the chick brain. *Brain Res.* 39, 449-465.

Booth, D. A. (1967) Vertebrate brain nucleic acids and memory retention. *Psychol. Bull.* 68, 149-177.

Bryant, R. C. (1971) Transfer of light-avoidance tendency in groups of goldfish by intracranial injection of brain extract. *J. Biol. Psychol.* 13, 18-24.

Byrne, W. L. (1970) Introduction. In *Molecular Approaches to Learning and Memory*, W. L. Byrne, Ed., Academic Press, New York, 11-29.

Byrne, W. L. (1972) presented at the Symposium on Memory and Transfer of Information, Göttingen, Germany, May 24-26 (to be published).

Byrne, W. L., Samuel, D., Bennett, E. L., Rosenzweig, M. R., Wasserman, E., Wagner, A. R., Gardner, R., Galambos, R., Berger, B. D., Margules, D. L., Fenichel, R. L., Stein, L., Corson, J. A., Enesco, H. E., Chorover, S. L., Holt, C. E., III, Schiller, P. H., Chiapetta, L., Jarvik, M. E., Leaf, R. C., Dutcher, J. D., Horovitz, Z. P., and Carlson, P. L. (1966) Memory transfer. *Science* 153, 658-659.

Cherkin, A. and Lee-Teng, E. (1965) Interruption by Halothane of memory consolidation in chicks. Federation Proceedings, 1965, 24, 328.

Cohen, H. D. Learning, memory and metabolic inhibitors. In *Molecular Mechanisms in Memory and Learning*, (1970) F. Ungar, Ed., Plenum Press, New York, 59-70.

Collins, R. L. and Fuller, J. L. (1968) Audiogenic seizure prone (asp): A gene affecting behavior in Linkage group VIII of the mouse. *Science* 162, 1137-1139.

Corning, W. C. and Riccio, D. (1970) The planarian controversy. In *Molecular Approaches to Learning and Memory*, W. L. Byrne, Ed., Academic Press, New York, 107-149.

Davis, R. E. (1968) Environmental control of memory fixation in goldfish. *J. Compar. Physiol. Psychol.* 65, 72-78.

Deutsch, J. A. (1969) The physiological basis of memory. *Ann. Rev. Psychol.* 20, 85-104.

De Wied, X. X. (1972) presented at the Symposium on Memory and Transfer of Information, Göttingen, Germany, May 24-26 (to be published).

Domagk, G. F., and Zippel, H. P. (1971) Chemical transfer of learned information in goldfish. In *Chemical Transfer of Learned Information*, E. J. Fjerdingstad, Ed., North-Holland Publ., Amsterdam, 183-189.

Domagk, G. F. and Thines, X. X. (1972) presented at the Symposium on Memory and Transfer of Information, Göttingen, Germany, May 24-26 (to be published).

Dyal, J. A. (1971) Transfer of behavioral bias: Reality and specificity. In *Chemical Transfer of Learned Information*, E. J. Fjerdingstad, Ed., North-Holland Publ., Amsterdam, 219-263.

Fjerdingstad, E. J. (1969a) Chemical transfer of alternation training in the Skinner box. *Scand. J. Psychol.* 10, 220-224.

Fjerdingstad, E. J. (1969b) Chemical transfer of learned preference. *Nature* 222, 1079-1080.

Fjerdingstad, E. J. (1969c) Memory transfer in goldfish. *J. Biol. Psychol.* **11**, 20-25.
Fjerdingstad, E. J. (1971a) Introduction. In *Chemical Transfer of Learned Information*, E. J. Fjerdingstad, Ed., North-Holland Publ., Amsterdam, 11-21.
Fjerdingstad, E. J. (1971b) The goldfish as an experimental subject in chemical transfer. In *Chemical Transfer of Learned Information*, E. J. Fjerdingstad, Ed., North-Holland Publ., Amsterdam, 199-209.
Fjerdingstad, E. J., Nissen, T., and Røigaard-Petersen, H. H. (1965) Effect of ribonucleic acid (RNA) extracted from the brain of trained animals on learning in rats. *Scand. J. Psychol.* **6**, 1-6.
Fjerdingstad, E. J., Byrne, W. L., Nissen, T., and Røigaard-Petersen, H. H. (1970) A comparison of transfer results obtained with two different types of extraction and injection procedures using identical behavioral techniques. In *Molecular Approaches to Learning and Memory*, W. L. Byrne, Ed., Academic Press, New York, 151-170.
Frank, B., Stein, D. G., and Rosen, J. (1970) Interanimal "memory" transfer: Results from brain and liver homogenates. *Science* **1969**, 399-402.
Fuller, J. L. and Collins, R. L. (1968) Mice unilaterally sensitized for audiogenic seizures. *Science* **162**, 1295.
Garcia J., Kimeldorf, D. J., and Koelling, R. A. (1955) Conditioned aversion to saccharin resulting from exposure to gamma radiation. *Science* **122**, 157-158.
Gay, R. and Raphelson, A. (1967) "Transfer of learning" by injection of brain RNA: A replication. *Psychonomic Sci.* **1**, 369-370.
Glassman, X. X. (1972) presented at the Symposium on Memory and Transfer of Information, Göttingen, Germany, May 24-26 (to be published).
Golub, A. M. and McConnell, J. V. (1971) Empirical issues in inter-animal transfer of information. In *Chemical Transfer of Learned Information*, E. J. Fjerdingstad, Ed., North-Holland Publ., Amsterdam, 1-29.
Gross, C. G. and Carey, F. M. (1965) Transfer of learned response by RNA injection: Failure of attempts to replicate. *Science* **1165**, 150, 1749.
Guttman, X. (1972) presented at the Symposium on Memory and Transfer of Information, Göttingen, Germany May 24-26 (to be published).
Henry, K. R. (1967) Audiogenic seizure susceptibility induced in C57BL/6J mice by prior auditory exposure. *Science* **158**, 938-940.
Henry, K. R. and Bowman, R. E. (1969) Effects of acoustic priming on audiogenic, electroconvulsive, and chemoconvulsive seizures. *J. Compar. Physiol. Psychol.* **67**, 401-406.
Herblin, W. F. (1971) The validity and reproducibility of the chemical induction of a position habit. In *Chemical Transfer of Learned Information* E. J. Fjerdingstad, Ed., North-Holland Publ., Amsterdam, 51-63.
Huff, S. D. and Huff, R. L. (1962) Dilute locus and audiogenic seizures in mice. *Science* **136**, 318-319.
Hydén, H. (1967) Biochemical changes accompanying learning. In *The Neurosciences, A Study Program*, G. C. Quarton, T. Nelnechuk, and F. O. Schmitt, Eds., Rockefeller Univ. Press, New York, 765-771.
Hydén, H. (1972) presented at the Symposium on Memory and Transfer of Information, Göttingen, Germany, May 24-26 (to be published).
Ingle, D., Ed. (1968) *The Central Nervous System and Fish Behavior*, Univ. of Chicago Press, Chicago.
Jacobson, A. L. (1971) Progress in the study of learning and chemical transfer in planarians. In *Chemical Transfer of Learned Information*, E. J. Fjerdingstad, Ed., North-Holland Publ., Amsterdam, 211-217.
Jarvik, M. E. (1970) The role of consolidation in memory. In *Molecular Approaches to Learning and Memory*, W. L. Byrne, Ed., Academic Press, New York, 15-26.

Laskov, R., Margolias, E., Littauer, U. Z., and Eisenberg, H. (1959) High-molecular-weight ribonucleic acid from rat liver. *Biochim. Biophys. Acta* **33**, 247-248.

LeVan, H., Hebron, D. L., Moos, W. S., and Mason, H. C. (1969) Transferability of post-irradiation conditioned avoidance behavior by intraperitoneal injection of brain tissues. *Rad. Res.* **39**, Gc-7.

LeVan, H., Moos, W. S., Mason, H. C., and Hebron, D. L. (1970) Induction of post-irradiation conditioned avoidance behavior by intraperitoneal injection of brain tissues. *Experientia* **26**, 648-649.

Luttges, M., Johnson, T., Buck, C., Holland, J., and McGaugh, J. (1966) An examination of "transfer of learning" by nucleic acid. *Science* **151**, 834-837.

McConnell, J. V. (1962) Memory transfer through cannibalism in planarians. *Neuropsychiat.* **3** (suppl. 1), 42-48.

McConnell, J. V. (1972) presented at the Symposium on Memory and Transfer of Information, Göttingen, Germany, May 24-26 (to be published).

Moos, W. S., LeVan, H., Mason, B. T., Mason, H. C., and Hebron, D. L. (1969) Radiation induced avoidance transfer by brain extracts of mice. *Experientia* **25**, 1215-1219.

Nissen, T., Røigaard-Petersen, H. H., and Fjerdingstad, E. J. (1965) Effect of ribonucleic acid (RNA) extracted from the brain of trained animals on learning in rats. II. The dependence of the RNA effect of training conditions prior to RNA extraction. *Scand. J. Psychol.* **6**, 265-272.

Quarton, G. C. (1967) The enhancement of learning by drugs and the transfer of learning by macromolecules. In *The Neurosciences, A Study Program*, G. C. Quarton, T. Melnechuk, and F. O. Schmitt, Eds., Rockefeller Univ. Press, New York, 744-755.

Reinis, S. (1965) The formation of conditioned reflexes in rats after the parenteral administration of brain homogenate. *Activ. Nerv. Super.* **7**, 167-168.

Reinis, S. (1971) A derepressor hypothesis of memory transfer. In *Chemical Transfer of Learned Information*. E. J. Fjerdingstad, Ed., North-Holland Publ., Amsterdam, 109-142.

Revusky, S. H. and DeVenuto, F. (1967) Attempt to transfer aversion to saccharine solution by injection of RNA from trained to naive rats. *J. Biol. Psychol.* **9**, 29-33.

Rosenblatt, F. (1969) Behavior induction by brain extracts: A comparison of two procedures. *Proc. Nat. Acad. Sci.* **64**, 661-668.

Rosenblatt, F., and Rosen, S. (1971) Effects of trained brain extracts on behavior. In *Biology of Memory*, G. Ádám, Ed., Akadémiai Kiadó, Budapest, pp. 137-143.

Rucker, W. B. (1971) Factors controlling interanimal transfer effects. In *Chemical Transfer of Learned Information*, Ed., North-Holland, Publ., Amsterdam, pp. 97-108.

Røigaard-Petersen, H. H., Fjerdingstad, E. J., and Nissen, T. (1968) Effect of ribonucleic acid (RNA) extracted from the brain of trained animals on learning in rats. III. Results obtained with an improved procedur. *Scand. J. Psychol.* **9**, 1-16.

Shashoua, V. E. (1968) The relation of RNA metabolism in the brain to learning in the goldfish. In *The Central Nervous System and Fish Behavior*, D. Ingle, Ed., Chicago Press, Chicago, pp. 203, 213.

Smits, S. and Takemori, A. E. (1968) Lack of transfer of morphine tolerance by administration of rat cerebral homogenates. *Proc. Soc. Exper. Biol. Med.* **127**, 1167-1171.

Ungar, G. (1970) Role of proteins and peptides in learning and memory. In *Molecular Mechanisms in Learning and Memory*, G. Ungar, Ed., Plenum Press, New York, pp. 149-176.

Ungar, G. (1971) Bioassays for the chemical correlates of acquired informaation. In

Chemical Transfer of Learned Information. E. J. Fjerdingstad, Ed., North-Holland, Publ., Amsterdam, pp. 31-49.

Ungar, G. and Oceguera-Navarro, C. (1965) Transfer of habituation by material extracted from brain. *Nature* 207, 301-302.

Ungar, G., Galvan, L., and Clark, R. H. (1968) Chemical transfer of learned fear. *Nature* 217, 1259-1261.

Ungar, G. (1972) presented at the Symposium on Memory and Information Transfer, Gottinger, Germany, May 24-26 (to be published).

Ungar, G. and Fjerdingstad, E. J. (1971) Chemical nature of the transfer factors; RNA or Protein? In *Biology of Memory,* Ádám, Ed., Akadémiai Kiadó, Budapest, pp. 137-143.

Ungar, G. Desiderio, D. M., and Parr, W. (1971) Identification and synthesis of a behavior-coded brain peptide. *Proc. Internat. Union Physiol.* Scientists, XXV. *Internat. Congress* (Munich 1971), 9, 575.

Ward, R. (1971) Unilateral susceptibility to audiogenic seizure impaired by contralateral lesions in the inferior colliculus. *Exper. Neurol.* 32, 313-316.

Weiss, K. P. (1971) Information specificity in memory transfer. In *Chemical Transfer of Learned Information,* E. J. Fjerdingstad, Ed., North-Holland, Publ., Amsterdam, pp. 85-95.

Yager, D. (1969) Behavioral measure of spectral sensitivity in the goldfish following chromatic adaptation. *Vision Res.* 9, 179-186.

Zippel, H. P. and Domagk, G. F. (1969) Versuche zur Chemischen Gadachtnisubertragung von farbdressierten Goldfischen auf underessierte Tiere. *Experientia* 25, 938-940.

CHAPTER 5

Neurochemical Correlates
of Brain Activities

YASUZO TSUKADA

1. INTRODUCTION

It is one purpose of this chapter to discuss some of the biochemical bases of higher nervous activities which may not be directly related to the encoding process of memory or learning. It appears necessary to have more precise information concerning biochemical events in the brain. For example, the finding that RNA or protein synthesis in the brain changes during learning is in itself not sufficient to relate RNA and protein changes unequivocally to the learning process, although it may indicate the importance of these processes in the functioning nervous system. It is certain that many biochemical changes occur in the brain following learning and performance, other than, or in addition to, changes in RNA or protein metabolism. However, one cannot eliminate the possibility that some of these results derive from emotional responses or an arousal state. It is possible that the role of macromolecules in the brain may plan an important part in regulating the efficiency of synaptic transmission.

To investigate functional metabolism which is closely related to higher nervous activities, two different approaches have been adopted; 1) to determine what chemical changes occur in brain following the alteration

99

of brain activities and 2) to evaluate changes in the learning ability of animals following an experimentally produced metabolic disorder in the brain.

2. AMMONIA METABOLISM IN RAT BRAIN AND CONDITIONED REFLEX

The first procedure was to measure ammonia content in the rat brain during various activity states. It is well known that extensive ammonia formation occurs in the brain after electric shock with consequent convulsive seizures and death. This finding is specific for brain tissue and is not seen in other tissues. Ammonia ions have been thought to be of special importance because of their unique functions, and glutamine may be induced in the detoxication of ammonia in the brain. The content of ammonia and glutamine can now be estimated accurately in living rat brain during various states of cerebral activity. The ammonia level of the brain has been regarded as a reliable biochemical index of the state of in vivo physiological activity of the brain.

Experimental arrangements are shown in Figure 1. The experiment was conducted in a dark, quiet room, the left compartment being used for

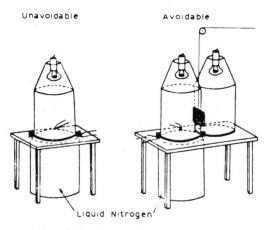

Fig. 1 Apparatus for Experimental Conditioned Reflex Studies

active defense reflex and the right one for an avoidance reflex. The rat was put into the experimental chamber, and an electric shock of 30-50 Vac was applied to the paws through a grid as an unconditioned stimulus. A 60 W electric lamp was used as a conditioned stimulus. In order to obtain the rat immediately at the time corresponding to various states of behavior, an electric magnet was instantaneously switched off at the corresponding point of task activity and the animal was then dropped into liquid nitrogen and frozen. The frozen brain was rapidly chiseled out, ground to a powder in the frozen state, and homogenized after weighing in 10% trichloroacetic acid. Determination of ammonia and glutamine were carried out in accordance with Conway's microdiffusion method.

A mean value of 0.36 μmol/g was obtained for the ammonia content of rat brain in the resting state. Electrical stimulation for 5 sec, which caused an active defense reflex, resulted in a significant increase of the ammonia content of the rat brain to a mean of 0.45 μmol/g, as shown in Table 1. With continuous stimulation longer than 5 sec (for example, 30, 60, 120

Table 1

Mean ($\pm\sigma$) Ammonia and Glutamine
Concentration in Rat Brain after Electric Shock

DURATION OF STIMULATION (SEC)	NO. OF EXPERIMENTS	AMMONIA (μMoles/g)	GLUTAMINE (μMoles/g)
RESTING	14	0.38 (0.06)	0.21 (0.07)
5	11	0.49 (0.01)*	0.20 (0.04)
15	4	0.37 (0.10)	0.20 (0.03)
30	4	0.45 (0.05)	0.24 (0.07)
60	4	0.40 (0.01)	0.22 (0.01)
120	5	0.41 (0.07)	0.19 (0.05)
1800	11	0.38 (0.06)	0.35 (0.02)**

*p <.01
**p <.02

sec and longer) no increase of ammonia level was observed, although rats showed active defense reflex behavior during stimulation.

If the rat was stimulated continuously for 30-60 min with electric current, the brain glutamine content increased significantly, although the ammonia level remained constant as did the resting level. With this kind of stimulation, the rats displayed a peculiar posture during the stimulation phase. They stood on their hind legs on one grid in order to avoid electric shock for 30-60 min. Their behavior appears to correspond to strong defense inhibition. This would be a result of learning to avoid the shock. From these results, one can assume that the ammonia forming process in the brain appears to accompany the excitatory state, and glutamine accumulation as a detoxication mechanism of ammonia relates to the inhibitory state of brain activity.

The next experiment was designed to study the effect of a second 5 sec electrical stimulus on rat brain ammonia level. A second electrical stimulus was applied within 120 min after the first one of 5 sec. This did not induce any increase whatsoever in ammonia content in the naive animal. However, at 150 min, after the first stimulation, an increase of ammonia induced by electrical shock was again observed.

It would appear that the initial stimulus affected chemical processes concerned with brain ammonia metabolism for a long period of time. In other words, the first stimulus produces an after effect which inhibits an elevation of ammonia in living brain (Table 2.)

Table 2

Mean (±σ) Concentration of Ammonia and
Glutamine in Rat Brain After a Second Electric Shock
(Numbers in parentheses = No. of Experiments)

Time After First Stimulation (Min.)	Ammonia (μMoles/g)		Glutamine (μMoles/g)	
0.25	0.47 ± 0.10* (6)	0.42 ± 0.04 (5)	0.35 ± 0.06 (6)	0.34 ± 0.02 (5)
1	0.35 ± 0.002 (4)	0.36 ± 0.01 (5)	0.31 ± 0.05 (4)	0.34 ± 0.01 (5)
2	0.385 ± 0.045 (4)	0.39 ± 0.04 (4)	0.31 ± 0.05 (4)	0.30 ± 0.07 (4)
10	0.42 ± 0.04 (4)		0.31 ± 0.04 (4)	
60	0.42 ± 0.03		$0.40 \, {}^{-0.05}_{+0.10}$ (4)	
120				
150	0.55 ± 0.04 (4)		0.30 ± 0.03 (4)	

*p < .01

When a 60 W lamp was lit for 5 sec and applied to the reinforced rat as a conditioned stimulus instead of an electric shock, similar results were obtained as those for electric shock (shown in Table 3). But, when the

Table 3

Changes of Ammonia and Glutamine in
Rat Brain After the Application of
the Conditioned Stimulus

Condition	Expts.	NH_3 (μmoles/g) (mean±S.D.)	Glutamine (μmoles/g) (mean±S.D.)
Resting state	8	0.35±0.03	3.41±0.38
5-sec cond. stim.	8	0.42±0.03*	3.19±0.41
60-sec cond. stim.	4	0.35±0.03	3.25±0.28
Elect. stim. 60 min after cond. stim.	5	0.41±0.02*	3.51±0.39
Twice cond. stim. with 60-min interval	7	0.39±0.05**	3.13±0.44
Three times cond. stim. with 60-min interval	6	0.35±0.35	3.18±0.25
Elect. stim. 10 min after lighting (unconditioned)	9	0.43±0.03*	3.40±0.41

*P < 0.01.
**P < 0.05.

conditioned stimulus became weaker as a stimulus for ammonia increase. This biochemical change could be related to the extinction phenomenon for behavioral performance in reinforced animals.

The ammonia response caused by a 5 sec stimulus in rat brain was also different in naive and conditioned animals. In the case of reinforced rats which had learned a defense reflex, the second stimulation was sufficiently effective to increase brain ammonia level by 60 min after the initial stimulation, although in naive rats ammonia response appeared at 150 min after the first stimulation. This indicates that the duration of the silent period during which the elevation of ammonia occurred following stimulation (experience) was shortened as a result of repeated stimulation. Futhermore, when the rat was conditioned to the light for an avoidance reflex (operant rather than classical conditioning), the ammonia response caused by the second stimulus appeared 30 min after the first stimulation, as shown in Table 4.

If ammonium chloride, 20 mg/kg, was repeatedly injected, the same effect as that when the rat was trained by electric shock could be observed. Here again, the ammonia response caused by the second stimulation appeared 60 min after the first stimulation (Table 5).

From these results, the effect of reinforcement might be attributed to a

Table 4

Mean (±σ) Concentration of Ammonia (A) and
Glutamine (G) in Rat Brain under Several Conditioning Procedures
(Numbers in Parentheses = No. of Experiments;
values are expressed as μMoles/g).

| Time After First or Second Stimulation (Min.) | STIMULUS CONDITION | | | | | |
| | Unconditioned | | Unavoidable | | Avoidable | |
	A	G	A	G	A	G
Resting		0.32 ± 0.07 (14)		0.35 ± 0.06 (14)	0.35 ± 0.02 (10)	0.32 ± 0.06 (10)
10	0.40 ± 0.03 (4)	0.31 ± 0.04 (4)			0.31 ± 0.03 (4)	0.35 ± 0.01 (4)
30			0.37 ± 0.03 (4)	0.35 ± 0.03 (4)	0.42 ± 0.05 (7)	0.32 ± 0.03 (7)
60	0.42 ± 0.05 (4)	0.40 ± 0.10 (4)	0.52 ± 0.06 (6)	0.40 ± 0.04 (6)	0.44 ± 0.02 (3)	0.33 ± 0.04 (3)
120	0.45 ± 0.12 (4)					
150	.55 ± 0.00 (4)	0.30 ± 0.04 (4)				

Table 5

Effect of a Second Electric Shock
Upon Ammonia and Glutamine
Content of Rat Brain After
Repeated NH_4Cl Injection

Condition	Exp. No.	NH_3	Glu-NH_2
Resting State	14	0.37±0.06	3.40±0.55
2nd Stim after 1st Stim (Naive)	6	0.37±0.05	3.35±0.28
2nd Stim 60 min after 1st Stim (NH_4Cl Inj)	11	0.46±0.10*	3.80±0.14
2nd Stim 60 min after 1st Stim (H_2O Inj)	7	0.41±0.06	3.40±0.33

*$P < 0.02$ μmol/g (Mean±S.D.)

repeated increase of brain ammonia represented as a biochemical code. It seems that brain ammonia metabolism may be closely related to the learning process. We have, thus, examined ammonia metabolism in the brain biochemically, but the source of ammonia in the functioning brain still remains obscure.

3. LEARNING ABILITY IN THE PHENYLKETONURIC MONKEY

Another approach to the study of brain functions involves the question of whether brain activities are altered when metabolic changes occur in the brain. As is well known, in the genetic abnormality of phenylalanine metabolism in which there is a defect in the metabolic pathway of one of the essential amino acids, severe mental retardation results in the syndrome known as "Phenylketonuric Oligophrenia". In this condition, phenylalanine is found at an unusually high level in the blood and cerebrospinal fluid. On the other hand, the blood tyrosine level is very low. Phenylpyruvic acid, a metabolite of the amino acid, is excreted in abnormally high quantities (0.7–2.8g) in the urine. The cause of this disorder is a genetically conferred deficiency of phenylalanine hydroxylase in the liver, which serves to catalize the conversion of phenylalanine to tyrosine by a normal metabolic route (Figure 2). At the present time, therapeutic treatment can be successfully accomplished by limiting the intake of phenylalanine at an early stage of development.

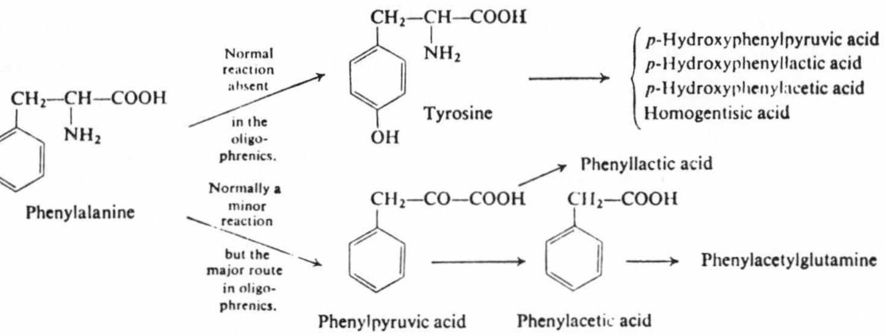

Fig. 2 Pathway for Phenylalanine metabolism.

Biochemical approaches to mental retardation have been attempted using the experimentally induced phenylketonuric monkey as a model of higher nervous activity dysfunction. Five month old infantile monkeys *(Maccaca fuscata)* were given high L-phenylalanine loaded diets that approximated 2 g/kg body weight. Plasma phenylalanine was consistantly elevated, and phenylpyruvic acid was excreted in the urine, as shown in Table 6.

Due to the overload of phenylalanine in the monkey, *de novo* sysnthesis

Table 6

Plasma and Urinary Phenylalanine and
Phenylpyruric Acid Concentration (mg/ml)
in Monkeys Loaded with L-phenylalanine.

Day	Urinary PPA	Serum Phenylalanine	Serum Tyrosine
0	0	0	0
5	100	75	10
10	105	70	15
15	100	40	20
100	95	70	17
200	105	65	19

of liver phenylalanine hydroxylase seems to be inhibited as a feedback process. Consequently, it was thought that phenylalanine metabolism would become abnormal just as in the phenylketonuric patient. It is possible that phenylalanine itself or its derivatives might cause disturbances in developing nervous tissue.

At 200 days after continuous adminstration of L-phenylalanine, intellectual development and neurochemical changes were evaluated in the experimental phenylketonuric monkeys. As shown in Table 7, phenylalanine hydroxylase activity in the liver of the experimental monkey was reduced to 20% of normal. Blood tyrosine level was kept fairly constant in spite of phenylalanine loading.

The intellectual development of monkeys was tested by a light-dark discrimination learning task or O-X figure discrimination learning using a Skinner-type test instrument, as shown in Figure 3. When the correct stimulus shown on the screen, the monkey was able to obtain food by pulling out the bar. The acquisition training was carried out by giving each monkey 100 trials per day. The learning measures are shown in Table 8. In the light-dark discrimination task, a normal monkey learned to almost 100% criterion performance within 3 days, although a phenylketonuric monkey learned to only 70%. In the case of O-X discrimination learning, a

Table 7

Enzyme Activity in Monkey Liver
After Phenylalanine Treatment

Enzyme Activities in the Liver of Monkey

Diet	Phe hydro-xylase*	Phe α-keto-glutarate trans-aminase**	Phe-Pyr trans-aminase**	Tyr-α-keto-glutarate trans-aminase***	p-HPPA oxidase****
Control	1.78	52.0	12.6	21.6	204.0
High Phe	0.34	63.7	16.0	26.6	216.0

Enzyme activities are indicated as the amounts of

 * tyrosine
 ** phenylpyruvic acid
 *** p-hydroxyphenylpyruvic acid formation (μmoles/g liver/h)
 **** p-Hydroxyphenylpyruvic acid oxidase activities are indicated as the amounts of
 p-hydroxyphenylpyruvic acid consumption (μmoles/g liver/h).

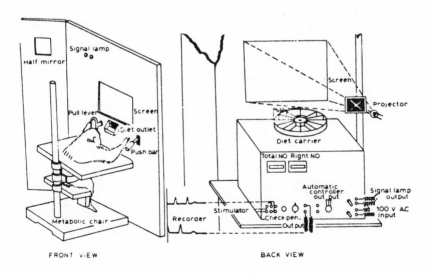

Fig. 3 Apparatus for testing learning ability in monkeys.

Table 8

Per Cent Learning Scores
for PKU and Control Monkeys Tested on
Light-Dark Discrimination and O-X Discrimination Tasks

Light-Dark Discrimination	% Correct DAY										% Error DAY									
	1	2	3	4	5	6	7	8	9	10	1	2	3	4	5	6	7	8	9	10
Control	50	99	99	99	99	99	100	99	99	99	45	51	80	80	70	55	40	25	15	8
PKU	8	70	68	65	90	95		85	80	70	90	60	100	100	85	75	90	45	30	30	35

O-X Discrimination	DAY							
	1	2	3	4	5	6		
Control	34	60	50	90	95	95		- - -
PKU	5	2	2	9	5	10		- - -

dramatic difference was found between normal and phenylketonuric monkeys. An experimental monkey was not able to demonstrate any additional learning of this more complicated test. This finding indicates that the intellectual development of the phenylketonuric monkey was highly disturbed. The somatic development of the phenylketonuric animal was almost normal in terms of body weight, and it had a good appetite throughout the experiment. On EEG examination, nothing of interest was found. However, when the retarded monkey was fed a normal diet for three months, it was again able to learn other figure discrimination learning tasks as well as did the normal control. This demonstrates that this kind of metabolic disorder can be reversible and that metabolic disorders in the brain can produce behavioral abnormality.

In the next phase of the study, biochemical analyses in monkey brain were conducted. Among the free amino acids in the cerebral cortex, GABA and cystathionine were considerably decreased as compared with the normal control, as shown in Table 9, although the RNA, DNA, protein and lipid content of the experimental monkey's brain were not significantly changed. It was interesting that changes in concentration of particular amino acids, such as GABA and cystathionine, which are found only in brain tissue, were observed.

These findings suggest that regional amino acid metabolism in the brain can be related to higher nervous activities in some way. These attempts along with those mentioned above might contribute to our understanding of the relationship between chemical changes and brain activities.

Interdisciplinary approaches to memory storage appear now to be required so that a wide variety of techniques can be brought to bear on these complicated problems.

Table 9

Brain Amino Acid Content
in a Phenylalanine-Loaded
Monkey

Condition	Asp	Glu	GABA	Crystathionine	Phe
Control	3.42	9.46	1.90	1.38	<0.01
PKU	1.64	7.37	1.43	0.27	1.42

μmoles/g w.w.

REFERENCES

Tsukada, Y. (1966) *Prog. Brain Res.* 21A, 268-291.

The editors and publisher wish to thank Igakushion, Ltd., Tokyo for permission to reproduce figures used in this chapter. These were originally published in:
Shinkei kenkyu no shimpo, 1962, *6*, 631.
Shinkei kenkyu no shimpo, 1963, *7*, 721.
Noh to shinkei, 1963, *16*, 747.

CHAPTER 6

Cholinergic Mechanisms in the Regulation of Learning and Memory

R. YU. ILYUTCHENOK,
M. A. GILINSKY,
AND G. V. ABULADZE

1. INTRODUCTION

Current concepts have postulated several possible bases for engram formation; these have included reverberation, the formation of cell assemblies, potentiation and structural changes of synapses, conformational changes of proteins of the subsynaptic membrane, and the activation of the synthesis of nucleic acids leading to increased function of mediator enzymes. All these changes may constitute the basis for the facilitation of subsequent impulse transmission along certain channels of communication in neuronal circuits.

However, the rate of the formation and storage of the engram depends not only upon these mechanisms, but also upon the activity of systems regulating memory. The elucidation of principles of the neurocytochemical architecture of these systems and of their functional capacities is necessary for investigating the mechanisms of electrographic and behavioral responses and predicting the efficiency of psychotropic drugs for the processes of learning and memory. In recent years, neuropharmacological analysis has become one of the major approaches used in studies of intercellular and intracellular processes, and adaptive mechanisms as well as behavior and memory.

Useful investigations have used agents that interfere with the metabolism, storage and uptake of endogenous substances, primarily those which provide for chemical synaptic transmission.

The body of evidence accumulated in the literature, along with the data we have obtained (see Ilyutchenok, 1972), demonstrate that of the drugs which act specifically on neurochemical substrate-specific regions, those influencing cholinergic receptors exert an extremely potent effect on memory trace formation.

In studies concerned with the role of cholinergic mechanisms in memory processes, interesting results have been obtained with anticholinergic drugs. Such data permit evaluation of the contribution of cholinergic mechanisms to each of the three stages of memory trace formation: registration, consolidation, and retrieval.

When anticholinergic drugs were administered before learning amnesic effects were observed, but this effect was not found if they were given promptly after learning. This may be ascribed to drug influence on registration, the earliest stage of memory formation. However, it should be kept in mind that the action of anticholinergic drugs develops slowly. Clear-cut EEG effects are displayed 2-4 min after the intravenous injection of benactizine and 1.5-2 min after scopolamine administration. A decreased firing rate of the neurons of the cortex, hippocampus, amygdaloid complex and the blockade of the reticulocortical evoked potentials occur with a similar latency (Ilyutchenok & Gilinsky, 1971).

Thus, before marked blockade of the cholinergic structures results, even when drugs are administered intravenously, not less than 1-2 min elapse during which the crucial period of consolidation passes. In fact, even electroconvulsive shock may not produce an amnesic effect for certain types of behavior if delivered more than 8 sec after a learning event (McGaugh, 1968).

We have obtained direct evidence that the action of anticholinergic drugs on memory is not due to their interference with registration. The engram may be formed when the blockade of cholinergic structures is time limited by the registration stage. Such a model was produced by taking advantage of the antagonism between anticholinergic drugs and anticholinesterases. The administration of the anticholinesterase galanthamine in appropriate doses may deblock a receptor when required (Ilyutchenok & Eliseyeva, 1972).

2. CONDITIONED RESPONSE ACQUISITION AND RETENTION: CHOLINERGIC BLOCKADE

Passive avoidance conditioned response (PACR) was elaborated in mice while under the effect of the anticholinergic drug scopolamine. In order to abolish the anticholinergic drug effect during the early period of consolidation, galanthamine, which acts rapidly with almost no latent period, was administered intravenously immediately after the training trial. In a previous study it was found that a 15-fold dose of galanthamine is required to abolish the EEG effects of scopolamine. At such doses, however, galanthamine evoked lethal seizures in waking animals. For this reason, the dose of galanthamine had to be reduced. Even incomplete abolition of the cholinergic blockade instantaneously after registration made the elaboration of the conditioned response possible (Fig. 1).

In this experiment, the process of registration was certainly altered with a blackade of muscarinic cholinergic receptors. However, this did not prevent the trace from being laid down, provided that the blockade was subsequently abolished and the crucial period of the consolidation proceeded in the presence of active cholinergic receptors. Therefore, the amnesic effect of anticholinergic drugs appears not to be due to their effect upon the registration stage, but upon the fixation and retrieval of memory trace. When training was carried out under the influence of anticholinergic drugs, memory trace fixation becomes feasible if the intensity of the conditioning foot shock is increased or the number of trials are increased. In untreated cats a fear response is acquired after an auditory stimulus has been paired 3-4 times with unavoidable electric shock. During fear conditioning given following treatment with the anticholinergic drugs benactizine or benzacine, at doses of 1-20 mg/kg, there were no manifestations of the conditioned response whatsoever; the animals did not respond to the conditional stimulus even after 10 paired stimulus presentations. The unconditioned response to electric stimulation remained unimpaired. However, 24 hrs later, when the test was performed in the absence of the drug, effect, the conditioned response was expressed fully and was retained for a long period of time. These results can be integrated with the supporting data of other workers (Meyers, 1965; Ricci & Zamparo, 1965; Oliverio, 1968). With increasing doses of benzacine

114   ILYUTCHENOK, et al

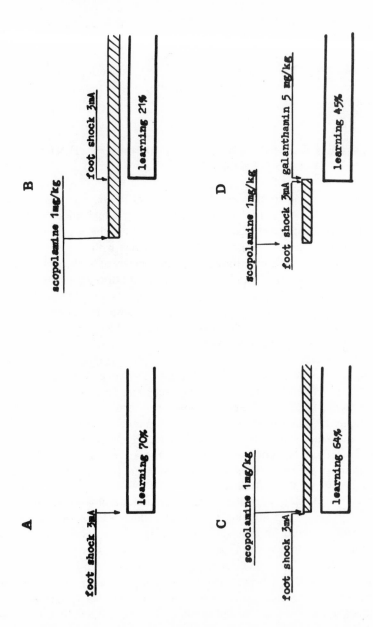

Fig. 1. Amnesic effect of scopolamine and its abolition by galanthamine: (A) control;
(B) PACR blockage by scopolamine given 5 min before single training trial;
(C) no amnesic effect of scopolamine administered immediately after trial;
(D) abolition of amnesic effect of scopolamine by galanthamine administered
immediately after trial.

(1-30 mg/kg) the acquisition of a conditioned emotional response is attenuated and at maximum dose it was not acquired at all, although the unconditioned response was exhibited during conditioning.

Hence, under conditions of learning with stimulus intensification, short-term inhibition of cholinergic structures was insufficient to impair the trace. Such learning may be the consequence of the involvement of previously nonfunctioning synapses during the intense secretion of endogenous acetylcholine. Consequently, when animals are trained under the influence of anticholinergic drugs, the outcome of the competition for the cholinergic receptor determines whether the response will become manifest at the time of conditioning and thereafter. The possibility of abolishing cholinergic blockade at the neuronal level by anticholinesterases supports this suggestion (Ilyutchenok & Gilinsky, 1971). Deutch's hypothesis implying that learning increases the number of functioning synapses is relevant to this issue.

When usual tests fail to provide evidence for a memory trace, it is difficult to decide which mechanism has been impaired; the consolidation of the trace or its retrieval. It may be said that the retrieval mechanism is disrupted only when a consolidated response is not emitted. Kryglikov and Dolganov (1972) have shown that when acquisition of a learned response occurs in the presence of cholinergic blockade (2.5 mg/kg of scopolamine injected i.p. to mice), the trace is not retrieved; it is, however laid down, since it is possible to subsequently recover it by a reminder shock. However, with more profound scopolamine induced blockade (5 mg/kg) memory trace formation is permanently disrupted, because the reminder stimulus no longer serves to mediate retrieval. In this instance it is impossible to determine if the trace has been lost as a result of the impairment either of consolidation or retrieval.

An amnesic effect is attributable to impairment of retrieval, assuming that the retrieval program is established simultaneously with the formation of memory trace. The possibility of impaired retrieval has been demonstrated in our laboratory by Vinnitsky in rats with bilateral amygdalectomy given a single task acquisition training trial. In these animals the memory trace is not retrieved after single trial avoidance conditioning training using a strong pain reinforcement, whereas it is retrieved if repeated, although weaker, reinforcements are given. The apparently nonlearned avoidance behavior by rats trained with a single strong reinforcement showed memory retrieval after a shock reminder. Furthermore, in subsequent days the PACR was more overtly expressed in these animals.

116   ILYUTCHENOK, et al

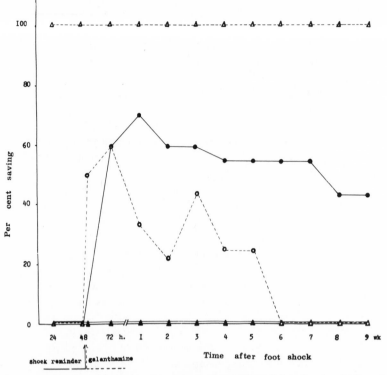

Fig. 2. Galanthamine effect on the retrieval of PACR conditioned under cholinergic
blockakde in mice: (△———△) control training (3 mA, 1 sec); (△———△)
control training under scopolamine (2.5 mg/kg); (o———o) training under
scopolamine (2.5 mg/kg) + shock reminder (10 mA, 1 sec.); (o————o)
training under scopolamine (2 mg/kg) + galanthamine (1 mg/kg).

3. MEMORY TRACE RETRIEVAL: A CHOLINERGIC APPROACH

At present, no data are available which permit us to define the
neurochemical mechanisms for memory trace retrieval, but some observations may shed light on this problem. It has been found that retrieval may
be produced by a "chemical reminder," like that brought about by a shock
reminder. Chemical memory retrieval has been achieved in our laboratory
by Chaplygina utilizing the model of scopolamine amnesia (Kryglikov &
Dolganov, 1972). In this model no evidence for the retrieval of the trace
itself was found if the animals were trained under the influence of 2.5
mg/kg scopolamine injected i.p., but retrieval could be elicited by a shock
reminder. In Chaplygina's experiments mice trained following scopolamine
treatment according to the procedure of Essman and Alpern (1964) did
not show a conditioned passive avoidance response 24-48 hrs after
training. Twenty minutes after the administration of the anticholinesterase

galanthamine (1 mg/kg i.p.) the PACR was retrieved in 50% of the mice (Fig. 2). However, the PACR retrieved by galanthamine persisted for a shorter time than in animals trained without drugs. After 2-4 weeks the response remained in 20% of the mice only, whereas for a control group the incidence of response preservation was 100%. In scopolamine treated animals, amnesia persisted throughout the entire observation period (several weeks).

The data indicate that the prospects for the development of pharmacological approaches for the facilitation of retrieval are encouraging.

4. RETRIEVAL MECHANISMS AND CHOLINERGIC ACTIVITY

The participation of cholinergic events in mechanisms of retrieval was analyzed based upon electrical correlates of the formation of temporary connections in acute experiments conducted with cats and rats. For this purpose, the model of delayed conditional evoked potential was used (Adam & Kukorelli, 1965). After habituation to the conditional stimulus, the CS, (light flash, threshold stimulation of the paw) was paired with the unconditional stimulus, the US (a series of electrical stimuli to the paw, single pulse stimulation of the hypothalamus, thalamus, and the midbrain). As a result of this procedure, the delayed evoked potential (DEP) was registered in the cortex, midbrain reticular formation, posterior hypothalamus and other brain structures. Figure 3 shows the evoked potentials recorded during the habituation procedure (A), the pairing of the CS with US (b), and the DEP in tests omitting the US (C); it may be observed that the DEP occurs in that portion of the curve where the response to the US was previously recorded. In shape, the DEP is similar to the late components of the potential evoked by the US. In some cases, the DEP was represented by a complex of two or even three waves. The appearance of the DEP with a delay identical with the time lag between the CS and the US, its retention, the possibility to extinguish it after change in time lag, all indicate the possibility that the DEP may be an electrical index of the consolidated memory trace.

As in the behavioral experiments, analysis of the hypothalamocortical DEP has shown that changes in cholinergic activity affect the retrieval of memory trace. When the DEP failed to occur after 200 or more pairings, galanthamine administration was sometimes capable of retrieving the DEP. In other experiments 0.75% of the anticholinergic drug benactizine was applied to the somatosensory cortex from which responses to the US were recorded. In this case, the DEP recorded from the auditory cortex of both hemispheres was reduced or disappeared (Fig. 4). Concomitantly, the DEP appeared in the midbrain reticular formation in instances where it has not previously been recorded. (Fig. 5).

The reports of Buser et al. (1969), Rabin (1965), & Lindsley et al.

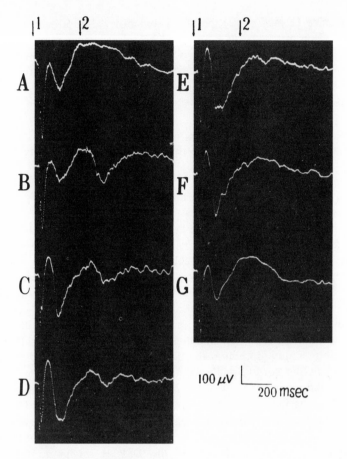

Fig. 3. Delayed evoked potential and increase in late components of the potential evoked by CS in auditory cortex: (A) habituation; (B) 1-20 pairings of CS with US; (C) 181-200 pairings; (D) test; (E) extinction (1-20 presentations of CS 1 hr after test); (F) 81-100 extinctions; (G) 281-300 extinctions. 1,2: marks of presentation of CS and US.

(1972) have demonstrated that the somatosensory cortex is the most influential cortical area for changes in the activity of the reticular formation (RF). These data are in agreement with our results and permit us to explain the appearance of the DEP in the RF after the application of benactizine to the somatosensory cortex and blockade of the descending inhibitory influence.

The reciprocal relationship between the cerebral cortex and the RF may constitute a basis for why the DEP is rarely observed (18% of the experiments) simultaneously in these regions. Moreover, it has been a common observation that the DEP, which has been generated in the RF,

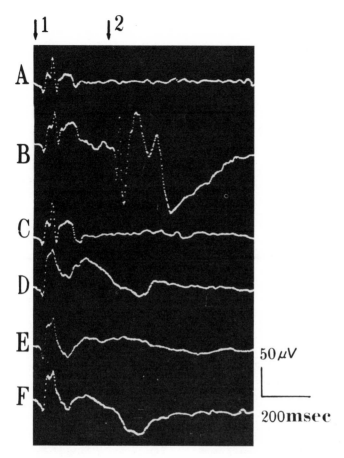

Fig. 4. Manifestation of the delayed evoked potential in the midbrain RF when benactizine is applied to the somatiosensory cortex. (A) habituation; (B) 141-160 pairings; (C) test before application; (D) test during application; (E) test after washing drug away; (F) test during repeated application. 1,2: marks of presentation of CS and US.

started to disappear with further pairings of the CS with the US and simultaneously appeared in the auditory cortex. The possibility of an inhibitory cortical influence on the midbrain reticular formation has been confirmed by the data of Adam and Markel (1969) who have recorded DEP of increased amplitude in the midbrain RF, after precollicular section. It is not clear whether these findings reflect direct relationships between the RF and the cortex or whether they are the result of the regulatory influences of some intermediary structure.

Cooling of the somatosensory cortex also leads to a blockade of the DEP in the auditory cortex. After the cessation of cooling the DEP is

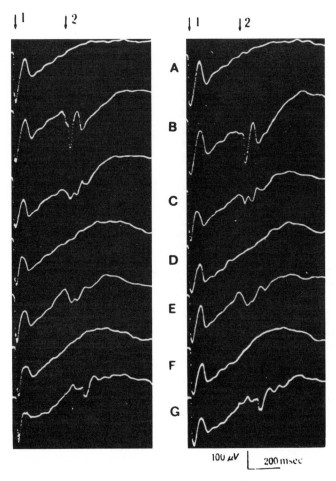

Fig. 5. Blockade of DEP registered from symmetrical points of the auditory cortex during benactizine application to the somatosensory cortex. Left: auditory cortex contralateral to the stimulated paw. Right: the ipsilateral cortex. (A) habituation; (B) 81-100 pairings; (C) test before application; (D) test during contralateral application. (E) test during ipsilateral application; (F,G) test after washing drug away. 1,2: marks of presentation of CS and US.

restored in this area. The cooling technique we have used does not appreciably alter the temperature of the deeper cortical layers. The similarity between the effects of benactizine application and surface cooling is indicative of the superficial localization of the cholinosensitive elements modulating the occurrence of the DEP in the cortex. After benactizine was washed away, the potential evoked (EP) by the US in the somatosensory area was rapidly restored; this was probably paralleled by a return of the descending corticoreticular influences to their initial level. In contrast, changes in the EP in the RF lasted up to 20 min. It may be thought that the persisting changes in the reticular EP are due to long-lasting modification in reticular neuropil activity which is mediated by neurohumoral factors.

5. ELECTRICAL COMPONENTS OF CORTICAL-SUBCORTICAL INTERACTIONS

The results of the experiments with the registration of the EP from symmetrically localized points on the auditory cortex (similar shape and amplitude of the late phases of the EP produced by the US and identical changes in response to paired stimulations) suggest that the sources generating the late components of EP are located in subcortical structures and that signals lose their sensory specificity upon entering into these structures. The bilateral manifestation of the DEP and its blockade on both hemispheres following unilateral application of anticholinergic drugs also supports the idea that nonspecific cortical structures are involved in the genesis of the DEP.

Our data should not be interpreted as indicating that the retrieval mechanism is exclusively cholinergic. Nevertheless, cholinergic structures do participate in this mechanism.

In order to understand the location of the cholinergic substrate which participates in mechanisms regulating the formation of a memory trace, it appeared useful to examine the possible neuronal mechanisms participating in the effect of anticholinergic drugs.

Anticholinergic drugs disrupt the transmission of neuronal impulses over cholinergic synapses in the neuronal circuits of the cerebral cortex. Certain drugs reduce the rate at which ascending reticular impulses occur. This is exemplified by the blockade of the reticulocortical EP (Ilyutchenok & Zinevich, 1970), neuronal responses (Spehlmann, 1971) and reticulocortical inhibition (Ilyutchenok & Gilinsky, 1969). Furthermore, anticholinergic drugs exert a blockade of recurrent inhibition presumably via the same neurons which transmit the reticular inputs. The abolition of the limiting influence of inhibitory cells widens the zone of cortical neurons involved in the response and decreases the contrast in the neuronal pattern.

The suppression of cholinergic activity in the limbic system or other structures, such as the cerebral cortex is probably critical to the effect of anticholinergic drugs on memory mechanisms. Thus, the regulatory mechanisms involved in memory trace formation may be switched off.

It is important to note that complete memory blockade by anticholinergic drugs is only possible with single trial training procedures. After repeated training the trace is laid down, though not overtly expressed during training.

The rate of memory trace formation, by inference, is determined by the emotional status of the animal during the time within which the learning occurs, independent of the neurochemical nature and type of such an emotional state. It is conceivable that the inhibitory action of anticholinergic drugs on memory is more potent if there is an emotional component involved with the response. It is hypothesized that the regulatory influence of "emotionogenic" structures on memory occurs through involvement of cholinergic substrates. If this were so, it would then explain why the blockade of central muscarinic cholinergic activity constitutes a formidable barrier for the appearance of a memory trace in single trial conditioning procedures but is no hindrance to trace formation when repeated trials are utilized.

In experiments utilizing dogs, an attempt was made to control a stable conditioned emotional fear response (Ilyutchenok & Chaplygina, 1970). Motor food conditioned responses were elaborated in freely moving dogs utilizing Beritashvili's method (1968). When the conditional stimulus was presented, the animal stepped down from a platform, directed itself towards the food cup—to the left cup in response to the buzzer and to the right one when the tone was sounded. Having eaten, the dog returned to the platform. When the conditioned response was stabilized, the buzzer was followed by an electric shock (110 V) delivered the moment the dog touched the cup. Henceforth, the animal did not approach the cup in response to the conditional stimulus not even when drawn towards the cup. The response to the stimulus, independent of the shock did not change in some dogs, while in others it was impaired. Once established after 1-2 shocks, the conditioned fear response persisted for several months.

One to two months after the acquisition of the emotional fear response, 1 mg/kg benactizine was given to the animals four times a day for three days. This resulted in the inhibition of the conditioned fear and food responses. The food conditioned responses were restored 14 days after cessation of drug treatment. Whereas most of the animals no longer showed the conditioned fear response, a few displayed some components of the emotional fear response. Further studies have shown that the traces for emotional memory were not affected at such dosage levels. Two to sixteen weeks after the return of the food approach response the animals were given a weak shock reminder (10 V) when trying to eat from a cup at which shock had never been given. After this reminder stimulus the fear response was restored. Initially, the response occurred to both conditional stimuli, but in subsequent sessions, the animals responded only to the stimulus which had been previously associated with the strong painful shock.

Emotional memory could be eliminated, if the central cholinoreactive structures were profoundly blocked. Three weeks after the dogs had acquired the conditioned emotional fear, response they were treated with 10mg/kg benzacine given twice a day for three days. Following this treatment, the conditioned fear response was not spontaneously restored nor could it be elicited by a reminder shock.

Thus, by means of profound cholinergic blockade we were able to thoroughly disrupt the conditioned emotional fear response in dogs several weeks after its acquisition.

Based upon the foregoing data, the efficiency of the cholinergic blockade was tested with respect to obsessive syndromes (Korolenko, 1973). The blockade of cholinergic brain structures by atropine has yielded favorable results in patients manifesting obsessive ideas based on long-term emotional memory (phobic syndrome, obsessive fear) in whom other therapeutic measures were unsuccessful.

The experimental data have suggested that the mechanisms of emotional memory differ from those underlying other types of memory. There is some basis for assuming that after the memory trace has been consolidated, the blockade of cholinoreactive structures provides for impairment of emotional memory for those responses which are based upon cholinergic mechanisms. However in the process of memory trace formation, anticholinergic drugs, by acting via regulatory mechanisms, may impair trace formation in response to stimuli of a neurochemical nature.

In single trial conditioning procedures where emotional arousal is essential for memory, the roles of the ascending reticular activation system (ARAS) and the limbic system are significant, since they determine the response capacity of the central nervous system and the emotional component of such responses, respectively. In tasks with repeated training trials and multiple emotional arousal the limbic system and the ARAS, accordingly, have less important roles in the fixation of the memory trace. It appears justified to consider that the limbic system and the ARAS are involved in the regulation of memory formation. Let us now discuss some neurochemical aspects of the activities of the ARAS and the limbic system.

6. CHOLINERGIC REGULATION OF REGIONAL RESPONSES

The ARAS may be activated by pharmacological excitation of adreno-, cholino- and/or serotoninoreactive structures via the brainstem, since ARAS excitation is not observed in animals with premesencephalic section. Our earlier electrographic studies suggested that the terminal link of the ARAS is cholinergic by nature. The hypothesis was further substantiated by investigations of single neurons as well as by the analysis of cortical responses evoked by the stimulation of the ARAS at different levels (Ilyutchenok & Gilinsky, 1971). It has been shown that intravenous injection and local cortical application of muscarinic anticholinergic drugs block the electrocorticographic response to high frequency stimulation of the midbrain RF, simultaneously abolishing the reticular inhibition of cortical neurons. Drug effects served to reduce the superficially generated reticulocortical responses (Fig. 6), while the primary responses recorded

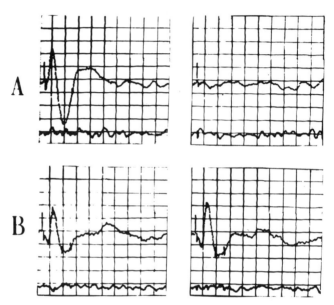

Fig. 6. Effect of intravenous benactizine on reticulocortical and primary sensory responses: (A) reticulocortical potential; (B) primary response. Left: before administration. Right: 5 mins after 3 mg/kg benactizine administration. Each square contains averaged evoked potentials to 20 stimulations and the functions of their standard deviations. Sides of square: X = 232 msec, Y = 117 mV, calculated by "Dnepr-1" computer.

from this point were enhanced. It is interesting to note that cholinergic blockade inhibits not only reticulocortical responses, but also cortical responses to single pulse stimulation of nonspecific nuclei of the thalamus and hypothalamus (Fig. 7). The cholinosensitive elements of the cortex are, therefore, of importance in the genesis of these nonspecific EP.

The transmission of excitation along specific sensory pathways and the integration of such excitation at the cortical level is an altogether different circumstance. Changes in the activity of cholinoreactive structures do not prevent the propagation of sensory signals along specific pathways; they only modulate the transmission of afferent impulses.

An overall picture of the neurochemical organization of the limbic

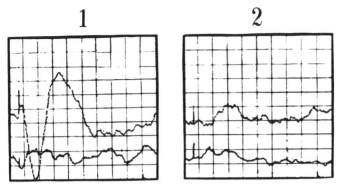

Fig. 7. Effect of epicortical application of benactizine on hypothalamocortical evoked potentials: (1) before application; (2) 7 min after application of 0.75% benactizine solution under recording electrode. Each square contains averaged evoked potentials to 20 stimulations and functions of their standard deviations. Sides of square: X = 309 msec, Y = 164 mV, calculated by "Dnepr-1" computer.

system, is as yet inconceivable, although some interesting data concerning the neurochemistry of the interaction between structures comprised by the limbic system and the neocortex have been obtained. Theta rhythm may arise in response to sensory stimulation as well as during the excitation of the central chemoreactive structures in the limbic system after premesencephalic section. Under such circumstances there is no cortical EEG activation, which seems to indicate that the ascending limbic-cortical influences are propagated through the ARAS (Ilyutchenok & Bannikov, 1968). In fact, premesencephalic section sharply decreases the facilitatory influence of the hippocampus on the activity of the cortical neurons. On the other hand, the hippocampus also exerts an ARAS-independent influence on the cortex; this is confirmed by the persistence of hippocampal-cortical inhibition after mesencephalic section. This inhibition is effected by the cholinosensitive elements of the cortex (Ilyutchenok & Jivotikov, 1972).

7. INTRALIMBIC RELATIONSHIPS AND MEMORY FORMATION

Data on intralimbic interrelationships, particularly those between the hippocampus and the amygdala, aid in our understanding of the role of the limbic system in behavior and memory. In our laboratory Wolf has demonstrated that EP and responses of amygdala neurons to hippocampal stimulation change under the influence of anticholinergic drugs. Hippocampal inhibition of amygdala neuron firing is abolished by the administration of anticholinergic drugs. Such abolition is paralleled by an increase in the hippocampal-amygdaloid EP, which is observed not only after systemic drug administration but also after its microinjection into the amygdala. Consideration of possible intralimbic relationships provided particular relevance for these data, inasmuch as no cholinergic outputs from the hippocampus have been identified histochemically (Shute & Lewis, 1965). The conclusion is that the hippocampal influence of the amygdala is modulated by the cholinergic character of the amygdala itself. Microelectrophoretic drug application has confirmed the presence of a high percentage (46.5) of cholinosensitive neurons in the basolateral nuclei of the amygdala. (Gilinsky & Wolf, 1972). Figure 8 illustrates how the firing rate of a neuron has been increased following the injection of acetylcholine from one barrel of a five-barreled glass microelectrode. Atropine injected from another barrel exerts an opposite effect. Other patterns were observed, with the general finding that decreased the rate of neuronal firing and atropine increased it (Fig. 9).

The amygdaloid complex exerts a more profound influence upon mechanisms of emotion and memory than other limbic structures. It is known that electrical and chemical treatments leading to changes in amygdala activity elicit violent emotional responses. During emotional excitation specific burst activity arises in the amygdala (Lesse. 1960; McLennan & Grastone, 1965; Oniani, et al., 1969). Moreover, it has been shown that the involvement of the amygdala with seizure activity is the condition required for amnesia to occur (Kesner & Doty, 1968).

It may be thought then that the "pacing" of amygdala neurons by different rhythms might qualitatively modify the influence of the amygdaloid complex on memory trace formation. In our laboratory, Vinnitsky used a stepdown platform technique in studies of the effects of different stimulus frequencies on the amygdala of rats. Six or more daily sessions were required for 100% of the rats to learn after a foot-shock with a current intensity of 0.75 mA. In two experimental groups a 10 sec (square wave pulses 0.3 msec., 20 mA) at frequencies of 60 and 200 pulses/sec was given to the amygdala immediately after foot-shock. Stimulation at 200 pulses/sec decreased the incidence of single trial conditioned response acquisition. The rate of single trial avoidance conditioning was increased after amygdala stimulation at a frequency of 60 pulses/sec. Most of the animals showed criterion performance after the first session (Fig. 10).

It is difficult to determine the optimum parameters of stimulation that provide for learning in all animals through the use of a single training procedure. Perhaps in addition to the close time proximity of the provoked emotional event, there is an additionally required emotional orientation towards the event which is difficult to reproduce in experiments utilizing electrical stimulation.

The influences of limbic structures upon memory may occur in several

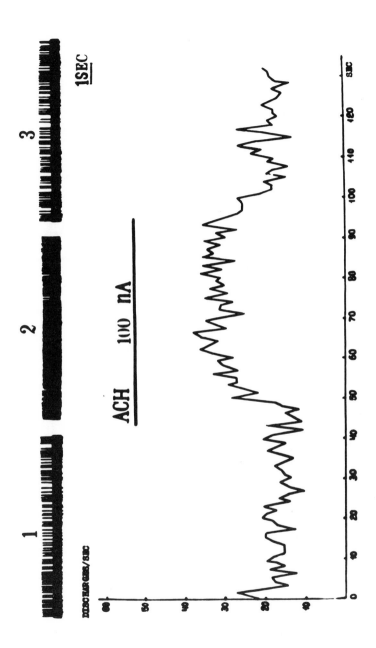

Fig. 8. Acetylcholine effect on neuronal activity in amygdaloid complex: (1) background activity; (2) 27 sec after acetylcholine microelectrophoretic application; (3) 20 sec after electrophoretic current has been switched off. The time of acetylcholine application is marked by a horizontal bar.

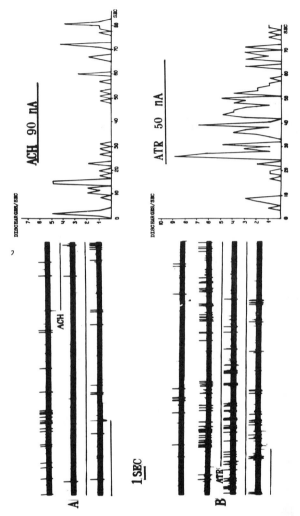

Fig. 9. Neuronal responses in the amygdaloid complex to microelectrophoretic application of acetylcholine and atropine: (A) decrease in discharge rate of the
neuron under acetylcholine; (B) increase in discharge rate under atropine. The
time of microelectrophoretic drug application is marked by a horizontal bar
in the oscillograms and figures.

ways. The formation of a memory trace may be facilitated by increased
reverberation in neuronal circuits (Beritashvili, 1968) which enhance, and
possibly also accelerate consolidation. Contrast among neuronal patterns
or blockade of the retroactive interference of acquired information with
subsequent sensory flow are the other possibilities. The latter two may be
accomplished through cortical inhibition evoked by nonspecific systems,

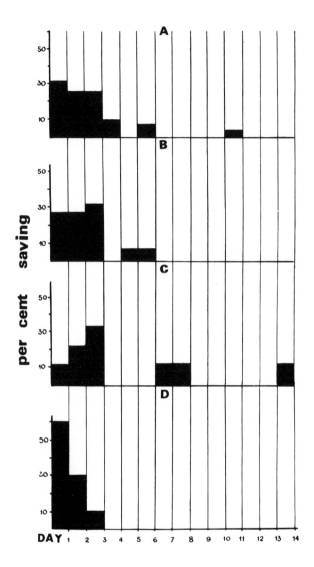

Fig. 10. Effect of unilateral stimulation of basolateral nuclei in the amygdaloid complex on PACR in rats: (A) control; (B) control, rats with implated electrodes; (C) stimulation, 200 pulses/sec, 0.3 msec, 20 mA, 10 sec (signification of differences, on day one P<0.05); (D) stimulation 60 pulses/sec, 0.3 msec, 20 mA, 10 sec (signification of differences, on day one P < 0.05).

such as the limbico-cortical and reticulocortical. As mentioned earlier, cholinergic mechanisms are instrumental in bringing about such types of inhibition, as well as inhibition within the limbic system.

REFERENCES

Adam, G. and Kukorelli, T. (1965) Conditioned evoked potential, a model experiment of learning. *Acta Physiol. Acad. Sci. Hung.* **26**, 47-51.

Adam, G. and Markel, E. (1969) Mesencephalic conditioned evoked potentials. *Acta Physiol. Acad. Sci. Hung.* **36**, 1-2, 179-182.

Beritashvili, I. S. (1968) Memory, its characteristics and origin in vertebrates. *Tbilisi,* USSR (in Russian).

Buser, P., Richard D. and Lescop J. (1969) Controle, par la cortex sensorimoteur, de la reactivite de cellules reticularies mesencephaliques chez la chat. *Exper. Brain Res.* **9**, 83-95.

Deutsch, J. A. (1966) Substrates of learning and memory. *Dis. Nerv. Syst.* **27**, 20.

Essman, W. B. (1965) Facilitation of memory consolidation by chemically induced acceleration of RNA synthesis. *XXIII Int. Congr. Physiol. Sci.,* Tokyo, p. 1128.

Essman, W. B. and Alpern, H. (1964) Single trial learning: methodology and results with mice. *Psychol. Rpts.* **14**, 731-740.

Gilinsky, M. A. and Wolf, N. V. (1972) Microelectrophoretic study of cholinoceptive amygdaloid neurons. *Neurophysiolgy,* **4**, 645-650.

Ilyutchenok, R. Yu. (1972) Pharmacology of behavior and memory. In *Novosibirsk,* "Nauka," USSR (in Russian).

Ilyutchenok, R. Yu., and Bannikov, G. N. (1968) The effect of cholinergic substances on the bioelectric activity of the limbic system. *Bull. Exper. Biol. Med.,* **66**, 55-59.

Ilyutchenok, R. Yu. and Gilinsky, M. A. (1969) Anticholinergic drugs and reticulocortical interaction. *Pharmacol. Res. Commun.* **1**, 242-248.

Ilyutchenok, R. Yu. and Chaplygina, S. R. (1970) Participation of cholinergic brain structures in the mechanism of emotional memory. *J. Vish. Nerv. Deiatelnosty,* **20**, 176-184.

Ilyutchenok, R. Yu. and Zinevich, V. (1970) Short latency reticulocortical potentials: Effect of muscarinic anticholinergic drugs. *Neuropharmacology* **9**, 433-440.

Ilyutchenok, R. Yu. and Gilinsky, M. A. (1971) *Design and Mediators for Reticulo-Cortical Connections.* Nauka, Leningrade.

Ilyutchenok, R. Yu. and Eliseyeva, A. G. (1972) Cholinergic mechanisms of memory: Analysis of the amnesic effect or anticholinergic drugs. *Int. J. Psychobio.* **1**, 177-192.

Ilyutchenok, R. Yu. and Jivotikov, B. P. (1972) Activity of cortical neurons in response to hippocampal stimulation. *J. Vish. Nerv. Deiatelnosty,* **22**, 136-139.

Kesner, R. P. and Doty, R. W. (1968) Amnesia produced in cats by local seizure activity initial from amygdala. *Exper. Neurol.* **11**, 58-68.

Korolenko, R. Yu. (1973) Some pathogenetic mechanisms of atropine therapeutic efficiency in obsessive states. *Psychiatria Polska* No. 1.

Kryglikov, R. and Dolganov, G. (1972) Effect of scopolamine on the formation, preservation and reproduction of temporary connections. *J. Vish. Nerv. Deiatelnosty,* **22**, 837-842.

Lesse, H. (1960) Rhinencephalic electrophysiological activity during "emotional" behaviour in cats. *Psychiat. Res. Rep.* **12**, 224-237.

Lindsley, D. F., Ranf, S. K. and Barton, R. J., (1972) Corticufuqal influences on reticular formation evoked activity in cats. *Exper. Neurol.,* **34**, 511-521.

McGaugh, J. L. (1968) A multi-trace view of memory storage processes. In *Recent Advances on Learning and Retention,* D. Bovet, F. Bovet-Nitti and A. Oliverio Eds. Roma, pp. 13-24.

McLennan, H. and Grastone, P. (1965) The electrical activity of the amygdala and its relationship to that of the olfactory bulb. *Can. J. Physiol. Pharmacol.* **43**, 1009-1017.

Meyers, B. (1965) Some effects of scopolamine on a passive avoidance response in rats. *Psychopharmacology,* **98** ,111-119.

Oliverio, A. (1968) Effects of scopolamine on avoidance conditioning and habituation of mice. *Psychopharmacology,* **12**, 214-226.

Oniani, T. N., Naneishvili, T. L., and Koridze, M. G. (1969) The dynamics in the background electrical activity of limbic structures in cats during wakefulness and sleep. *Soobsh. Akad. Nauk Gruzinsk SSR,* **56**, 429-432.

Phillis, J. W. and York, D. H. (1967) Cholinergic inhibition in the cerebral cortex. *Brain Res.,* **6**, 517-526.

Rabin, A. G. (1965) Selective cortical control of activity from reticular structures of the brain. *Fisiol. J. I. M. Sechenova,* **51**, 159-163.

Ricci, G. F. and Zamparo, L. (1965) *Electrocortical Correlates of Avoidance Conditioning in the Monkey and their Modifications with Learning and Retention.* M. Ya. Mikhelson, V. G. Longo, and Z. Votava, eds., Oxford, pp. 269-285.

Shute, C. C. D. and Lewis, P. R. (1965) The ascending cholinergic reticular system: neocortical, olfactory and subcortical projection. *Brain* **3**, 497-520.

Spehlmann, R. (1971) Acetylcholine and the synaptic transmission of nonspecific impulses to the visual cortex. *Brain,* **94**, 139-150.

CHAPTER 7

Biochemical Disruption of Memory: A Re-examination

SHINSHU NAKAJIMA

1. INTRODUCTION

Studies dealing with the biochemical basis of learning and memory can be classified into three categories: 1) Correlational studies, 2) transfer studies, and 3) interference studies. Bogoch trained pigeons by operant conditioning, and found an increase in glycoproteins in the brain of trained birds. Valzelli kept mice in isolation which caused aggressiveness and poor learning ability, and suggested that monoamines may be involved in learning. Izquierdo selectively bred rats with poor learning ability, and found less release of K^+ from the hippocampal neurons of these animals. Tsukada analyzed the concentration of ammonia and amino acids in the brain of rats and monkeys immediately after learning, and suggested the involvement of these chemical substances in the process of learning. Many other experiments (Hydén & Lange, 1968; Bowman & Strobel, 1969; etc.) fall into this category of correlation studies.

The experimenter takes a measure of learning on one hand, and correlates it with a biochemical change on the other. The major role of the correlational studies is to determine possible substances (or chemical reactions) which may be involved in learning. Once a correlation is found, it becomes critical to demonstrate that the chemical changes occur as a result of learning, rather than as a result of sensory, motor, or motivational changes unrelated to learning.

The elimination of factors outside learning is most important in transfer studies, in which chemical substances are extracted from the brains of trained animals and injected into naive animals. Fjerdingstad trained rats to press the left-side bar or the left and right alternately. In his study, changes due to the sensory stimulation and motor activity are well controlled. Transfer studies in general (Rosenblatt et al., 1966; Ungar et al., 1968) assume that the information acquired by the donor is somehow coded into a chemical substance which is stored in the recipient's brain without any alteration in the code. Fjerdingstad suggested that such a substance may be a peptide.

The converse of correlational study is interference study. In this type of study, biosynthesis of a putative memory substance is blocked, usually by a drug. Essman found that intrahippocampal injection of 5-hydroxy-tryptamine, which inhibited cerebral protein synthesis, produced a retrograde amnesia in the rat. There are a number of experiments reporting similar interference studies which seem to indicate that the synthesis of new proteins in the brain is necessary for the neuronal events underlying learning to be consolidated into a more permanent form. The idea that macromolecules constitute long-term memory appeals to us because it is consistent with the classical two-factor theory of memory proposed by Hebb (1949). However, before drawing definite conclusions, it may be necessary to re-examine the present evidence. The following is a report of re-examinations performed in our laboratory.

2. ACTINOMYCIN D

We have been interested in the finding that actinomycin D injected into the hippocampal area of the rat brain interferes with the performance of a previously learned task (Nakajima, 1969). Since actinomycin inhibits the synthesis of ribonucleic acid (RNA), and later regulates the synthesis of proteins as well, it was thought that the drug may disrupt memory by limiting the availability of materials with which permanent memory traces are built. If this assumption is correct, it would be expected that 1) tasks that were learned when the synthesis of RNA or proteins was absent would not be retained at a later time, and that 2) tasks that were learned long before injection of the drug would be well retained. However, the results of experiments performed in our laboratory did not support this reasoning (Nakajima, 1972).

The performance of a previously learned position discrimination task was only slightly impaired when rats were tested within a few days of actinomycin injection into the hippocampal area, regardless of whether the task had originally been learned long before injection or after injection.

Performance was severely impaired if the animals were tested more than four days after injection, again regardless of when the task had been originally learned. The behavioral effect of actinomicyn D, therefore, is more likely to be a proactive interference with performance at the time of retention test, rather than retroactive interference with some aspect of memory. These findings led us to consider the validity of previously reported effects of puromycin.

3. PUROMYCIN DIHYDROCHLORIDE

Flexner et al., (1963) reported that injection of puromycin into the temporal area of the mouse brain blocked the memory of a task learned one day before injection, but not a task learned seven days before. Since puromycin suppresses protein synthesis, they thought that continuous synthesis of new proteins in the brain is essential in maintaining memory for a long period of time after learning. Supplementing findings of Flexner et al., Barondes and Cohen (1966) found that there is a period of a few hours during which memory can survive under the influence of puromycin. Presumably, short-term memory does not require synthesis of new proteins.

Later, Flexner and Flexner (1967) found that the memory blocked by puromycin could be restored by an injection of physiological saline, and suggested that memory was not really lost, but its "expression" was suppressed by peptidal puromycin. However, when they injected puromycin 5 hr before or 8 min after original learning, later injection of saline failed to restore the expression of memory (Flexner & Flexner, 1968). They concluded that consolidation of memory is disrupted by puromycin if it is injected before or immediately after original learning.

Experiment 1: Radioautographic study

Before conducting any behavioral experiment, it is important to know the extent and time course of the drug effect after its injection into the temporal area. Flexner et al. (1964) used a liquid scintillation method to measure protein synthesis in various regions in the brain after puromycin injection. In the present experiment, a radioautographic method was used to demonstrate the extent of the drug effect more clearly.

Method

Fourteen male Swiss albino mice (Charles River) were unilaterally implanted with stainless steel cannulae (23 gauge) into the left hippocampal area under pentobarbital anesthesia (70 mg/kg, i.p.). The animal was placed in a stereotaxic instrument in such a way that the incisor bar was on the same horizontal plane as the interaural line. The tip of the cannula was placed 1.0 mm anterior to the interaural line, 3.0 mm lateral to the midsagittal plane, and 3.0 mm below the cortical surface. These coordinates approximately correspond to the "temporal site" of Flexner et al. (1963), and were uniformly used for hippocampal injections in the subsequent experiments. After about one week of recovery period, a small volume of drug solution could be injected, without anesthetizing the animal, by means of a 30-gauge needle connected to a microsyringe with polyethylene tubing.

Puromycin dihydrochloride was dissolved in physiological saline solution and neutralized with 0.3N NaOH to a final concentration 7.5 mg/ml. Twelve microliters of the drug solution (containing 90 μg of puromycin) was injected into the left hippocampus at a rate of approximately 2 μl/min.

The slow rate of injection was very important to ensure uniform diffusion of the drug without causing massive draining into the ventricles. No injection was given into the right hippocampus so that the uninjected side would serve as a control. Tritiated leucine (L-leucine-4,5-H^3 58.2-59.1 Ci/mmole, New England Nuclear) was injected intraperitoneally at a dosage of 8 mc/kg, 5, 24, 48, or 72 hr after puromycin injection. After 3 hr of incorporation, the animals were anesthetized with pentobarbital (70 mg/kg, i.p.) and perfused with physiological saline followed by 10% neutral formalin. The brains were excised and fixed in formalin, and paraffin sections were cut at 8 μ. Hydrated sections were washed in a mixture of chloroform and methanol (2:1) followed by a cold 0.2N perchloric acid solution, and processed for radioautography by a dipping method (Kopriwa & Leblond, 1962).

Results

Radioautographic sections are shown in Figure 1. In the animals injected with radioactive leucine 5 hr after puromycin, there was virtually no trace of radioactivity in the left hippocampus, while the right side

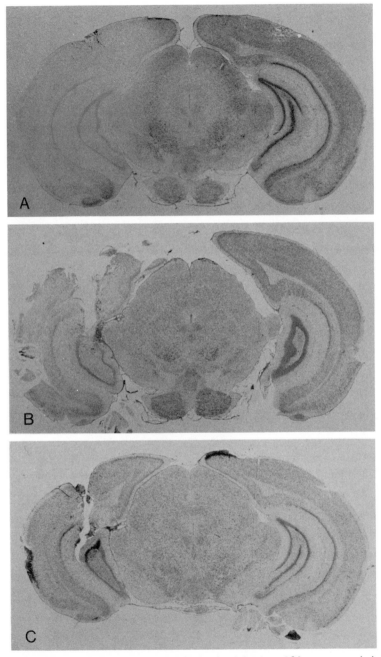

Fig. 1. Radioautography of the mouse brain after injection of 90 μg puromycin into the left hippocampus. (A) Radioactive leucine was injected 5 hr after puromycin and incorporated for 3 hr, (B) leucine 24 hr after puromycin; (C) leucine 72 hr after puromycin.

showed heavy labeling. The radioactive labeling was absent in the neocortex and entorhinal cortex surrounding the hippocampus, except in the superficial layer.

The central gray substance was also affected by the drug, suggesting some diffusion of the drug into the cerebrospinal fluid passing through the third ventricle. There was no sign of chromatolysis or necrosis in the injected area at this stage. Twenty-four hours later, protein synthesis started again in the drug-affected structures, except in a part of the hippocampus close to the injection site where neurons now showed chromatolysis. By the third day, protein synthesis was quite normal. There was a small area in the vicinity of the cannula tip where neurons were necrotic and glia were more numerous.

Experiment 2: Learning in the Absence of Protein Synthesis

The radioautographic experiment demonstrated that 90 μg of puromycin suppresses protein synthesis in the hippocampus and the surrounding structures. If protein synthesis in these regions is essential for the formation of long-term memory, tasks that are learned in the absence of protein synthesis would be retained for only a short period of time (Barondes and Cohen, 1966).

Method

Stainless steel cannulae were implanted bilaterally in the hippocampal area of male Swiss albino mice. After about 7 days of recovery they were divided into 8 groups of 8 animals. Four groups were bilaterally injected with puromycin through the cannulae, 90 μg into each hippocampus.

The animals were trained in a T-maze 5 hr after injection and then tested for retention 0.08, 3, 24, or 72 hr later. The other 4 groups were injected with 12 μl of physiological saline through each cannula, trained 5 hr later, and tested 0.08, 3, 24, or 72 hr after the training.

The T-maze consisted of a 30-cm stem and two 20-cm arms, 10 cm wide throughout. All walls were painted gray, and the grid floor was wired to give scrambled 0.7-mA foot shocks. Each animal was first placed at the starting point of the maze and allowed to explore it. When the animal entered either one of the arms, a sliding door was closed, and the animal was gently lifted out of the maze with a plastic scoop. The arm which the animal entered in this free choice trial was designated as incorrect, and the other arm as correct. in other words, the animal was trained against its initial choice. A wooden floor was placed over the grid of the correct arm, and training trials were started. The animal was placed at the starting point, and 5 sec later a foot-shock was delivered. The shock was continued until the animal entered the correct arm, where it was confined for approximately 60 sec before the next trial. The training was terminated when the animal reached a criterion of 9 correct choice in 10 consecutive trials.

In the retention test, the animal was again trained to the same criterion. The mice were kept in their home cages for at least 24 hr after puromycin injection if retention tests were finished earlier, so that the chromatolytic change could be observed in the brain. They were then anesthetized with pentobarbital (70 mg/kg), and their brains fixed with 10% formalin.

Those tested 24 and 72 hr after original learning were similarly processed after the last test trial. The brains were embedded in gelatin, sectioned, and stained with thionin.

Results

Brains fixed one day after puromycin injection showed clear chromatolysis of the hippocampal neurons; brains fixed 3 days after injection had a necrotic region surrounded by a chromatolytic area in the hippocampus. There were 6 mice which showed these histological changes only on one side of the brain, suggesting that the drug solution had escaped into the ventricles and was diluted. These animals were discarded and replaced with new animals.

Behavioral results are shown in Figure 2. During the original learning of the task, the drug-injected mice made more errors than the saline control animals (Mann-Whitney U test, $p < 0.001$), but they all learned the task and reached the criterion. The retention-test scores for the control groups indicated that there was some forgetting with saline injection. Compared with saline, puromycin had virtually no effect up to 3 hr, but at 24 hr, some animals began to show errors. At 72 hr, some of the puromycin-treated animals made an extremely large number of errors, while others still showed good performance.

The general trend of the present results agrees with the findings of Barondes and Cohen (1966), in that the errors in the retention test increased as a function of the time interval between original learning and the retention test (Kruskal-Wallis analysis of variance, $\chi^2 = 7.96$, d.f. = 3, $p < .05$). It should be noted, however, that the learning-test interval paralleled the injection-test interval, and that the errors may have increased as a function of time after puromycin injection.

Experiment 3: Learning before Puromycin Injection

If the errors in a retention test at 72 hr indicate the failure to form long-term memory, then the tasks that were learned long before drug

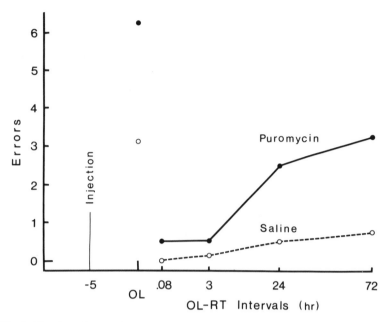

Fig. 2. Number of errors in original learning and in retention test of Experiment 2. Puromycin or physiological saline was injected 5 hr before original learning.

injection should be remembered well. In fact, Flexner et al. (1963) reported that puromycin had no effect on retention if injected 7 days after original learning.

Method

In this experiment, mice were first trained in the T-maze to the 9-out-of-10 criterion. Seven days after learning in one group, and one day after in another group, the animals were anesthetized with pentobarbital (70 mg/kg) and 90 µg was injected into the hippocampal area of each side by means of a 30-gauge needle held in a stereotaxic instrument. Two other groups were similarly injected with physiological saline. The coordinates, the drug concentration, and the rate of injection were all identical to those in the preceding experiments. The animals were tested for retention 3 days after injection. There were 8 mice in each group after discarding 3 animals that showed the signs of asymmetric injections.

Results

The number of errors made are shown in Figure 3. There was no statistical difference among the four groups in original learning. For the

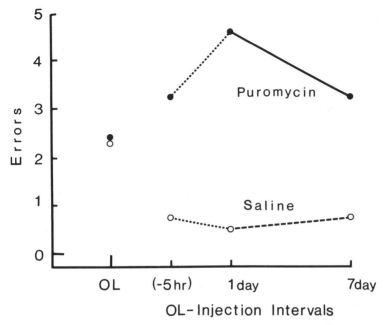

Fig. 3. Number of errors in original learning and in retention test of Experiment 3. Retention tests were given 3 days after injection. The retention-test scores of the 72 hr groups of Experiment 2 (−5 hr) are also included for comparison.

retention test, the puromycin group made significantly more errors than the saline-treated control groups (Mann-Whitney U test, $p < 0.001$). The scores of the 72 hr groups of Experiment 2 are included in Figure 3 to facilitate comparison. There was no significant difference in the retention-test scores among the three puromycin groups (Kruskal-Wallis analysis of variance, $\chi^2 = 0.195$, d.f. = 2). The performance was very poor regardless of whether the task had been learned 7 days before, 1 day before, or 5 hr after puromycin injection, as long as retention tests were conducted 3 days after injection.

These results disagree with the findings of Flexner et al. (1963). Their failure to find behavioral deficits in the animals injected 7 days after learning may have been the result of asymmetric injection of the drug. There is a high probability that the injected solution escapes into the lateral ventricle when the rate of injection is too rapid. If this happens on one side, the animal tends to turn contralaterally regardless of previous training. In the present experiments, the rate of injection was slow enough to allow good diffusion of the drug solution without draining it into the ventricles, and cases of asymmetric injections were eliminated on the basis of histological examination.

The results of the above three experiments can be summarized as follows: 1) a position discrimination task was learned and retained for many hours in the absence of protein synthesis in the hippocampus and surrounding structures. 2) Puromycin interfered with performance of the task a few days after injection, when protein synthesis returned to a virtually normal level. 3) The behavioral deficits were not dependent upon the time interval between original learning and drug injection. These findings are similar to previous results with actinomycin D, and suggest that the behavioral effects of puromycin injection into the hippocampus is not related to protein synthesis or even to memory.

The proactive explanation, proposed to account for the actinomycin data, would also be applicable to the puromycin data: puromycin interferes with the performance of discrimination at the time of retention test. The results of Experiment 2, as well as the results of Barondes and Cohen (1966), should be viewed as a gradual development of disruptive effect after drug injection, not as a decay of short-term memory. Strong support for the proactive explanation derives from the results of Experiment 3; even when mice were given sufficient time after original learning to form long-term memory, the behavioral deficits appeared three days after puromycin injection.

The cause of the interference could be necrotic lesions in the hippocampus, abnormal electrical activity (Cohen & Barondes, 1967; Cohen et al., 1966), or peptidal puromycin (Flexner & Flexner, 1968). It is not the absence of protein synthesis in the hippocampal area.

4. CYCLOHEXIMIDE

At present, the effect of cycloheximide on "memory" is under re-examination in our laboratory. Preliminary findings and tentative conclusions are presented here.

The "amnesic effect" of cycloheximide has been reported in an appetitive learning situation (Cohen & Barondes, 1968) and also in a number of aversive learning situations (Geller et al., 1969; Quartermain et al., 1970; Quinton, 1971). The underlying mechanism has been thought to be the same in all situations: cycloheximide disrupts the formation of long-term memory by suppressing cerebral protein synthesis (Barondes, 1970).

However, cycloheximide also causes diarrhea within several hours of injection. If a mouse experiences gastrointestinal discomfort after drinking water in the correct end of a maze, than the animal may respond to such "reinforcement" as if it were poisoned. If so, the animal would not run to the correct end of the maze when it is replaced in the same maze at a later time. Instead, it would explore the maze in order to obtain water elsewhere.

The whole situation becomes very similar to the conditioned aversion reported by Garcia et al. (1955), where sweetened water was used as a conditioned stimulus (CS) and gamma irradiation of the body as an unconditioned stimulus (US), such that the discomfort produced by the irradiation was conditioned to the taste of the water. A similar type of conditioned aversion has been observed with nongustatory CS (container and position of water) (Rozin, 1969).

It is, then, quite possible that the situational cues arising from the correct end of the maze become CS for the possible cycloheximide illness, and the mice develop a conditioned aversion to water in the correct end.

The following experiment was designed to demonstrate such a conditioned aversion.

Method

Male Swiss albino mice were water-deprived on day 1, and given 1 hr of access to water on day 2 in their home cages. On day 3, they were individually placed in a test box. The box had a 10 X 20 cm grid floor and 20 cm high grey walls, and a water spout protruded from one of the walls 6 cm above the floor. Water provided from the spout was the same tap water as that supplied in the home cages. At the moment when the animal started drinking, a timer was activated, and the total time it spent drinking in the subsequent 5-min period was recorded (Test 1). The volume of water each animal consumed was so minute that the drinking time, rather than the volume, was taken as a measure of drinking response. The mice were randomly distributed into 6 groups of 8, and each group was injected with either a cycloheximide solution or physiological saline 0.5 hr before, immediately after, or 3 hr after Test 1. The drug solution was prepared by dissolving cycloximide (Sigma) 7.5 mg/ml in physiological saline, and was injected subcutaneously into the neck region at a dose of 150 mg/kg. No water was given on day 3 in the home cages. Starting on day 4, the animals were given free access to water in their home cages, until water deprivation was reinstated on day 8. The animals were given water for 1 hr on day 9, and on day 10 they were allowed to drink in the test box for 5 min without any injection (Test 2).

Results

Each mouse was classified into either an Increased (more than 150%), Decreased (less than 50%), or Same (50-150%) category depending on the drinking time in Test 2 relative to that in Test 1. The distribution of the animals in the three categories is shown in Table I. Although the number of animals is insufficient for statistical analysis, 6 out of 8 animals injected with the drug 30 min before Test 1 acquired the conditioned aversion to water in the test box after a single pairing of drinking and injection.

TABLE I

Number of Animals in the Three Categories Classified According to the
Drinking Time in Test 2 Relative to the Drinking Time in Test 1

Categories (percent)	Increased (above 150%)	Same (150-50%)	Decreased (below 50%)
Cycloheximide			
0.5 hr before	0	2	6
immed. after	3	3	2
3 hr after	4	4	0
Saline			
0.5 hr before	2	6	0
immed. after	1	7	0
3 hr after	3	5	0

The results suggest that cycloheximide injection gives rise to an aversive aftereffect, and that a conditioned aversion to water in a particular place can be learned in one trial. The results also indicate that, in spite of cycloheximide injection, the mice formed the memory of the test box and retained it for seven days. Had they forgotten all about the test box, because of the drug injection, they would have shown the same drinking behavior in Test 2 as in Test 1. The mice in the Cohen-Barondes experiment (1966), therefore, must have remembered where they had water in the maze, and what happened after drinking it. When they were placed into the maze for the retention test, they avoided water in the correct end of the maze and explored elsewhere. Thus, the experiment was a demonstration of good memory, not amnesia.

The effect of cycloheximide in situations involving foot-shocks appears to be based on a different mechanism. Deficits in the performance of passive avoidance tasks (Geller et al., 1969; Quartermain et al., 1970; Quinton, 1971) and a T-maze based on shock escape (Barondes & Cohen, 1968) have been reported. The deficits in these aversive learning situations cannot be explained by conditioned aversion. Whether the deficits result from retrograde amnesia, as assumed by these investigators, or from some other mechanisms remains to be re-examined from a totally different view point.

5. CONCLUSIONS

The validity of macromolecular theory for memory processes was tested by the reexamination of experimental findings previously reported. The effects of actinomycin D and puromycin were found to be the gradual development of debilitation, not the loss of memory. The effect of cycloheximide in an appetitive learning situation was found to be a conditioned aversion, not retrograde amnesia. It is surprising to see how research workers have been misled by their findings. There are, of course, other chemical substances and other test situations which have not been examined in our laboratory.

At present, we have a long list of putative "memory substances"; we have a sufficient number of studies which "suggested" that these substances "may be involved" in learning and memory. It is, probably, no longer necessary to add more substances to the list. It is time to make certain that we are dealing with memory, not sensory or motor impairment or motivational changes.

This study was supported by National Research Council of Canada, Grant No. A0233. The author wishes to express his gratitude to Dr. B. Kopriwa for her advice on radioautography. Thanks are also due to N. Cullen, B. Greenberg, M. Li, and D. Ramusson, who assisted the author in various phases of this study.

REFERENCES

Barondes, S. H. (1970) Cerebral protein synthesis inhibitors block long-term memory. *Internat. Rev. Neurobiol.*, 12, 177-205.

Barondes, S. H. and Cohen, H. D. (1966) Puromycin effect on successive phase of memory storage. *Science* 151, 594-595.

Bowman, R. E. and Strobel, D. A. (1969) Brain RNA metabolism in the rat during learning. *J. Compar. Physiol. Psychol.* 67, 448-456.

Cohen, H. D., Ervin, F., and Barondes, S. H. (1966) Puromycin and cycloheximide: Different effects on hippocampal electrical activity. *Science* 154, 1557-1558.

Cohen, H. D. and Barondes, S. H. (1967) Puromycin effect on memory may be due to occult seizure. *Science* 157, 333-334.

Cohen, H. D. and Barondes, S. H. (1968) Cycloheximide impairs memory of an appetitive task. *Commun. Behav. Biol.* 1A, 337-340.

Deutch, J. A. (1969) The physiological basis of memory. *Annu. Rev. Psychol.* 20, 85-104.

Flexner, J. B., Flexner, L. B., and Stellar, E. (1963) Memory in mice as affected by intracerebral puromycin. *Science* 141, 57-59.

Flexner, L. B., Flexner, J. B., Roberts, R. B., and de la Haba, G. (1964) Loss of recent memory in mice as related to regional inhibition of cerebral protein synthesis. *Proc. Nat. Acad. Sci. U.S.*, 52, 1165-1169.

Flexner, J. B. and Flexner, L. B. (1967) Restoration of expression of memory lost after treatment with puromycin. *Proc. Nat. Acad. Sci. U.S.* 57, 1651-1654.

Flexner, L. B. and Flexner, J. B. (1968) Intracerebral saline: Effect on memory of trained mice treated with puromycin. *Science* 159, 330-331.

Garcia J. Kimeldorf, D. J. and Koelling, R. A. (1955) Conditioned aversion to saccarin resulting from exposure to gamma radiation. *Science,* 122, 157-158.

Geller, A., Robustelli, F., Barondes, S. H., Cohen, H. D., and Jarvik, M. E. (1969) Impaired performance by post-trial injections of cycloheximide in a passive avoidance. *Psychopharmacologia* 14, 371-376.

Hebb, D. O. (1949) *The Organization of Behavior,* Wiley, New York.

Hyden, H. and Lange, P. W. (1968) Protein synthesis in the hippocampal pyramidal cells of rats during a behavioral test. *Science* **159**, 1370-1373.

Jarvik, M. E. (1972) Effects of chemical and physical treatments on learning memory. *Ann. Rev. Psychol.* **23**, 457-486.

Kopriwa, B. and Leblond, C. P. (1962) Improvements in the coating technique of radioautography. *J. Histochem. Cytochem.* **10**, 269-284.

Nakajima, S. (1969) Interference with relearning in the rat after hippocampal injection of actinomycin D. *J. Compar. Physiol. Psychol.* **67**, 457-461.

Nakajima, S. (1972) Proactive effect of actinomycin D on maze performance in the rat. *Physiol. Behav.* **8**, 1063-1067.

Quartermain, D., McEwen, B. S., and Azmitia, E. C., Jr. (1970) Amnesia produced by electroconvulsive shock or cycloheximide: Conditions for recovery. *Science* **169**, 683-686.

Quinton, E. (1971) The cycloheximide-induced amnesia gradient of a passive avoidance task. *Psychonomic Sci.* **25**, 295-296.

Rosenblatt, F., Farrow, J. T., and Herblin, W. F. (1966) Transfer of conditioned responses for trained rats to untrained rats by means of a brain extract. *Nature* **209**, 46-48.

Rozin, P. (1969) Central or peripheral mediation of learning with long CS-US intervals in the feeding system. *J. Compar. Physiol. Psychol.* **67**, 421-429.

Ungar, G., Gelson, L. and Clark, R. H. (1968) Chemical transfer of learnined fear. *Nature* **217**, 1259-1261.

CHAPTER 8

Brain Glycoproteins and Learning: New Studies Supporting the "Sign-Post" Theory

SAMUEL BOGOCH

1. Introduction
2. Primary and Secondary Biochemical Processes
3. Phases of the Memory Process
4. Changes in Glycoprotein 11A in Relation to "the Amount of Learning"
5. Carbohydrate Constituents of Pigeon Brain Glycoproteins 10B and 11A
6. Incorporation of 14C-Glucose into Training
7. Glycoproteins at the Synapse
8. Conclusions
9. References

1. INTRODUCTION

In 1965 when it was first demonstrated that the glycoproteins of brain change in concentration during training, I proposed that the glycoproteins and related substances of the brain were involved in information, contact, and communication functions in the nervous system (Bogoch, 1965). The ten years of work preceding that study and several subsequent years of work on the subject, were summarized in the 1968 monograph *The Biochemistry of Memory; with an Inquiry into the Function of the Brain Mucoids* and the "Sign-Post" theory proposed (Bogoch, 1968). Thus, the concept that brain glycoproteins are involved in learning processes was

147

developed in studies beginning in the 1950's which examined the possibility that the macromolecular carbohydrates in brain have membrane, receptor, and recognition functions. It was demonstrated that a group of substances in the brain with carbohydrate end groups, including the aminoglycolipids and the glycoproteins, had the chemical structural properties which would make them suited to function at membrane surfaces and membrane interfaces (Bogoch, 1958c, 1960a, c, 1962) had the properties of viral receptors (Bogoch, 1957a; Bogoch et al, 1959), had pharmacological specificity (Bogoch et al., 1962) had molecular specificity related to antigen-antibody reactions (Bogoch, 1960c), occurred in high concentration in cerebrospinal fluid (Bogoch, 1960b) varied in concentration in cerebrospinal fluid with changes in the clinical and behavioral status of psychiatric patients (Bogoch, 1957b, 1958a, 1966; Bogoch et al., 1960, 1961; Campbell et al., 1967), occurred in high concentration in membranes and synaptosome fractions from brain (Quamina and Bogoch, 1966) showed changes in concentration with increasing developmental complexity of the nervous system (Bogoch, 1968), were disturbed when there was regression of higher brain functions (Bogoch, 1962; Bogoch and Belval, 1966), and showed increases in concentration in particular brain glycoprotein fractions in relationship to operant conditioning training of pigeons (Bogoch, 1965, 1968).

In more recent studies the fine structure of the carbohydrate and amino acid chains of the glycoproteins which appear to be most involved in the brain of the training pigeon were studied in detail (Bogoch, 1970). The function of glycoproteins in the formation of brain circuitry was discussed (Bogoch, 1969b), and the role of brain glycoproteins and brain tumors, where there is a regression of these postulated functions for brain glycoproteins (Bogoch, 1972a). Further to the study of brain glycoproteins in terms of *inter*cell recognition, studies on the brain glycoproteins in Tay-Sachs' disease have suggested that here there may be a disturbance in *intra*neuronal recognition (Bogoch, 1972b).

In studies of the glycoprotein 10B, an immunologically active component of this fraction has been purified and named astrocytin (Bogoch, 1973).

In the present chapter, further studies in training and learning pigeons will be reported. First, with a regard to the concentration of brain glycoproteins 10B and 11A achieved over a relatively long term series of learning trials, and second, with regard to the incorporation of radioactive carbohydrate constituents into brain glycoproteins in very short-term learning experiments, where that incorporation is measured in minutes. Both of these new lines of evidence support further the "Sign-Post" hypothesis that the brain glycoproteins are involved in memory and learning functions.

2. PRIMARY AND SECONDARY BIOCHEMICAL PROCESSES

I have pointed out elsewhere (Bogoch, 1968) that in examining biochemical processes for possible relevance to memory, an important distinction must be made between the primary or fundamental biochemical processes and secondary supportive processes. Our ignorance frequently prevents us from separating these two sets of phenomena. Thus, for example, when energy-generating or energy-storing mechanisms in the organism or cell are interfered with experimentally, and the processes of learning and memory are concurrently interrupted, one clearly cannot say that the energy mechanism is synonymous with the memory mechanism. Interference with the synthesis of adenosine triphosphate production may interfere with literally thousands of biochemical processes, the maintenance of cell membrane and cytoplasmic constituents of all types, and all of these may be essential to the maintenance of certain biological structures without which learning cannot occur. This, however, is a different matter from the identification of particular molecules which actually mediate the transmission of an electrical signal or facilitate storage in a nerve net. This subtle, demanding, and continuous task of distinction between primary and secondary supportive reactions is present in the experimental and the hypothetical aspects of all studies of learning and memory.

3. PHASES OF THE MEMORY PROCESS

Table I summarizes some of the major components of the memory process which, although overlapping in some parts, appear to require at least partially separate definition.

In addition, I have pointed out that there may well be different mechanisms for the retention of information which is to be held temporarily, but not "stored"; that is, held for seconds or minutes, as in the case of certain phone numbers, or held only for minutes or hours, as in the case of the departure time of an airplane. Both of these types of temporary retention of information may differ in quite fundamental or in only superficial ways from those which deal with storage for longer periods of time (Bogoch, 1968).

For long-term storage there may be distinctions between the mechanisms used for data which must always be readily available, and those used for data which may be required months or years later.

Are there macromolecules of the same or different types whose biosynthetic half-lives correspond to these various needs, or are there different anatomic subsystems performing these different functions, or both?

TABLE I

REQUIRED MECHANISM[a] FOR PROCESSING OF INFORMATION
IN THE NERVOUS SYSTEM: (PHASES OF THE MEMORY PROCESS)

1. Sensory input reception.

2. Encbding for transmission: Transduction from primary sensory modalities
   (sound, light, etc.) to electrochemical equivalents utilized by nervous system cells.

3. Association and Abstraction: Association with information previously stored,
   pattern recognition, abstraction, synthesis of new constructs: Conscious and
   unconscious.

4. Storage: (a) Further encoding, or same as 2?
            (b) Same process for short and long duration?

5. Retrieval: Remembering–forgetting.

6. Effector Consequences of Retrieval: Further association and abstraction; discharge in thought, language; motor and affective accompaniments.

7. Supporting chemical reactions for 1 through 6.

[a]Immediate chemical reactions are expected to be defined for each of the primary mechanisms 1 through 6. In addition, "second order" supporting reactions are
expected for each (7. Supporting Chemical Reactions).

The time frame for correlations is also important. Thus, many recent
biochemical studies on axonal transport of glycoproteins which attempt to
relate this to functional events fail to note that neurophysiological
transmission is measured in milliseconds, whereas axonal transport is
measured in hours.

Some of the brain glycoproteins, but not all of them, have been shown
by us to show changes in pigeon brain with training and learning (Bogoch,
1968). The most active of these glycoproteins in the training pigeon brain
are 10B, 11A, and Group 2. In their amino acid change, Group 2 and
Group 10B changes appear to be early reflections of the training process
but do not persist with time (Bogoch, 1968).

The brain mucoids demonstrate sufficient heterogeneity, fixed location,
appropriate development, change with pathology, recognition functions,
biosynthesis (resting, training, and puromycin-sensitive), change with
behavior, and change with learning, all consistent with the notion that
they are directly involved in the biochemistry of learning and memory
(Bogoch, 1968).

4. CHANGES IN GLYCOPROTEIN 11A IN RELATION TO "THE AMOUNT OF LEARNING"

Whereas many experimental protocols have been published for the
study of the "all-or-none" acquisition of information in a variety of

experimental animals, it is a more difficult task to express a graded response in terms of the amount learned in a given time by an individual subject. In order to approach this problem in the training pigeon, as it might relate to brain glycoproteins, we have done the following experiment. Eighteen experimentally naive pigeons were exposed to the following learning conditions. The pigeons were permitted to choose between two alternatives, one which, after a fixed delay interval, led to food reinforcement and the other which led only to the delay interval (without food). The percentage of time that the "food" condition is chosen is a function of the duration of the delay. Thus, at short delay intervals the food condition is exclusively chosen. At very long intervals, the pigeon is unable to discriminate between the two conditions (? forgets) and chooses equally between them.

When the delay interval was 20 seconds, some birds would learn to choose exclusively the food condition, some learned not al all and chose equally between the two conditions, and some were intermediate, preferring the food condition, but not exclusively.

The pigeons were male White Carneaux. They were maintained at approximately 85% of their free-feeding body weights. The apparatus used was a two-key operant chamber for pigeons according to Ferster and Skinner.

First, all birds were trained to peck equally at the two response keys in order to obtain food reinforcement. After this preliminary training, a concurrent VI 1 VI 1 schedule was instituted. On this schedule, responding on one key occasionally (on the average of once each minute) resulted in a delay interval of 20 seconds that was followed by food. Responding on the other key resulted only in the delay (again, on the average of once each minute). During the 20 second delay, the experimental chamber was completely dark, and responses were ineffective. Thus, responding on only one of the keys is effective in producing food.

The subjects were run for 21 sessions, each session terminating after 30 reinforcements were received. Following the last session, all subjects were sacrificed by dipping the pigeon into a Dry Ice-acetone bath. Each pigeon brain was coded and extracted individually for brain glycoproteins, and 13 groups separated on column chromatography with Cellex D as previously described (Bogoch, 1968).

The chemical analyses, Folin-Lowry quantitative determination of protein, were done "blind" with regard to the performance of each pigeon.

The degree to which the responses deviated from a random 50-50 response to the two keys represented the preference for the correct key. The result of this deviation from random are expressed in Table II as deviations from 50, the highest deviation being 50 and the lowest being zero. Table II shows the relationship of the concentration of brain glycoprotein 11A to the rank achieved in training. The pigeons were

152   BOGOCH

TABLE II

Relationship of Concentration of Brain Glycoprotein
11A to Rank Achieved by Pigeons in Training

| TRAINING DATA | | | NEUROCHEMICAL DATA | |
Last Day Rank	N	Score Mean Range	Brain Glycoprotein 11A, mg/g Mean Range	
Highest	5	38.2 (28-50)	2.63 (1.24-3.88)	
Middle	9	16.0 (10-24)	0.65 (0.40-1.39)	
Lowest	4	3.8 (0-9)	0.56 (0.32-0.83)	

ranked according to their scores and then divided into three groups: the highest group scoring in the range of 28-50, the middle group scoring in the range of 10-24, and the lowest group scoring in the range of 0-9. Because of the small numbers of subjects in each group, only a trend can be perceived, but this was fairly clear. Thus, those demonstrating the highest "amount of learning" had the highest mean amount of brain glycoprotein 11A, 2.63 milligrams per gram of wet weight of brain tissue. Those of the middle group had 0.65 milligram per gram and those of the lowest group had 0.56 milligram per gram. The concentration of brain glycoprotein 10B did not show any relationship to rank order. Since these were long-term results observed after 21 sessions of training, these results were in confirmation of the earlier results on the changes in brain glycoprotein 10B, which was elevated early, then normal later (Bogoch, 1968).

5. CARBOHYDRATE CONSTITUENTS OF PIGEON BRAIN GLYCO-PROTEINS 10B AND 11A

In earlier studies (Bogoch, 1970) it was shown that the carbohydrate constituents of glycoproteins 11A and 10B (10B has two separate fractions, 10B1 and 10B2, in the pigeon) are quite different from each other, although their amino acid chains appear quite close in composition. Thus, a change from 10B to 11A represents a major structural change interminal carbohydrate units, which would correlate with the notion that specific kinds of connections are being favored or that entirely new kinds of connections are being formed. Thus, 11A has considerably less hexose and hexosamine than does either 10B1 or 10B2. These differences are sufficient that specific antibodies can be made to these substances which distinguish between them. This type of specificity is therefore of a sufficiently high order that it might account for specificity of contact between neuronal membranes of two different neurons.

6. INCORPORATION OF ^{14}C-GLUCOSE INTO TRAINING AND RESTING PIGEON BRAIN GLYCOPROTEINS

Glucose labeled in the first carbon was injected intravenously into pigeons at rest. They were then allowed to rest, or to engage in a training procedure for varying periods of time before sacrifice in a Dry Ice-acetone bath. The brain glycoproteins were extracted and separated as previously described (Bogoch, 1965, 1968). Figure 1 summarizes the findings.

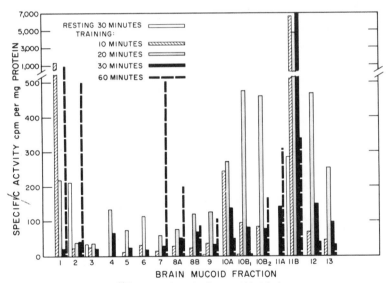

Fig. 1. Incorporation of ^{14}C-glucose into brain mucoids of pigeons.

At rest for 30 minutes, only slight incorporation was observed in groups 2, 3, and 11B. Much more incorporation was observed at only 10 minutes of training.

Furthermore, the nature of the most actively labeled groups was a function of time. Thus, at 10 minutes training, groups 1, 10A, and 10B were most prominently labeled. At 20 minutes, groups 10A, 10B, and 10B2, 11B, 12, and 13 were most active. At 60 minutes, groups 1 and 2 were again active, together with groups 7, 11A, and 11B. The fact that groups 1 and 2 are associated with the lateral dendritic processes (Bogoch, 1968) and that 10B proteins are associated with different cell types (glia and neurones) will require further individual examination.

What is clear is that there is an extremely active turnover of carbohydrates in the brain glycoproteins of training pigeons, and that much of this activity occurs within minutes. We had previously noted (Bogoch, 1965, 1968) that these changes occurred earlier than those times usually examined in such studies, and the present data confirms the importance of examining discrete and short time periods in relation where possible to specific glycoproteins and specific cell fractions.

7. GLYCOPROTEINS AT THE SYNAPSE

With the development of the new stains for the electron microscope which visualize large molecular weight carbohydrate materials, the periodic acid stains, it has been possible to demonstrate visually the presence in high concentration of glycoproteins at the synaptic cleft. Figure 2, on top, (periodic acid-silver methenamine, x 23,00) shows the dendrite of the nerve cell whose perikaryon is visible at the base outlined by stained material (arrows), which, in the neuropile separate nerve and glial processes from each other. Staining of the intercellular space is sharply increased in the region of the synaptic cleft (S). Some unspecific staining (without periodic acid oxidation) is present in the matrix of mitochondria (M) and in the rough endoplasmic reticulum (ER). At lower right, three intensely stained dense bodies are probably lysosomes (L) (from Rambourg & Leblond, 1967).

With phosphotungstic acid (lower picture), as with periodic acid-silver-methenamine, a stained layer outlines cell and nerve processes (arrow). Staining of the intercellular space is enhanced in the synaptic cleft (S). Unstained mitochondria are labeled M; at upper left, a densely stained multivesicular body (mv) may be seen in the perikaryon of a nerve cell (*J. Microsc.* **8**: 325-342, 1969). (Both of these electron photomicrographs are shown here through the courtesy of Dr. A. Rambourg.)

8. CONCLUSIONS

The studies herein reported support the "Sign-Post" theory of the function of brain glycoproteins in the establishment of brain circuitry and its relationship to learning and memory. The long-term learning experiment showed a correlation between the absolute amount of glycoprotein 11A and the "amount learned". This supports the earlier data in this

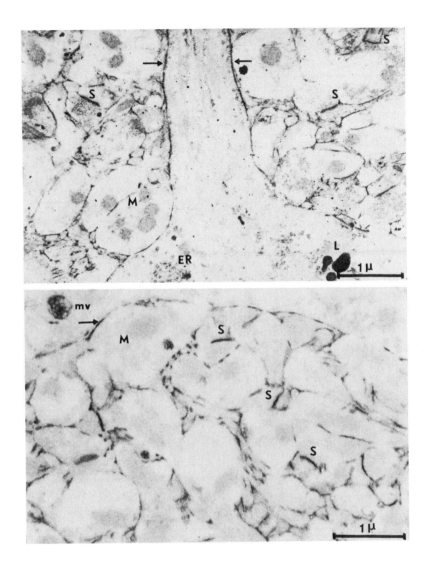

regard (Bogoch, 1968). The short-term learning experiments show that the incorporation of ^{14}C-glucose into all of the brain glycoproteins are indeed more active during training, and that marked incorporation occurs within minutes during training, in contrast to hours and days as reported for axonal transport.

The preceding studies provide evidence of the "expression" of function with reference to the proposed higher recognition functions of the brain glycoproteins. Other studies in our laboratory have demonstrated the

TABLE III

Carbohydrate Composition of Pigeon Brain Glycoproteins
(10B1, 10B11 and 11A, as % of protein Bogoch, 1970)

	10B1	10B11	11A
Hexose	11.1	16.7	10.9
Hexosamine	16.2	17.9	4.6
Neuraminic Acid	0.6	1.0	0

"regression" of these higher recognition functions in the loss of carbohydrate moieties of the brain glycoproteins occurring in brain tumors
(Bogoch, 1972a). This in turn has led to the extension of the "Sign-Post"
concept to the proposal (Bogoch, 1972a) that mucoid biosynthesis is
inversely related to DNA replication. That is, DNA and cell division are
inhibited during cell positioning and the formation of intercell contacts
(the proposed glycoprotein "Sign-Post" experiential function), and
mucoid biosynthesis is inhibited when DNA and cell division are active.

REFERENCES

Bogoch, S. (1957a) *Virology* **1**, 458.
Bogoch, S. (1957b) *Amer. J. Psychiat.* **114**, 122.
Bogoch, S. (1958a) *AMA Arch. Neurol. Psychiat.* **80**, 221.
Bogoch, S. (1958b) *Amer. J. Psychiat.* **114**, 1028.
Bogoch, S. (1958c) *Biochem. J.* **68**, 319.
Bogoch, S. (1960a) *Nature* **190**, 153.
Bogoch, S. (1960b) *J. Biol. Chem.* **235**, 16.
Bogoch, S. (1960c) *Nature* **185**, 392.
Bogoch, S. (1962) *Cerebral Sphingolipidoses,* S. M. Aronson and B. W. Volk, Eds.
  Academic Press, New York, p. 249.
Bogoch, S. (1965) *Neurosci, Res. Prog. Bull.* **3**, 38.
Bogoch, S. (1966) In *Biological Treatment of Mental Illness,* M. Rinkel, Ed., Farrar,
  Straus and Giroux, New York, p. 406.
Bogoch, S. (1968) *The Biochemistry of Memory: With an Inquiry into the Function
  of the Brain Mucoids,* Oxford University Press, New York.
Bogoch, S. (1969a) Nervous system proteins. In *Handbook of Neurochemistry,* Vol.
  I, A. Lajtha, Ed., Plenum Press, New York.
Bogoch, S., Ed (1969b) *Future of the Brain Sciences,* Plenum Press, New York, pp.
  104-113.
Bogoch, S. (1970) In *Protein Metabolism of the Nervous System,* A. Lajtha, Ed.,
  Plenum Press, New York, pp. 535-569.

Bogoch, S. (1972a) Brain glycoprotein 10B: Further evidence of the 'Sign-Post' role of brain glycoproteins in cell recognition, its change in brain tumor, and the presence of a 'Distance Factor'. In *Structural and Functional Proteins of the Nervous System*, A. N. Davison, I. G. Morgan, and P. Mandel, Eds. Plenum Press, New York, pp. 39-54.

Bogoch, S. (1972b) In *Sphingolipids Sphingolipidoses and Allied Disorders*, B. W. Volk and S. M. Aronson, Eds., Plenum Press, New York, pp. 127-149.

Bogoch, S., Astrocytin: Purified immunologically active component of brain glycoprotein 10B. Published Abstract, Internat. Soc. Neurochem., 3rd Internat. Mtg., Tokyo, August 1973.

Bogoch, S. and Bogoch, E. S. (1959) *Nature* **183**, 53.

Bogoch, S., Lynch, P., and Levine, A. S., (1959) *Virology* **7**, 161.

Bogoch, S., Dussik, K. T., Fender, C., and Conron, P. (1960) *Amer. J. Psychiat.* **117**, 409.

Bogoch, S., Dussik, K. T., and Conran, P., (1961) *New Eng. J. Med.* **264**, 521.

Bogoch, S., Paasonen, M. K., and Trendelenburg, U. (1962) *Brit. J. Pharmacol.* **18**, 325.

Bogoch, S., Rajam, P. C., and Belval, P. C. (1964) *Nature* **204**, 73.

Bogoch, S. and Belval, P. C. (1966) In *Inborn Disorders of Sphingolipid Metabolism*, S. M. Aronson and B. W. Volk, Eds., Pergamon Press, New York, p. 273.

Bogoch, S., Belval, P. C. Sweet, W. H., Sacks, W., and Korsh, G. (1968) In *Proc. XVth Collog., Brugge, Protides of Biilogical Fluids*, H. Peeters, Ed., Elsevier, Amsterdam, p. 129.

Campbell, R., Bogich, S., Scolaro, N. J., and Belval, P. C. (1967) *Amer. J. Psychiat.* **123**, 952.

Quamina, A. and Bogoch, S. (1966) In *Proc. XIIIth Colloq., Protides of Biological Fluids, Brugge*, H. Peeters, Ed., Elsevier, Amsterdam, p. 211.

Rambourg, A. and Leblond, C. P. (1967) *J. Cell Bio.* **32**, 41.

CHAPTER 9

Experimentally Induced Retrograde Amnesia: Some Neurochemical Correlates

WALTER B. ESSMAN

1. INTRODUCTION

The behavioral effect of agents and/or events presented in close temporal proximity with a learning experience has been a consequent retrograde amnesia for that experience. Several site-specific biochemical alterations in the central nervous system have also been shown to be related to such amnesic stimuli. One consistent finding within this context which has served to clarify the role of several molecular events probably

159

involved with short-term memory fixation, has been an alteration in brain 5-hydroxytrptamine (5-HT) content and/or metabolism; such changes appear dependent upon the time following the amnesic stimulus when such measures are assessed. A change in brain 5-HT has been particularly apparent following a single electroconvulsive shock (ECS), a well established amnesic stimulus that provides for a temporal gradient of retrograde amnesia, depending upon its proximity in time with the learning experience; i.e., as the interval between a learning experience and ECS is increased, the probability of consequent retrograde amnesia for that experience is decreased. A more precise role of brain 5-HT in amnesia has been evaluated for conditions which confer changes in its brain level or turnover, indicating that such factors as age, pharmacological treatment, environmental interactions, and endogenous molecular interactions may all, independently or interactively, serve to alter the incidence or time course over which retrograde amnesia may occur (Essman, 1970a, b).

Cellular and subcellular changes related to the regulation of cerebral protein synthesis have been associated with several events which may be significant for the mediation of amnesic processes that can interfere with short-term memory fixation. 5-HT content and 5-hydroxyindoleacetic acid (5-HIAA) levels of glia have been significantly elevated following a single ECS sufficient to effect a retrograde amnesia; a cellular increment in these substrates may persist to permit protein synthesis to be affected. Moreover, at the presynaptic nerve ending (synaptosome) the rate of protein synthesis measured for both the cerebral cortex and limbic system has been shown to be significantly inhibited by 5-HT at concentrations approximating the elevation resulting from amnesic treatments such as ECS (Essman, 1970b). In parallel with the amnesic effect of ECS there is an inhibition of cerebral protein synthesis, ranging from 4 to 42%; the reduced incorporation of amino acids into proteins occurs within seconds after ECS administration and then becomes less pronounced by approximately 60 minutes postshock. Maximal inhibition of protein synthesis has been shown to occur in the basal ganglia and diencephalon; by five minutes following ECS (60%), protein synthesis measured in synaptosomes of these regions was inhibited by approximately 41% (Essman, 1971). Similar findings have been reported for whole brain protein synthesis which was inhibited in mice within minutes following ECS (Cotman et al., 1971). More precise definition of the temporal relationship and subcellular sites of ECS-induced inhibition of regional brain protein synthesis has also been described (Heldman and Essman, 1971).

The synthesis of macromolecules at specific sites within the central nervous system may represent one system within which molecular changes attending experimentally induced amnesia can be assessed. The possible relevance of macromolecular synthesis to memory fixation and storage processes has essentially evolved from studies utilizing synthesis inhibitors as tools for the induction of learning and memory deficits (Barondes, 1970); however, these avenues of investigation have frequently failed to specify regions, cell sites, or subcellular loci within which altered synthesis has occurred; there is also the more obviously pragmatic issue that the fixation or disruption of memory processes as endogenous intracellular central nervous system events does not utilize antibiotics, antimetabolites, or other pharmacological agents, but probably depends more intimately upon the utilization of endogenous substrates by which such synthetic events are regulated.

2. INTERACTION OF 5-HT AND RNA

Some support for a molecular interaction related to ECS-induced retrograde amnesia has been the significant negatively correlated changes in brain 5-hydroxytryptamine and ribonucleic acid. The magnitude of such changes decreased as a function of time after ECS. Previous date (Essman, 1970b) have shown that the time course of such correlated consequences of ECS relate to the cellular specificity of such effects over time. Examination of this relationship on a gross tissue level rather than a cellular basis, indicates a rapid decrease in this molecular interaction after treatment, such that by 15 minutes after a single ECS, the trend remains but the significance of the effect is questionable. As an example of this relationship, a reduced level of forebrain RNA persists ($\sim$6%) although not significantly, for 15 minutes after treatment and an increase in forebrain content of 5-HT ($\sim$50%) was also indicated. The interval after a single ECS where such changes appear to be maximal is within 5 to 8 minutes wherein both changes occur at a magnitude sufficient to yield statistically significant differences from concentrations obtained in sham-treated controls.

The interrelationship between forebrain RNA content and 5-HT concentration as measured at 8 minutes after a single ECS was investigated for several brain regions dissected after the animal was killed by cervical dislocation following overt recovery from the post-ictal phase of the convulsion. The areas samples included the corpus callosum, cerebral cortex, hypothalamus, thalamus, and structures of the limbic system (hippocampus, fornix, amygdala, and septal region). A highly significant negative correlation between RNA decrements and 5-HT increments may be observed in these regional data summarized in Figures 1 and 2. One suggestion that might be highly consistent with such a regional relationship could be a physical interaction between 5-HT and RNA. Of course, one issue related to such an interaction is the extent to which endogenous increases in a biogenic amine having a putative central nervous system transmitter role may possibly account for a reduced level of a macro-

162   ESSMAN

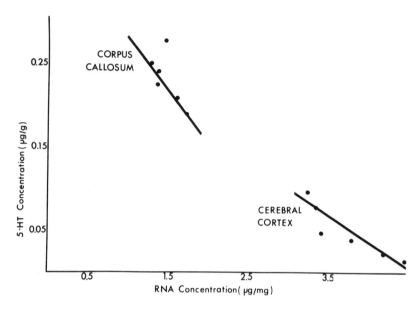

Fig. 1. Concentration of 5-hydroxytryptamine and ribonucleic acid in several regions of the mouse brain following a single electroconvulsive shock.

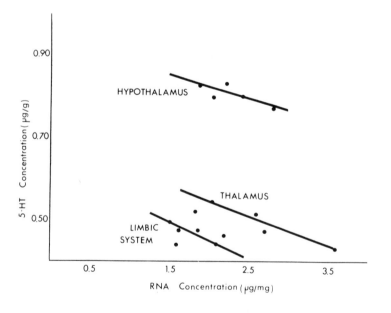

Fig. 2. Concentration of 5-hydroxytryptamine and ribonucleic acid in several regions of the mouse brain following a single electroconvulsive shock.

molecule critical to the synthesis of new proteins. Of such proteins or polypeptides, there may well be several, the presence of which is either demanded at the synaptic region or the synthesis of which may be at synaptic sites, in order for memory fixation and associated events to be successfully accomplished.

Supporting evidence has emerged for the hypothesis that brain 5-HT metabolism may serve as a molecular substrate for the mediation of macromolecular synthetic events of possible relevance to memory and amnesia processes. The interaction of 5-HT with other macromolecules such as RNA, nucleotides, etc. and the regulation of these interactions through endogenous changes in ionic strength have all served as a basis for reinforcing the significance of indoleamines in the regulation of macro-molecular synthesis significant for memory fixation and storage processes (Bittman et al., 1969; Bittman and Essman, 1970; Essman, 1970b; Essman et al., 1971).

3. BIOCHEMICAL EVENTS IN AGE-DEPENDENT AMNESIC EFFECTS

One point that has emerged from previous studies has concerned biomolecular changes related to memory fixation in an age-dependent manner during the early development of the male CF-1s strain mouse. It has been previously shown (Essman, 1970b) that 17 day old CF-1s mice have significant resistance to the retrograde amnesic effects of a single ECS presented at varying intervals following a conditioning procedure. Mice of 15, 16, or 18 days of age, or older, showed a characteristic retrograde amnesia resulting from such treatment. Also, 17 day old CF-1s mice have low whole brain levels of 5-HT, as compared with younger or older animals, and as compared with these other groups they show a higher brain 5-HT turnover rate and significantly lower turnover time.

As an example of the differences in susceptibility or resistance to the amnesic effect of posttraining ECS between CF-1s strain mice of different ages, reference is made to the data summarized in Figure 3. Mice of either 17, 25, or 33 days of age, trained for acquisition of a passive avoidance response, utilizing a standardized conditioning technique (Essman and Alpern, 1964) were given a signle ECS (10 mA, 200 msec, 400 V) at either 10 sec, 2 min, 4 min, 8 min, or 16 min following the training trial. A testing trial, given 24 hours later was used to assess the incidence of conditioned response retention (avoidance of a shock chamber for 120 sec or more after providing for entry) or retrograde amnesia (entry into the chamber in which prior foot-shock was given, within 20 sec after being provided with this option). The data clearly indicate that, for each of the respective post-training ECS intervals, the 17 day old mice showed a significantly greater conditioned response retention (rate constant for

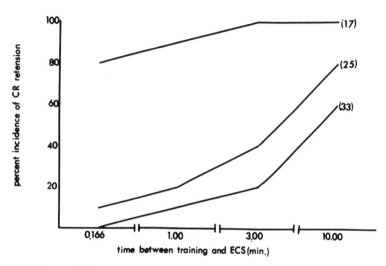

Fig. 3. Percent incidence of conditioned response retention as a function of the time interval between training and electroconvulsive shock in mice of three differing age populations.

consolidation, based upon temporal gradient (K_c) = 33.33) than did the 33 day old animals $(K_c$ = 5.65). These data suggest that the rate of memory consolidation as defined by a temporally linked susceptibility to retrograde amnesia, can differ appreciably at select ages wherein differences in brain 5-HT turnover occur. It became apparent, therefore, that several rather well defined relationships were obtained during critical periods of early development; the CF-1s mouse showed an age-specific resistance to the amnesic effects of a treatment which differed from mice of other ages, did not lead to changes in brain 5-HT level or metabolism.

4. AMNESIA-RELATED CHANGES AT THE SUBSYNAPTIC LEVEL

In view of previous results indicating a critical age in the developmental sequence where both the behavioral as well as biochemical requisites for resistance to an amnesic treatment occur, further experiments were carried out in order to explore some of the related considerations in greater detail. One such issue concerned ECS and its effects upon brain RNA level. In earlier studies, it has been shown that ECS, among several amnesic treatments, can lead to a reduction of whole brain and regional RNA levels (Essman, 1965, 1967), and that under conditions wherein such ECS-induced decrements are blocked either by acceleration of brain RNA synthesis, and/or elevation of RNA level, the susceptibility to the ECS-induced amnesic effect was significantly reduced (Essman, 1966;

Essman & Essman, 1969). Evidence in support of the interaction of RNA with 5-HT in the brain (Essman et al., 1971) and the relevance of this interaction for memory processes provided for several experiments carried out to assess changes in RNA level synaptic subcellular sites of the mouse cerebral cortex following ECS. Three age populations were used in order to test the hypothesis that the stability of the RNA molecule in 17 day old mice given ECS would be increased because of the specific serotoninergic character of the brain at that critical age. Such increased resistance of brain RNA to the effects of ECS relate to the observation that at 17 days of age the CF-1s mouse has higher endogenous RNA levels and lower 5-HT content than older animals. It was further assumed that resistance to the amnesic effect of ECS depends in part upon the integrity of such molecules such that ECS-induced changes might relate to ECS-induced amnesia. Behavioral data have consistently indicated that 17 day old mice show a marked resistance to the amnesic effect of ECS and it was assumed that this might represent the extent to which such molecules as RNA changed in regional concentration in response to the central effect of ECS. Male CF-1s strain mice from laboratory bred litters of either 17, 25, or 33 days of age were given a single transcorneal ECS (10 mA,200 msec, 400 V), with differences in transcorneal resistance taken into account. Ten minutes after treatment, the cerebral cortex, scraped free of underlying myelin, was obtained. A 10% tissue homogenate was prepared in 0.32M sucrose and was then fractionated, utilizing differential and gradient centrifugation to yield several subcellular fractions (Whittaker et al., 1964). The homogeneity of these fractions was estimated utilizing both enzyme marker assays and electron micrographs of material, fixed in 2.5% gluteraldehyde, and embedded and sectioned (Whittaker, 1969).

   A typical electron micrograph of a synaptosome fraction isolated from the mouse cerebral cortex by the techniques indicated is shown in Figure 4. This section illustrates a relatively uncontaminated synaptosome fraction, which with occasional mitochondria and membrane fragments, consists largely of intact sealed presynaptic nerve endings. In order to illustrate the external morphology of the isolated synaptosomes more comprehensively, pelleted synaptosome fractions fixed in gluteraldehyde were shadowed with gold and examined under a scanning electron microscope at maximum magnification. A single synaptosome, with a horizontal diameter of approximately 0.9μ is shown in Figure 5. The components of these synaptosomes, as utilized for analysis in the experiments described, were obtained by rupturing the external synaptic membrane of the synaptosomes by osmotic shock, whereby their contents were released and dispersed on a sucrose density gradient, which upon further centrifugation provided for a separation of these organelles. Figure 6 shows an example of an osmotically ruptured synaptosome examined under the scanning electron micorscope. From this illustration, one may

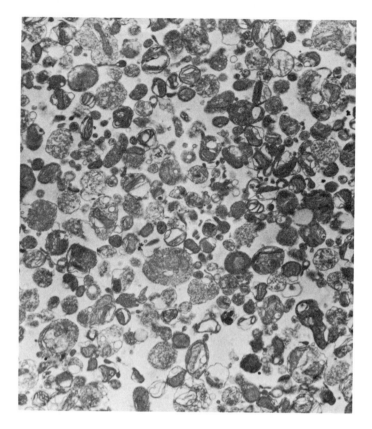

Fig. 4. Representative electron micrograph of a synaptosome fraction isolated on a sucrose density gradient. Magnification, 27,500X.

visualize the external synaptic membrane, from which, in subsequent studies, proteins were extracted.

The differences in RNA concentration associated with subcellular fractions between control ($\overline{\text{ECS}}$) and ECS-treated animals occurring as a function of age have been summarized and are listed in Table I. For the 33 day old mice particularly, and to a lesser degree among 25 day old animals, RNA levels decreased significantly for several subcellular sites. For 17 day old mice, those ECS-induced changes observed for older animals did not occur at all, or were appreciably less marked. The marked change in RNA content was in the synaptosome fraction, which although characterized by low levels of RNA, was reduced in RNA content as a consequence of ECS in 25 and 33 day old mice; 17 day old mice did not show such an ECS-induced change, and the basal RNA level associated with synaptosomes ($18.61 \pm 1.38\,\mu\text{g/mg}$) was slightly higher than that of 25

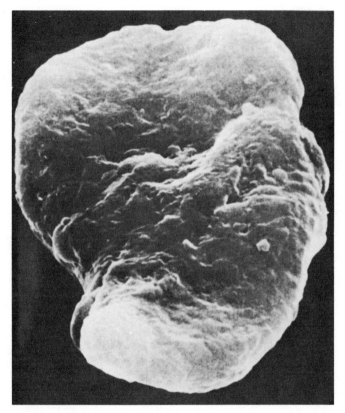

Fig. 5. Scanning electron micrograph by a single synaptosome isolated following density gradient centrifugation.

(12.94 ± 0.61) or 33 day old (11.68 ± 0.14) animals. When these synaptosomes were osmotically ruptured and their contents dispersed on a density gradient to yield several constituent fractions, the RNA content of these synaptic constituents was consistently higher for the 17 day old animals, and the ECS-induced changes in RNA content occurred in all but one of these synaptic constituents—the external synaptic membrane.

5. CEREBRAL PROTEIN SYNTHESIS: ALTERATIONS WITH ECS

The relationship between ECS treatment, temporally dependent retrograde amnesia production, and cerebral protein synthesis appears fundamental to the postulation of macromolecular substrates for memory fixation. This hypothesis is bounded by those conditions through which the memory fixation process can be approached and defined according to

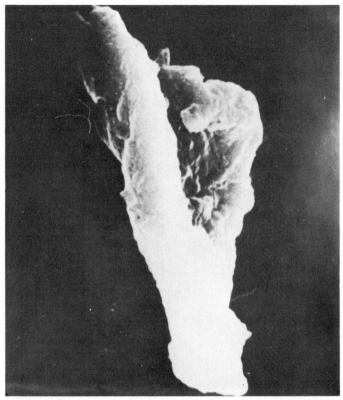

Fig. 6. Osmotically ruptured single synaptosomes shown in scanning electron micrograph.

those changes which lead to its disruption. ECS constitutes one means by which such disruption may occur and there are several neurochemical consequences of ECS that have been defined and summarized (Essman, 1972). ECS alters protein synthesis in the whole brain as well as in several regions of the mouse brain.

Groups of male CF-1s strain mice were given intracranial injections of C^{14} leucine providing for a 10 minute labeling pulse contiguous with a single transcorneal ECS (10 mA, 200 msec, 400 V). The animals were killed by cervical section either at zero time (within 10 sec following ECS administration) or at 5, 10, 15, 30, 60, 120 or 240 minutes after treatment. Total proteins were extracted and quantitatively assayed and the amino acid precursor incorporated into the protein was counted for the respective post-ECS times. The results are summarized in Table II where, based upon specific radioactivity of the precursor incorporated into whole brain protein, the percent inhibition of protein synthesis was derived from

TABLE I

Mean (±σ) Difference (Δ) in RNA Concentration
(μg/mg Protein) and Percent Change as a Consequence
of Electroconvulsive Shock

	AGE (DAYS)					
	17		25		33	
SUBCELLULAR FRACTION	RNA Δ	%Δ	RNA Δ	%Δ	RNA Δ	%Δ
Small Myelin Fragments	0.44 (0.05)	3	0.94 (0.07)	5	0.42 (0.04)	2
Synaptosomes	0.72 (0.04)	4	5.56* (1.02)	75	6.52* (1.03)	56
Mitochondria	0.62 (0.05)	37	1.45 (0.44)	46	2.25 (0.52)	50
Soluble Cytoplasm	0.69 (0.20)	2	5.98* (0.52)	59	7.77* (0.24)	45
Synaptic Vesicles	0.77 (0.16)	8	1.09 (0.16)	27	4.34* (0.62)	82
External Synaptic Membrane	0.64 (0.16)	2	1.53 (1.03)	8	0.99 (0.44)	5
Incompletely Disrupted Endings	0.07 (0.11)	0	11.83* (1.66)	55	10.22* (0.76)	52
Intraterminal Mitochondria	6.17 (1.96)	17	4.69 (0.24)	37	3.92 (0.54)	39

*$p < .01$

a baseline defined from groups of mice treated with sham-ECS ($\overline{ECS}$), wherein there was no posttreatment precursor incorporation variability. The inhibition of protein synthesis by ECS occurred mainly within the first 20 minutes; however maximum inhibition was within 5 minutes after treatment. By 60 minutes or more after ECS, protein synthesis was not altered in whole brain.

Protein synthesis in several brain regions after ECS was assessed after posttreatment dissection and separation of the tissue into several major regions. These data, summarized in Table III, indicate that a considerable extent of the ECS-induced protein synthesis inhibition occurs in the cerebral cortex and basal ganglia and diencephalon; the maximum effect was apparent in the latter regions, particularly by 5 minutes following treatment.

The initiation of regional inhibition of protein synthesis over a time course not inconsistent with the temporal dependency for the amnesic effect of ECS treatment does not necessarily suggest more than a tentative relationship and at this juncture does not constitute a causal relationship.

TABLE II

Percent Incorporation of C^{14} Leucine into
Whole Brain Proteins as a Function of Time After ECS

TIME AFTER ECS (MIN.)	PER CENT INCORPORATION OF C^{14} LEUCINE INTO PROTEINS
0.166	50
5.0	70
10.0	75
15.0	80
30.0	90
60.0	95
120.0	100
240.0	100

TABLE III

Percent Incorporation of
C^{14} Leucine into Proteins of
Several Brain REgions At Several Post-ECS Times

TIME AFTER ECS (MIN.)	BRAIN REGION			
	CEREBRAL CORTEX	BASAL GANGLIA & DIENCEPHALON	MIDBRAIN	CEREBELLUM
0.166	75*	75*	100	100
5.0	80	40*	90	95
30.0	100	100	100	100
*p <.01				

The issue of cerebral protein synthesis alterations by other agents or events which can effect a retrograde amnesia within a well defined temporal sequence also remains prominent. It has been suggested (Cotman et al., 1971) that protein synthesis inhibition by ECS may depend upon the convulsion rather than the current delivered through the tissue. Should a convulsion be the only requsite for a retrograde amnesia, then the current alone should not exert amnesic effects. This, however, does not appear to be the case; mice in which drug-induced anticonvulsant treatment blocked seizure onset after electroshock or pentylenetetrazol still showed a retrograde amnesia for behavior to which previous training had been given (Essman, 1968a,b.) Other treatments producing a retrograde amnesia, such as ether anesthesia (Essman & Jarvik, 1961) or hypothermia (Essman & Sudak, 1962) do not initiate seizure activity, yet effect a temporally dependent retrograde amnesia in rodents.

6. CEREBRAL PROTEIN SYNTHESIS: SITES OF ECS EFFECT

One of those issues raised in the foregoing data is the specificity of the changes induced by electroconvulsive shock in cerebral protein synthesis. At the level of the presynaptic nerve ending, the issue is precisely concerned with those proteins derived from either the soluble pool within the synaptosome or the insoluble constituents which represent some contribution to membrane structure at that site. Proteins derived from the soluble cytoplasm of the synaptosome were subjected to disc-gel electrophoresis on a polyacrylamide gel and the constituent proteins and/or polypeptides were dispersed along such gel columns in accordance with their molecular weight. In Figure 7, a schematic representation of the migrated bands of the soluble protein pool is shown where these were derived from the cerebral cortex of electroconvulsive shock treated or

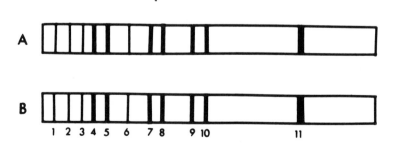

Fig. 7. Schematic representation of bands of electrophoretically isolated proteins developed on polyacrylamide gel. Parent proteins were derived from soluble synaptosomal pool. (A = control; B = electroconvulsive shock).

control-treated animals 5 minutes following treatment. There do not appear to be any qualitative differences between the migration of these protein bands.

Experiments were carried out wherein mice were given an intracranial injection of C^{14} leucine simultaneous with electroconvulsive shock or control treatment and the labeling of proteins was allowed to proceed for 5 minutes, after which disc-gel electrophoresis was done, and the protein bands were eluted and radioactivity was counted; these results are summarized in Table IV. These data indicate that a highly significant inhibition of the incorporation of the labeled amino acid into soluble

TABLE IV

Mean ($\pm\sigma$) Incorporation of C^{14} Leucine
into Electrophoretically Isolated Bands
from Soluble Synaptosomal Proteins

	TREATMENT	
BAND	$\overline{ECS}$	ECS
1	515 ± 11	175 ± 10*
2	101 ± 9	85 ± 12
3	90 ± 6	80 ± 4
4	105 ± 7	73 ± 6*
5	121 ± 10	89 ± 5*
6	92 ± 4	93 ± 4
7	128 ± 5	82 ± 17
8	73 ± 10	67 ± 8
9	60 ± 4	53 ± 7
10	118 ± 6	72 ± 11*
11	122 ± 9	73 ± 16

*$p < .01$

protein fractions occurred particularly for the high molecular weight proteins in the first 12 segments of the polyacrylamide gel, suggesting very strongly that it was these proteins that were affected by a single electroconvolsive shock.

The external synaptic membrane which has previously been illustrated in the scanning electron micrograph shown in Figure 6 also provides a source of insoluble proteins, the synthesis of which probably occurs intrasynaptosomally. In several experiments the proteins derived from this source were electrophoretically separated on a polyacrylamide gel upon which qualitative differences produced by electroconvulsive shock did not emerge (Fig. 8) When, as in the previous experiment, the incorporation of

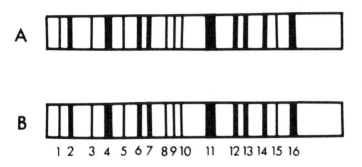

Fig. 8. Schematic representation of bands of electrophoretically isolated proteins developed on polyacrylamide gel. Parent proteins were derived from nonsoluble synaptosomal pool. (A = control; B = electroconvulsive shock).

C^{14} leucine was examined for 5 minutes following electroconvulsive shock and these proteins were again electrophoretically migrated, the results shown in Table V were obtained. A comparison of the electroshock conditions with those of the control conditions clearly suggests the synthesis of low molecular weight insoluble proteins was significantly interpreted by electroconvulsive shock treatment.

The relationship between amnesic agents or events, macromolecular changes, and protein synthesis has been explored on several further grounds. One approach has been based upon observations that one factor common to experimentally induced amnesia and antagonism of such amnesia relates to alterations in regional 5-hydroxytryptamine (serotonin) activity.

7. AMNESIC EFFECTS OF 5-HT AND INHIBITION OF CEREBRAL PROTEIN SYNTHESIS

Changes in RNA concentration associated with constituent subsynaptic organelles may be similarly effected in guinea pigs by the intracranial

TABLE V

Mean (±σ) Incorporation of C^{14} Leucine
into Electrophoretically Isolated Bands
from Insoluble Synaptosomal Proteins

BAND	TREATMENT	
	$\overline{ECS}$	ECS
1	75 ± 10	30 ± 4
2	48 ± 13	31 ± 3
3	36 ± 5	38 ± 4
4	50 ± 3	50 ± 4
5	50 ± 2	50 ± 3
6	80 ± 4	75 ± 6
7	100 ± 4	77 ± 5*
8	85 ± 6	77 ± 9
9	75 ± 6	70 ± 5
10	104 ± 6	78 ± 14
11	106 ± 10	102 ± 6
12	140 ± 15	80 ± 4*
13	125 ± 11	50 ± 8*
14	304 ± 18	75 ± 16*
15	52 ± 6	54 ± 10

*p <.01

administration of 5-HT in doses leading to the whole brain changes produced by ECS (Essman et al., 1971). Considering previous data supporting a potentially amnesic effect of intracranial 5-HT (Essman, 1970b), several experiments were conducted to assess the effects of intracranial 5-HT introduced in close temporal proximity with a learning experience and the production of a time-dependent interruption of memory trace fixation.

Male CF-1s strain mice (35 days of age) were trained, with the avoidance technique previously described, and 10 seconds later were given either an injection of 2 μg of 5-HT in 10λ of 0.9% NaCl, or 10λ of NaCl alone; the amine or control injection was given with a Hamilton Microliter syringe through a 30 gauge needle and adaptor which, utilizing midline and lateral coordinates and penetration of the skull, was inserted to a depth of the medial hippocampus. Twenty-four hours later, animals were tested in the same apparatus for retention of the conditioned avoidance response. Appropriate control groups were included in the experiment to obviate the possiblity of locomotor or performance changes by the intracranial 5-HT. The results of such control studies indicated that by 24 hours following intrahippocampal 5-HT administration, there were no overt behavioral effects beyond those with which the specific training-injection contingency was concerned.

A response latency difference between the testing and training trial response latency was obtained; this median value for the saline-treated controls was 115.5 seconds, whereas for the 5-HT treated animals this same value was 22.0 seconds. Eighty-seven percent of the control animals showed conditioned response retention, as measured on the testing trial, but only 12% of the 5-HT treated animals showed comparable retention. These findings support our earlier observations of the amnesic properties of intracranial 5-HT and indicated further investigation of: 1) endogenous 5-HT levels in brain following intrahippocampal 5-HT administration, and 2) the specificity of the observed amnesic effect for the 5-HT molecule.

The level of 5-HT in whole brain following intrahippocampal 5-HT injection was determined at three doses of 5-HT (0.5 - 2μg) and compared with a control (0.9% saline in an equivalent volume); 5-HT determinations were made for whole brain at 30 minutes following injection. The results, summarized in Figure 9, indicate significant 5-HT increases following intrahippocampal injections of this amine in the young adult mouse.

The specificity of posttreatment intrahippocampal injection of 5-HT for the amnesic effect was studied using several equimolar concentrations of related and/or control substances which were administered (10λ), post-training, to 35 day old mice in an equivalent behavioral paradigm. The choice of 5-HT dose in this experiment (0.46 μmoles) was based on the titration of intrahippocampally injected 5-HT, required to cause a twofold increase in tissue 5-HT level. Other compounds were chosen on

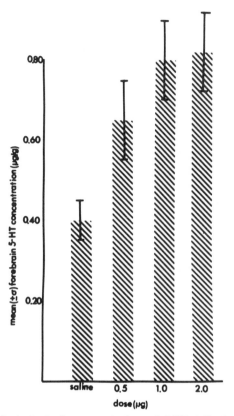

Fig. 9. Mean (±σ) forebrain concentration of 5-HT following intrahippocampal injection of this amine at different doses.

the basis of findings (Essman et al., 1971) that there were differences in the affinity of binding of indole derivatives binding to nucleic acids and nucleotides, suggesting that the interaction could serve as a model for predicting the significance of such molecules for neurobiological activity. For example, when tryptamine derivatives and t-RNA were interacted and the number of binding sites (n) and intrinsic association constants (k) were derived from Scatchard relationships, 5-HT had a greater affinity (n k = 7.7 × 10^4) than either 5-methoxy-1-methyltryptamine (n k = 1.2 × 10^4) of N-acetyl-5-hydroxytryptamine (n k = 5.9 × 10^3). It was therefore hypothesized that the latter two compounds should not have the same amnesic properties as 5-HT. Norepinephrine does not show affinity for macromolecules relevant to the regulation of protein synthesis, and therefore would not be expected to have an effect comparable to that of 5-HT.

The results summarized in Figure 10 indicate that intrahippocampal

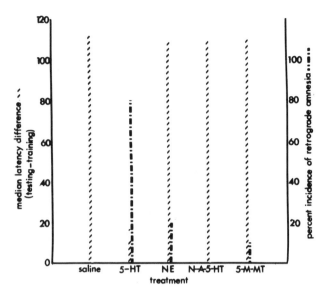

Fig. 10. Mean latency difference between testing and training trials and percent incidence of retrograde amnesia in mice intrahippocampally injected with 5-hydroxytryptamine or related amines and analogs.

5-HT, given within 10 seconds of a training trial, produced a retrograde amnesia for the conditioned response in mice. Equimolar quantities of analogs of 5-HT or norepinephrine, did not impair conditioned response retention.

A relationship between intrahippocampal 5-HT increases and retrograde amnesia in mice suggested that the experimentally induced amnesia was comparable in magnitude to that produced by ECS, provided that both treatments occurred within 10 seconds after a training experience. The temporal relationship between posttraining 5-HT treatment and retrograde amnesia remained to be explored. Some evidence for a temporal gradient of 5-HT-induced retrograde amnesia has been previously provided (Essman, 1971); these studies were extended to include the premise that a temporal gradient for the retrograde amnesic effects of intrahippocampal 5-HT can be demonstrated in mice.

CF-1s strain mice of approximately 35 days of age were trained for the acquisition of a passive avoidance response, as previously described; within 10 seconds following the training trial, medial intrahippocampal injections were given with 0.9% saline (10λ) or 5-HT (2 μg); other groups of mice were given intrahippocampal injections of 5-HT at the same dose and volume, either 1, 2, or 3 minutes posttraining. A comparison of response latency differences between the training and testing trial was used as a measure of the incidence of conditioned response retention for a testing trial given 24 hours following training. The data have been summarized in Figure 11 and illustrate a short temporal gradient for 5-HT-induced retrograde amnesia; the maximum effects for posttraining 5-HT were noted within the first minute following the training trial, with some indication of

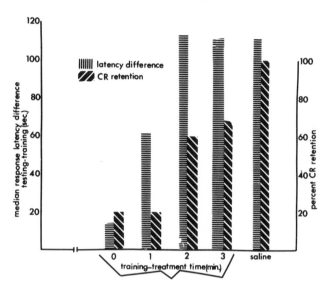

Fig. 11. Median response latency difference and percent incidence of conditioned response retention in mice as a function of the time between training and intrahippocampal 5-HT injection.

an amnesic effect with 2 minutes posttreatment and reduced retention, as compared with saline treated controls, if treatment occurred by 3 minutes posttraining. These data support the amnesia-mediating role of exogenously introduced 5-HT for passive avoidance behavior. The amnesic effects of 5-HT and the short temporal gradient for retrograde amnesia observed in the present study, should be reconciled with the prolonged period over which brain 5-HT level is elevated following intracranial injection at the same dose; these data, shown in Figure 12, indicate that brain 5-HT level was elevated by 105% for at least 30 minutes following intrahippocampal injection. Such a prolonged period of elevation of this amine may constitute a requisite for those significant central effects which regulate the process of memory fixation and its disruption; there are several alternatives

8. SITES OF 5-HT ACTION ON CEREBRAL PROTEIN SYNTHESIS

Consideration has been given to 5-HT mediated inhibition of cerebral protein synthesis and the sites at which such effect are manifest. To

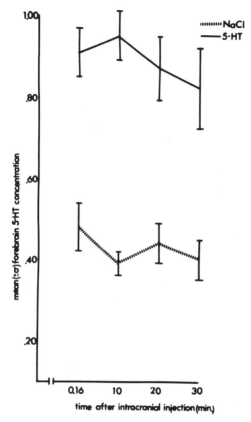

Fig. 12. Changes in forebrain 5-hydroxytryptamine concentration as a function of time after intrahippocampal 5-HT injection.

provide a more comprehensive evaluation of the sites at which 5-HT-induced effects occurred, three regions of the mouse brain were used 5 minutes after a unilateral injection of 10λ of 5-HT in 10λ of 0.9% NaC1. The cerebral cortex, basal ganglia and diencephalon, and brainstem were obtained after either 5-HT or saline injection concomitant with the intracranial injection of C^{14} leucine. Subcellular fractions were obtained from each of the regions by differential and density gradient centrifugation. The protein in each fraction was precipitated and the specific radioactivity of incorporated leucine was determined. These studies are summarized in Table VI. The most extensive degree of inhibition occurred in all fractions derived from the cerebral cortex, and the changes observed in the synaptosome fraction may account for a large proportion of the inhibition effected with a single intrahippocampal injection of 5-HT.

Changes in cerebral protein synthesis, notably for synaptosomes derived from several brain regions presumably related to having cognitive and

Table VI

Per Cent Inhibition of
C^{14}-Leucine Incorporation into Protein in
Subcellular Fractions from
Several Regions of the Mouse Brain

SUBCELLULAR FRACTION	BRAIN REGION		
	CEREBRAL CORTEX	BASAL GANGLIA & DIENCEPHALON	BRAIN STEM
MYELIN	58	18	27
SYNAPTOSOMES	72	42	35
MITOCHONDRIA	92	44	18

memory functions, have been indicated by several of the previous experiments. Several in vitro studies were carried out to further consider the relationship between 5-HT availability and synaptosomal protein synthesis. Synaptosome fractions, separated by differential and denisty gradient centrifugation from cerebral cortex and structures of the limbic system (including hippocampus, fornix, amygdala, and septal region) were incubated with either 5-HT or 0.9% saline in the presence of C^{14} leucine for 10 minutes. The fractions were then osmotically ruptured, the proteins were precipitated, and radioactivity of incorporated leucine was determined. The rate of C^{14} leucine incorporation under control conditions and under treatment conditions wherein 5-HT was used are summarized in Figure 13; it is apparent from these data that from about 26 to 32% of the incorporation of amino acid into protein was significantly reduced as a consequence of the presence of 5-HT. The findings are consistent with earlier data which have indicated that the in vivo effects of intrahippo-campal 5-HT treatment as well as those produced as a consequence of a single electro-convulsive shock inhibit cerebral protein synthesis, and more specifically, bring about such inhibition to an appreciable degree within sites related to the synaptic region.

One further consideration concerns the relationship between critical ages for the memory fixation process in the CF-1s strain mouse, its dependency upon endogenous 5-HT levels, and turnover, and the extent to

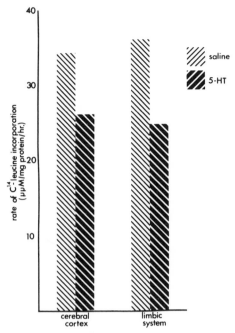

Fig. 13. Rate of C^{14} leucine incorporation into proteins of synaptosomes isolated from the cerebral cortex and limbic system structures and the effects of 5-Hydroxytryptamine.

which such dependencies may be altered by amnesic agents or events; another issue concerns the specific effect of elevated brain 5-HT upon the synthesis of the macromolecules of possible significance for memory fixation processes.

9. AGE DETERMINANTS OF THE AMNESIC AND NEUROCHEMICAL EFFECTS OF 5-HT

There are certain similarities between the time course of 5-HT-induced retrograde amnesia and the temporal gradient for this same phenomenon that has been observed with ECS. Previous observations of 1) an age-dependent temporal gradient for ECS-induced retrograde amnesia (Essman, 1970b), and 2) an age-related difference in endogenous 5-HT level and metabolism and age specific macromolecular changes as a consequence of ECS (Essman, 1970a), have provided further basis for experiments in which the age-dependent amnesic effects of 5-HT were studied. Male CF-1s strain mice, selected from matched litters of 15, 16, 17, 18, 20, 25 and 30 days of age, separate groups at each age, were given the training experience described above, followed by intrahippocampal administration of 2 μg of 5-HT in 0.9% saline (10λ). For each age group, the posttraining injection was given either 0 (within 10 sec) 2, 4, 8, or 16 minutes following the training trial. All animals were tested for conditioned passive avoidance response retention at 24 hours following the training trial.

The data in Figure 14 show that 5-HT-induced retrograde amnesia yielded a temporal gradient for mice of 20 days of age, or more; i.e., as the

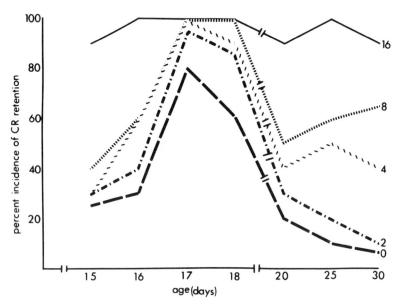

Fig. 14. Percent incidence of conditioned response retention as a function of the interval between training and intrahippocampal 5-hydroxytryptamine injection in mice of several ages.

time between the training trial and 5-HT treatment was increased, the incidence of retrograde amnesia decreased. These data agree with the findings of previous experiments. The present results also suggest that a high incidence of 5-HT-induced retrograde amnesia could be effected in 15 and 16 day old mice without appreciable differences in the incidence of retention; i.e., these findings suggest that 5-HT treatment in 15 and 16 day old animals, within the 8 minutes following training, leads to a retrograde amnesia for conditioned avoidance behavior and did not produce differences in amnesia incidence as a function of treatment time. A significant ($p < 0.01$) reduction in 5-HT-induced retrograde amnesia occurred among 17 and 18 day old animals. A small, statistically significant incidence of retrograde amnesia was observed within these two age populations for treatment given within 10 seconds following training, but there was no amnesic effect from such treatment given 2 minutes or more posttraining. These findings agree in several respects with those obtained with ECS; an antagonism for the amnesic effects of ECS was also found among 17 day old animals, where this was correlated with low endogenous levels of brain 5-HT and turnover differences at this specific age.

The similarity in the behavioral effect of posttraining ECS and increaased posttraining brain 5-HT warranted an age-related comparison in CF-1s mice between ECS and intracranial 5-HT. Should critical age factors regulate the response of those endogenous ECS-or-5-HT-responsive systems in terms of the 5-HT elevation and turnover change common to both treatments, then a reduced magnitude of such effects would be consistent with those ages at which the amnesic effects of these treatments are similarly minimized, antagonized, or attenuated. Seven age groups of mice ranging from 15 to 30 days of age were used; ECS (10 mA, 200 msec, 400 V) leading to a full clonic-tonic convulsion was given and these mice were compared with control animals given sham-ECS ($\overline{ECS}$); this consisted of the transcorneal electrodes without passage of current. Mice of each of the respective ages were given an intracranial injection of 5-HT (2 μg in 10λ of 0.9% saline) into the region of medial hippocampus or a control injection of saline only. The whole brain was removed 10 minutes following treatment and was solvent extracted and assayed spectrofluorometrically for 5-HT content.

The data summarized in Figure 15 indicate that mice of 20 days of age or older, as well as animals of 15 or 16 days of age, showed a statistically significant increase in whole brain 5-HT content within 10 minutes after either ECS or intracranial 5-HT treatment. It is apparent that 17 and 18 day old mice of this strain had lower endogenous 5-HT levels under control conditions than younger or older animals. It was further apparent that either ECS or intracranial 5-HT in these two age populations did not lead to appreciable increases in 5-HT level, or if such 5-HT elevation did, in fact, occur as a consequence of these treatments, was certainly no longer in evidence by 10 minutes following treatment. Further support for the present data derives from those observations indicating an age-related resistance to those amnesic treatments which lead to increased brain 5-HT concentration. It may be that the 17 and/or 18 day old mouse undergoes a critical neurodevelopmental alteration in 5-HT metabolism and 5-HT metabolic effects; this possibility has been suggested by previous findings (Essman, 1970b) and appears to be specific to this age interval and this specific amine, and not others that may be involved in the memory fixation process. The more obvious common ground upon which amnesic treatment conditions providing for modified brain 5-HT level or metabol-

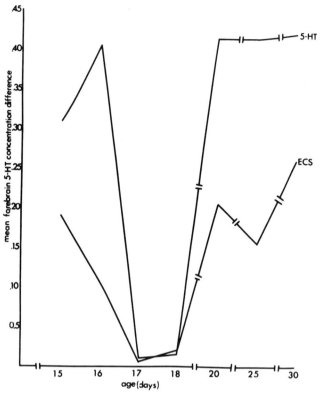

Fig. 15. Mean forebrain 5-hydroxytryptamine concentration difference in mice of different ages given either electroconvulsive shock or intrahippocampal 5-HT injection.

ism may relate to the memory fixation processes could well be represented by the effects upon cerebral protein synthesis.

Previous studies have considered the relationship between brain 5-HT and cerebral protein synthesis, particularly with reference to synaptic effects (Essman, 1970a), subcellular localization (Essman et al., 1971) and age factors (Essman, 1971). It was the purpose of the present experimental series to study the effects of regional increases in brain 5-HT concentration upon protein synthesis in these brain areas and to assess these effects as a function of age. Male CF-1s strain mice from matched litters were randomly assigned to groups ranging from 15 to 30 days of age. Ten animals of each age were intracranially injected with 2 μg of 5-HT dissolved in 0.9% saline into the region of the medial hippocampus. Mice at each of these respective ages were similarly injected with an equivalent volume (10λ) of 0.9% saline. Within 15 minutes after the concurrent intracranial injection of C^{14} leucine, brain tissue was carefully dissected into several discrete regions consisting of cerebral cortex, basal ganglia and diencephalon, midbrain, and cerebellum. Tissue proteins were assessed for incorporation of the labeled amino acid and a comparison of the differences in the rate of incorporation under control conditions were made with those rates obtained after intrahippocampal 5-HT treatment; this determination was made for each brain region at each age. From these data the rate of protein synthesis following intrahippocampal 5-HT treatment at each age was obtained, and these findings are summarized in Figure 16. There were no appreciable differences between 5-HT-treated and control-treated mice over those ages studies for the cerebellum, whereas significant inhibition of protein synthesis was indicated for other brain regions. Seventeen day old mice, however, did not show appreciable changes in cerebral protein synthesis from 5-HT treatment.

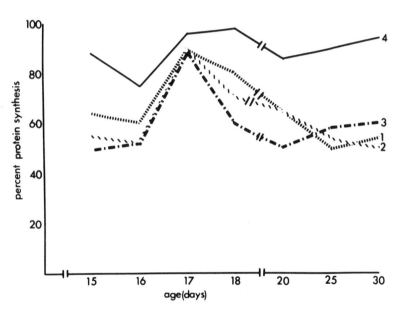

Fig. 16. Percent protein synthesis in several regions of the mouse brain for animals of different ages treated with intrahippocampal 5-HT. (1) = cerebral cortex; (2) = basal ganglia and diencephalon; (3) midbrain, (4) = cerebellum.

Age variables constitute a significant factor in the regulation of the susceptibility and/or resistance to the effects of molecular changes which alter memory consolidation upon cerebral protein synthesis. The present study offers data consistent with previous findings that: 1) parallel age-dependent inhibition of protein synthesis is brought about by electroconvulsive shock, wherein the time course for brain 5-HT elevation follows the time course for 5-HT-induced changes in protein synthesis; 2) an age-dependent resistance to both ECS as well as 5-HT-induced brain 5-HT elevation, and at the same ages, a failure to induce inhibition of protein synthesis by either of such treatments; 3) the temporal gradient for both ECS, as well as 5-HT-induced retrograde amnesia is also age dependent; at those ages where maximum resistance to the amnesic effects of either treatment occurs, this also represents the age at which brain 5-HT elevation does not appear to occur, and no inhibition of brain protein synthesis related to such 5-HT concentration increases in brain occurs.

10. SUMMARY AND PERSPECTIVES

A series of experiments have been presented in which it has been shown that the experimental induction of retrograde amnesia in mice may be effected by the intrahippocampal injection of 5-hydroxytryptamine (5-HT); this represents an endogenous event which similarly occurs, following the presentation of electroconvulsive shock, or other amnesic agents or events. Changes in the concentration and metabolism of brain 5-HT have been related to the acquisition of new behaviors and the fixation of representative stimulus traces for such experiences; a consideration of stored retrievable memories has been explored in previous reports (Essman, 1970a,b); physiological, pharmacological, biochemical, and environmental effects which modify either 5-HT content and/or metabolism or alter the tissue amine response to retrograde amnesic treatments have direct applicability to issues of the regional, cellular, and subcellular localization of 5-HT-related regulatory processes critical to memory consolidation. The events to which such central nervous system sites have been directly or indirectly related by both conceptual arguments or data involve brain protein synthesis, which, when prevented or modified, appears to interfere with the acquisition or retention of new behaviors. Support for the hypothesis that the regional modulations of protein synthesis may not only be related and/or dependent upon altered 5-HT content, and temporally bound to its retrograde amnesic effect, has emerged in the foregoing studies. The effects of ECS and intrahippocampal 5-HT upon memory consolidation are age-related to the extent that the 17 day old male CF-1s strain mouse demonstrates a reduced degree of brain 5-HT elevation consequent to ECS or intrahippocampal 5-HT in animals of the same strain at other ages. Seventeen day old animals given amnesic treatments also did not show any appreciable inhibition of protein synthesis, as did mice at other ages. Other substrates of brain metabolism of possible import for the process of memory consolidation may also rest upon age dependencies comparable to those that have so consistently emerged in the present studies; for example, the regional subcellular content of RNA, as affected by ECS, have illustrated that age-related changes may well have functional relevance for memory-related processes, at least in so far as at least one amnesic treatment, ECS, becomes capable of modifying such organelle-specific macromolecular levels.

The data presented have been intended to serve as one illustration of the potential interrelationships between memory-consolidation-dependent events, requirements for interruption of such events, and associated biochemical changes. Such changes involve regional, cellular, and subcellular sites in the nervous system, which in turn extends a challenging invitation to further experimental investigation of cellular specificity and subcellular participation. The temporal character of the memory consolidation process is such that the nature of those molecular events modified by memory-specific stimuli may be further relied upon for the specification of the molecular foundations upon which the memory traces are built. In the present discussion, we have dealt with only a limited molecular relationship for memory processing, but one to which clinical as well as experimental investigation of amnesic phenomena and information processing may be relevant. It remains for further aspects of such relevance to be studied and amplified.

The research reported herein was supported in part by a Grant from the Council for Tobacco Research, U.S.A. The author would like to acknowledge the technical assistance provided by E. Heldman and C. Antzelevitch.

REFERENCES

Barondes, S. H. (1970) Cerebral protein synthesis inhibitors block long-term memory. *Internat. Rev. Neurobiol.* 12, 177-205.

Bittman, R. and Essman, W. B. (1970) 5-Hydroxytryptamine-nucleic acid interactions: Implications for physical and in vivo studies as a model for neural function. *Abstr. of Papers, Third Ann. Winter Conf. Brain Research*, Snowmass-at-Aspen, Colo.

Bittman, R., Essman, W. B., and Golod, M. I. (1969) Studies of the interaction of 5-hydroxytryptamine with nucleic acids. *Abstr. Amer. Chem. Soc.* 1969, 330.

Cotman, C. W., Banker, G., Zornetzer, S. F., and McGaugh, J. L. (1971) Electroshock effects on brain protein synthesis: Relation to brain seizures and retrograde amnesia. *Science* 173, 454-456.

Essman, W. B. (1965) Facilitation of memory consolidation by chemically induced acceleration of RNA synthesis. *Proc. XXIII Internat. Congr. Physiol. Sciences* p. 470.

Essman, W. B. (1966) Effect of tricyanoaminopropene on the amnesic effect of electroconvulsive shock. *Psychopharmacologia* 9, 426-433.

Essman, W. B. (1967) Changes in memory consolidation with alterations in neural RNA: *Proc. Coll. Internat. Neuropsychopharm* pp. 108-113.

Essman, W. B. (1968a) Retrograde amnesia in seizure-protected mice: Behavioral and biochemical effects of pentylenetetrazol. *Physiol. Behav.* 3, 549-552.

Essman, W. B. (1968b) Electroshock-induced retrograde amnesia in seizure-protected mice. *Psychol. Rep.* **22**, 929-935.

Essman, W. B. (1970a) The role of biogenic amines in memory consolidation. In *The Biology of Memory* G. Adam, Ed., Akademiai Kiado Publ., Budapest, p. 213.

Essman, W. B. (1970b) Some neurochemical correlates of altered memory consolidation. *Trans. N. Y. Acad. Sci.* **32**, 948-973.

Essman, W. B. (1971) Retrograde amnesia and cerebral protein synthesis: Influence of age and drug factors. *Proc. XXV Int. Congr. Physiol.Sci* **9**, 166.

Essman, W. B. (1972) Neurochemical changes associated with ECS and ECT. *Semin. Psychiat.* **4**, 67-79.

Essman, W. B. (1973) *Neurochemistry of Cerebral Electroshock*, Spectrum publ., New York.

Essman, W. B. and Jarvik, M. E. (1961) Impairment of retention for a conditioned response by ether anesthesia in mice. *Psychopharmacologia* **2**, 172-176.

Essman, W. B. and Sudak, F. N. (1962) Effect of body temperature reduction on response acquisition in mice. *J. Appl. Physiol.* **17**, 113-116.

Essman, W. B. and Alpern, H. (1964) Single trial learning: Methodology and results with mice. *Psychol. Rept.* **14**, 731-740.

Essman, W. B. and Essman, S. G. (1969) Enhanced memory consolidation with drug-induced regional changes in brain RNA and serotonin metabolism. *Pharmako-Psychiat. Neuropsychopharm.* **12**, 28-34.

Essman, W. B., Bittman, R., and Heldman, E. (1971) Molecular and synaptic modulation of RNA 5-HT interactions *Abstr. of Papers, Fourth Ann. Winter Conf. Brain Research*, Snowmass-at-Aspen, Colo.

Heldman, E. and Essman, W. B. (1971) 5-Hydroxytryptamine-related changes in cerebral protein synthesis. Presented at 1st Annu. Meeting of the Soc. of Neurosciences, Washington, D. C., October 28, 1971.

Whittaker, V. P. (1969) The synaptosome. In *Handbook of Neurochemistry* Vol. 2 A. Lajtha, Ed., Plenum Press, New York, pp. 327-364.

Whittaker, V. P., Michaelson, I. A., and Kirkland, R. J. A. (1964) The separation of synaptic vesicles from disrupted nerve-ending particles ('synaptosomes'). *Biochem. J.* **90**, 239-305.

Author Index

189

Subject Index

197

Scotophobin, 82, 93
Scotophobin, 82, 93
Seizure activity, 14, 15
Seizure discharges, 51
Seizures, 56, 59, 63, 64, 86, 100, 113,
  126, 171
Seizure threshold, 51
Sensory stimuli, 56, 60
Sensory stimulation, 134
Sephadex column, 79
Septal region, 161, 180
Serotonin (5H7), 34, 35, 41
Shock avoidance response, 10
Shock-avoidance task, 10, 11
Shock-avoidance training, 6, 8, 10, 11
Short-term memory, 74, 135, 160
Shuttle box, 32, 33, 36, 40, 54, 61, 63,
  86, 88, 89, 92, 94
Shuttle-box avoidance, 37, 39
Sign-post, 156
Sign-post hypothesis, 148
Sign-post theory, 147, 154
Single trial avoidance conditioning, 115,
  126
Single trial conditioned response, 126
Single trial conditioning, 123
Single trial conditioning procedures, 122
Skinner box, 77, 78, 92, 93
Sleep, 53
Social behavior, 30
Sodium, 66
Sodium-potassium-magnesium-ATPase,
  62
Soluble cytoplasm, 171
Somatosensory, 2
Somatosensory cortex, 117, 118, 119,
  120
Sound, 85
Sound stimulus, 10
Spatial visual maze, 2
Specificity, 77, 93
Spreading depression, 10, 51
State-dependent learning, 12
Stereotaxic instrument, 62, 136, 140
Stimulants, 12
Stimulation, 34, 59
Stimulus recognition, 61
Storage, 150
Stress, 29
Stressful stimulation, 7
Strychnine, 2, 11
Subcellular changes, 160

Subcellular fractions, 165, 166, 179
Subcellular localization, 184, 186
Subcellular sites, 165, 187
Subcortical structures, 121
Subsynaptic membrane, 111
Subsynaptic organelles, 173
Superior quadrigeminal bodies, 37
Sucrose density gradient, 165, 166
Synapses, 94, 111, 114
Synaptic cleft, 154
Synaptic currents, 61
Synaptic knobs, 65
Synaptosome fraction, 165, 166, 179,
  180
Synaptic function, 60
Synaptic membrane, external, 31
Synaptic membranes, 57
Synaptic region, 163
Synaptic site, 3, 12, 16, 163
Synaptic transmission, 99, 112
Synaptosome, 148, 167, 168, 171, 181
Taste discrimination, 93
Tay-Sachs' disease, 148
TCAP, 11
Tempora-ammonic tract, 57
Temporal area, 135
Temporal gradient, 160, 177, 178, 181
  182, 184
Temporal lobes, 37, 50
Temporal summation, 57
Tetraethylammonium, 59
Thalamus, 117, 124, 161
Theta rhythm, 51, 56, 58, 59, 125
Theta waves, 8, 52, 53
Thionin, 139
Third ventricle, 138
Thirst, 32, 33
Thyroid, 55
Tissue cultures, 57
T-Maze, 15, 138, 140, 144
Trace retrieval, 115
Trained animals, 134
Transduction, 150
Transfer, 8, 75, 76, 77
Transfer effect, 73, 74, 92, 94
Transfer factor, 82, 89, 93
Transfer of alternation, 80
Transfer of habitation, 10
Transfer of information, 75, 79
Transfer studies, 133, 139
Transmitter released, 65
Transmitter substances, 17